Americanizing Britain

MODERNIST LITERATURE & CULTURE

Kevin J. H. Dettmar & Mark Wollaeger, Series Editors

Americanizing Britain

*The Rise of Modernism in the Age
of the Entertainment Empire*

Genevieve Abravanel

OXFORD
UNIVERSITY PRESS

OXFORD

UNIVERSITY PRESS

Oxford University Press, Inc., publishes works that further
Oxford University's objective of excellence
in research, scholarship, and education.

Oxford   New York
Auckland   Cape Town   Dar es Salaam   Hong Kong   Karachi
Kuala Lumpur   Madrid   Melbourne   Mexico City   Nairobi
New Delhi   Shanghai   Taipei   Toronto

With offices in
Argentina   Austria   Brazil   Chile   Czech Republic   France   Greece
Guatemala   Hungary   Italy   Japan   Poland   Portugal   Singapore
South Korea   Switzerland   Thailand   Turkey   Ukraine   Vietnam

Published by Oxford University Press, Inc.
198 Madison Avenue, New York, New York 10016
www.oup.com

Oxford is a registered trademark of Oxford University Press

A CIP record is available from the Library of Congress.
ISBN 978-0-19-9754458

9 8 7 6 5 4 3 2 1

Printed in the United States of America
on acid-free paper

Contents

Series Editors' Foreword

There are many things we love about editing the Modernist Literature & Culture series: one of those is nicely represented in Genevieve Abravanel's *Americanizing Britain: The Rise of Modernism in the Age of the Entertainment Empire*. To wit: it's a thrill to encounter the work of new scholars in modernist studies, and to allow their work to mess with your head.

For us, the central paradox of *Americanizing Britain* is this: if Abravanel's claim is correct—if much about British modernism can be understood only by restoring the dynamic relationship of British and American to those various other vectors along which we've become used to performing our analyses (high vs. low, art vs. entertainment, center vs. margin)—then surely we would have known of it before now. A claim as bold as this is almost certain not to prove out.

But when it does … well, it's a beautiful thing; and for that reason, this is a beautiful book. In it, Abravanel unravels, with extraordinary patience and clarity, the absolutely articulate (if largely unconscious) history of twentieth-century British culture's simultaneous invention and demonization of "the American Age." The "Americanizing" trope from her title is not her coinage, it turns out, but instead floated through British cultural discourse in the early decades of the twentieth century to identify a force akin to what Matthew Arnold had, a half-century earlier, dubbed "Philistinism." "Early twentieth-century British writers, scholars, and commentators," Abravanel explains, "had a name for what was happening to England and the world: they called it 'Americanisation.' " Arnold had spotted it "on the French coast," whereas Kipling and Wells and Woolf and Leavis saw it instead across the Atlantic: but both generations understood themselves as standing on "a darkling plain / Swept with confused alarms of struggle and flight, / Where ignorant armies clash by night."

As Abravanel unfolds her tale, Britain's fear of Americanization is seemingly everywhere. It's bound up intimately, if secretly, with its fears of loss of empire, with "a collapse from Britishness to Englishness, a shift from imperial confidence to pride in local customs and national traditions." And as Britain lost her grip on her empire, and was poised to shrink from Great Britain to a modest, nostalgically reduced state of "merrie England," so she began reactively to identify imperialism in the form of American popular entertainment—what Abravanel calls the American Entertainment Empire. Hence the oft-voiced fears that "England was being colonized internally by American cinema" or—even worse—that Britain's own colonies were being recolonized by the American "talkies," putting, as Abravanel writes, "England in the role of colony to America's new media empire." In another era, such nefarious influence might have been troped in terms of viral infection; during the Cold War, it would likely have manifested in fantasies of zombie takeover. Abravanel quotes from a rather fantastic speech given in the House of Commons in 1927: "We have several million people, mostly women, who, to all intents and purposes, are temporary American citizens." He was talking, of course, about American movies, but not *Invasion of the Body Snatchers*.

One of the admirable features of *Americanizing Britain* is the way that Abravanel draws from both canonical and noncanonical texts and treats a wide range of writers, including those conventionally considered "minor," to illustrate her thesis. H. G. Wells and Rudyard Kipling are both put in the dock, and testify as vividly as Virginia Woolf, T. S. Eliot, or the editors of *Close Up* to the pervasive fear of Americanization. Wells actually championed a version of Americanization—what he referred to as "The United States of Everywhere"—as an antidote to the retrogressive embrace of an ersatz Englishness he saw taking hold. This kind of proposal Abravanel reads under the banner of "Ameritopia," a distinctive thread in the texts she explores; somewhat surprisingly, she finds Woolf, in an essay written for the American *Cosmopolitan* magazine, one of its breathless exponents. Breathless but not guileless: "Woolf can write so cunningly about the United States without ever needing to visit," Abravanel points out, "because as she well understands, by the late thirties Ameritopia exists nowhere so potently as in the British imagination." In the discourse of Americanization, we learn, what matters is not so much the "actual" effect of American cultural production on an embattled British way of life, but instead British perceptions of that impact.

Abravanel's treatment of the Leavises, especially F. R., is one of the book's real treats, as she seeks to understand the response of English criticism to the menace posed by the American Century. What she discovers is that "Leavis's influential role in the development of English as a discipline follows from his desire to design a field of study that would save England from Americanization." She even suggests—though it's left at the level of suggestion—that literary studies in the United States itself imbibed Leavis's fear of Americanization, a type of literary self-loathing that must have taken a toll on the shape and trajectory of U. S. literary study. Most surprising of all—though we'll leave you to read the details yourself—Abravanel shows how the British "anti-Leavis," Richard Hoggart, founder of the Birmingham School of cultural studies, himself replicates Leavis's anti-Americanism.

For us, the book's most surprising argument, and the one most likely to provoke response, is Abravanel's reading of *Four Quartets* as a poem of beginnings and endings that silently elides...well, the United States. This closing chapter demonstrates most fully the heuristic power of Abravanel's critical lens; "In *Four Quartets*," she argues, "Eliot resolves the dilemma between modern Britain and the United States by refusing them both, returning instead to the moment in colonial history when America was part of Great Britain. In so doing, *Four Quartets* produces a specifically transatlantic nostalgia that recalls the golden age of British imperialism through its colonial relationship with America." It's a tour de force reading of a poem that's been much read—but never quite like this.

When a book articulates a thesis with this kind of analytical power, it seems almost to generate its own examples and case studies: one puts down the book still wearing its lenses, and looks at English modernism altogether anew. The most charming example of this comes in the book's brief Afterword, and we won't spoil that lagniappe further than to say that its deft reading of the novels of J. K. Rowling absolutely "gets" the Harry Potter phenomenon, while at the same time presenting the most convincing argument to date for its curious force. For we Americans still carry a strong strain of Anglophilia, of course, and that same English culture, in its twentieth-century variety, is formed around an irritant grain of anti-Americanism.

Kevin J. H. Dettmar
and
Mark Wollaeger

Acknowledgments

A long project such as this one incurs many debts. It started at Duke, under the guidance of a fantastic committee. Toril Moi gave generously of her tremendous talent, reading countless drafts with precision and rigor. She has earned my lasting gratitude. Ian Baucom introduced me to Atlantic Studies and helped me to see how my work might transform assumptions in that field and others. I learned much from his ease with complexity. I am extremely grateful to Michael Moses for his encyclo-pedic knowledge and generous insights as well as to Houston Baker for inspiration. Thanks are also due to the fabulous Kathy Psomiades and my wonderful peers, espe-cially the gang-of-three: Lili Hsieh, Amy Carroll, and Julie Chun Kim. Special thanks to Jené Schoenfeld, who remains a superb interlocutor and treasured friend.

My new home at Franklin & Marshall College introduced me to support-ive, inspiring colleagues: Patrick Bernard, Katie Ford, Tamara Goeglein, Kabi Hartman, Emily Huber, Peter Jaros, Padmini Mongia, Nick Montemarano, Judith Mueller, Patricia O'Hara, Jeff Steinbrink, and Anton Ugolnick. Emily Huber, Kabi Hartman, and Giovanna Faleschini Lerner in particular went above and beyond to encourage the book's final revisions.

Across the academy, collegiality of the best sort has come from Paul Saint-Amour, Jessica Berman, Jim English, Michael Tratner, Priscilla Wald, Jed Esty, Brian Richardson, Peter Mallios, Jean-Michel Rabaté, Amardeep Singh, Rebecca Wanzo, Sonita Sarker, Mary Lou Emery, Judith Brown, Melba Cuddy-Keane, and Douglas Taylor. I also want to thank Gail Potter and Jennifer Davis for their friend-ship throughout these many years of writing.

This work greatly benefited from the support of the American Academy of University Women, the NEH Summer Stipend Program, the Penn Humanities

Forum, and the Franklin & Marshall College Faculty Research Fund. Thanks as well to Rita Barnard and Demi Kurz who, under the auspices of the Gender, Sexuality, and Women's Studies Program at Penn, offered me space to write at a crucial moment in the project's development. In addition, I feel fortunate to have had the opportunity to discuss some of the book's central ideas at Modernist Studies Association conferences over the years; those conversations have been integral to what follows.

At F&M, Andrew Yager was an outstanding, meticulous research assistant and research librarian Scott Vine came through in a pinch. I would also like to thank the librarians at the British Film Institute and the British Library for their assistance. A portion of chapter 3 first appeared in *Modernist Cultures* 5 (2010) and an earlier, partial version of chapter 4 in *Modernism/Modernity* 15, no. 4 (2008). I thank the editors of these journals for permission to reprint.

Mark Wollaeger and Kevin Dettmar are superlative series editors; it has been a true pleasure to work with them both. Thanks, Mark, for talking shop with me whenever I needed it. Shannon McLachlan and Brendan O'Neill at Oxford University Press are at once rigorous and humane. I couldn't have asked for better. I would also like to thank the anonymous readers whose detailed remarks informed and improved the finished book.

Last but never least: my family. I am grateful to Fred and Nancy Abt for their love and belief in me, always delivered with humor and grace. Bessie Abravanel at 104 years of age continues to inspire me. I would like to thank my father, Eugene Abravanel, for modeling academic rigor and for bringing a capacious curiosity to every topic of conversation. To my mother, Wendy Abt, who has been there for me throughout the writing of this book and beyond: there are no words to express how grateful I am. It is a blessing to be your daughter. To my husband, Johnny, let me here mark the enduring delight I feel at having you in my life. You are the best decision I ever made. And to Joshua, you arrived at the very end of this project, to make everything sweet.

Americanizing Britain

Introduction

Take up the White Man's burden!
Have done with childish days

—Rudyard Kipling, "The White Man's Burden," 1899[1]

The old Edwardian brigade do make their brief little world look pretty tempting. All home-made cakes and croquet...Always the same picture: high summer, the long days in the sun, slim volumes of verse, crisp linen, the smell of starch. If you've no world of your own, it's rather pleasing to regret the passing of someone else's. But I must say it's pretty dreary living in the American Age—unless you're an American, of course. Perhaps all our children will be American. That's a thought, isn't it?

—John Osborne, *Look Back in Anger*, 1956[2]

In John Osborne's landmark 1956 play, *Look Back in Anger*, the shopkeeper, Jimmy Porter, is struck by a disquieting thought. England, he reflects, is now living in the "American Age"—so much so that the next generation of English children may simply turn out to be Americans.[3] Yet only a few decades earlier, at the beginning of the century, many in Britain believed their nation to be the dominant world power, the empire on which the sun never set, and a highly developed society in contrast to which, in Rudyard Kipling's phrase, the United States appeared "childish." It is worth asking how, in roughly half a century, Britain managed the transition from Kipling's imperial confidence to Osborne's grim defeatism. How did the storyline shift from Britain's worldly predominance to its minor role in a global American Age? Who told the stories that made up the shift, and how were they told? Moreover, given that literary modernism came of age during this time, how have these stories not become much more familiar to literary critics, and how has Britain's invention of the American Age not become a common feature of the field?

To return, for a moment, to Jimmy Porter. What Jimmy laments, in backhanded fashion, is a world that has already been lost, a world of cakes and croquet, of the upper crust, and the empire. By midcentury, with the so-called high summer of British imperial supremacy chilled by the Cold War, such stories abounded of the displacement of Britain by its former colony across the Atlantic. These stories told of the rise of American capitalism and a shift in financial prowess from London to New York. They told of a world learning to speak American slang and placing their faith in the dollar rather than the pound. They told of the deluge of American mass entertainment—Hollywood movies and jazz recordings—even into the most rustic pockets of the English countryside. And in tones variously elegiac, bitter, and hopeful, they told of the end of England and the demise of the empire with the coming of this new American epoch.

The most apparent crux of these stories was the transition from the height of British imperial power to the dawn of the American Century. Still, the question arises, how can anyone tell the story of the passing of one age into the next, par-ticularly if an age is the kind of thing made up of stories in the first place? In Jimmy's case, he looks ahead to the generation that will be born into the brave new world of American pleasures, leisures, and commodities. At the same time, as Osborne's title implies, in order to tell of the present and future, Jimmy must look back. Jimmy's backward gaze takes him to the early twentieth century, to the precipitous decades when the coming of this American Age seemed at once impossible and inevitable. Such a backward glance provokes its own questions. How did the early twentieth century experience this epic shift? In what ways did this shift alter diverse British conceptions of their role in the world and their cul-ture at home? Why did that unusual practice of storytelling, literary modernism, come into its own at the beginning of the American Century? How did the shift itself lessen the chance that literary scholars would tell its story? If *we* look back, what will we find?

The answers will take us not only through literary modernism but also direct our gaze toward the rise of literary studies itself. After all, English studies in its modern form took root at the university during the early twentieth century. Developing concurrently as they did, literary modernism and English studies might be deemed separated at birth, their morphologies reflected in each other in relational and inverse fashion—fraternal twins born under the sign of the narrative of the

American Age. While this study will not be a history of our discipline, I will along the way briefly consider the stories we have told ourselves, as well as our attempts to escape what we thought we knew, namely, Anglo-American modernism. I do not wish to reinstate Anglo-American modernism as a central figure but rather to unpack it, to suggest that it remains a blind spot rather than a known quantity, such that our very attempts to escape it remain tacitly, even invisibly, guided by it. Increasingly in recent years, modernist criticism has taken important and vast strides beyond an undifferentiated Anglo-American modernism to consider transatlantic influence and exchange.[4] Such work takes part in what Doug Mao and Rebecca Walkowitz identified in 2008 as the "transnational turn" in modernist studies; that is, a movement away from nation-based epistemologies toward an interest in other networks of connection. Nonetheless, modernist studies remains tethered to the Anglo-American model, even its modes of resistance, in part because the elements of the imagined transition from Britain to America—ideas of high and low, of art and entertainment, of language and nation—were there from the beginning, helping to constitute what we now know as literary studies.

At the same time, the story of the Americanization of Britain is a transnational tale—and not only transatlantic—insofar as British anxieties about American influence participated in, and contributed to, conceptions of Britain's imperial scope and what it meant to have or be an empire. Rather than focusing primarily on artistic influence, shared artistic movements, or the migrations of individual writers—what might be deemed a model of transatlantic plenitude—I situate key texts and narratives within the broader cultural field of Americanization. This broader field in its turn allows me to consider that which studies of exchange and influence tend not to foreground; namely, the negative reactions and anxieties that narratives of Americanization often embody and provoke. *Americanizing Britain* is not a cultural history of Anglo-American relations nor of British responses to American mass culture. Rather, it is an exploration of how Britain reinvented itself in relation to its ideas of America, and how Britain's literary modernism developed and changed through this reinvention.

Americanization

Early twentieth-century British writers, scholars, and commentators had a name for what was happening to England and the world: they called it "Americanisation." Americanization (along with cognates such as the French "américanisation") was the neologism of the century in part because it seemed to name the century's profound transformation. As a rough synonym for standardization or what F. R. Leavis called "levelling down," Americanization generally referred to the rise and spread of American-style capitalism and the mass entertainment that often followed in its wake.[5] After the First World War, jazz music spread contagiously throughout Britain's cities and countryside at the same time that Hollywood films began to dominate their homegrown counterparts in British cinemas. Hollywood films in particular became such a ubiquitous feature of daily life that cultural critics lamented the extent to which England was being colonized internally by American cinema. To some, Americanization seemed capable of fulfilling Jimmy Porter's prophecy: turning the English into Americans, or at least into rampant, mindless consumers of American goods and media. Even more pervasively, Americanization seemed a subtraction, an erasure of cultural specificity and the history that produced it. During the interwar period, the United States was slowly becoming synonymous with the "modern," leading the British Empire—historically viewed as a vanguard of progress—to begin to seem old-fashioned and poised to decline.

Such an equation of America with the modern was not only a British dilemma. European responses to Americanization are revealing both for their consonances with and their differences from those in Britain. The very term "Americanization" can be traced back to an early and even a progenitive moment in the development of European modernism. Charles Baudelaire, often considered a direct ancestor of modernist writing, is also often given credit for coining the term "américanisation." In a grim prophecy, Baudelaire referred to the modern age as "the period we shall next be entering, of which the beginning is marked by the supremacy of America and industry."[6] Philippe Roger, who has called Baudelaire "the torch bearer of resistance to Americanization," noted how Baudelaire's thinking progressed from the image of reprehensible "Americanized" individuals to a nightmare vision of collective Americanization.[7] As Baudelaire wrote in 1861, "so far will machinery have Americanized us, so far will Progress have atrophied in us all that is spiritual, that no dream of the Utopians, however bloody...will be comparable to the result."[8] Although Baudelaire famously celebrated decadence and decline, he conceived of the rise of America as the death of humanity. The concept "américanisation" thus served Baudelaire as a diagnosis of the particular malady of the modern condition.

Baudelaire's fervent resistance to Americanization foreshadows the positions of twentieth-century European intellectuals such as the Frankfurt-school theorist Theodor Adorno and the French social commentator André Siegfried. These European responses signaled the widespread character of conceptions of Americanization while ultimately revealing the singular nature of Britain's relationship to its former colony. Whereas Adorno feared for the fate of art in the age of what he saw as a largely American "culture industry," Siegfried, in widely reprinted and translated works such as *America Comes of Age* (1927) and *Europe's Crisis* (1935), played on circulating fears that the United States might supplant Europe in worldwide stature and influence.[9] According to Siegfried, "To America the advent of the new order is a cause for pride, but to Europe it brings heart-burnings and regrets for a state of society that is doomed to disappear."[10] Siegfried's "heart-burnings and regrets" reflect a belief that the economic strength of the United States, often emblematized in the figure of Henry Ford, was setting the stage for the destruction of Europe's cherished values and traditions. Bertolt Brecht echoed such sentiments, though from a distinctly political vantage point, when in a 1929 poem referring to America's "films" "records" and "chewing gum," he ironically noted that Americans seem "destined to rule the world by helping it to progress."[11] At the same time, European support for the United States sometimes emerged from surprising quarters. For instance, the Italian Marxist Antonio Gramsci lamented the "anti-Americanism...of the European petty bourgeois" and wondered if Henry Ford's methods might be turned to socialist ends.[12] Ford's potential for socialism was taken with even greater seriousness in parts of the new Soviet Union, where workers celebrated Ford and even occasionally named their children after him.[13]

Although the British echoed the European range of attitudes about the threat or promise of the United States, the Anglo-American situation was distinct. First, as a former British colony, the United States represented a new, independent nation, not bound by the Commonwealth, born out of the British Empire. The failure of the British imperial project—or the possibility of its failure—was thus encoded into the very existence of the United States. Additionally, it was the legacy of British imperialism that Britain and the United States should have the great misfortune, according to some, of sharing a language. To those for whom American entertainment was becoming a global menace, the fact of a common language rendered Britain and its empire particularly vulnerable markets for American music and film. By viewing modern Britain in a transatlantic framework, it is possible to move beyond the familiar pairing of metropole and colony to suggest that British imperial anxieties not only emerged within the geographic bounds of empire but were also roused by the idea of the United States.

Texts of the period variously represent the United States as colonizing the future, interrupting British imperial teleologies of progress, and forcing redefinitions of Britain's place in the world. In some cases, these redefinitions entail a collapse from Britishness to Englishness, that is, a shift from imperial confidence to pride in local customs and national traditions. This ideological shift marks a turn from the vision of the vast and unshakeable British Empire toward a romanticized Englishness tied to tradition and the past. While reactions to American influence varied greatly throughout Britain—the working classes in Scotland and Wales, for instance, generally eschewed this romantic vision of Englishness, sometimes in favor of even greater alliance with an imagined America—those writers and intellectuals with connections to London found it hard to avoid the discourse of American threat and English resistance. The rise of what some critics have called "little Englandism" not only reflects British imperial decline but also the transatlantic comparison that throws this decline into ever sharper relief.[14] As a result, Englishness becomes a kind of consolation prize for the anticipated loss of imperial supremacy, and the virtues of the English past compensation for the ebbing power to produce the future.

The fictionality of this Englishness, and the impetus for its construction, becomes especially clear in the reactions of those outside the London elite: the English, Scotch, and Welsh working classes, especially the younger generation, and in some cases, those looking at England from other parts of the empire. To the extent that these groups tended (though never uniformly) to embrace American entertainment and absorb aspects of its culture, they lent urgency to the invention of Englishness as an imagined center. While the pages that follow often turn to this dominant narrative of Englishness, the reader will also find persistent, if periodic, reference to the modes of resistance, exclusions, and fragmentation that made the consolidation of Englishness feel all the more necessary. After all, throughout Britain, America's rise to global power had its champions. British newspapers widely cheered the victory of the United States in the Spanish-American War of 1898, viewing their former colony as a possible strategic ally. After the American intervention in the First World War, such hopes appeared borne out. The very idea of the United States, especially as embodied in the figure of Woodrow Wilson, briefly but potently raised mass enthusiasm. And although they were in the minority, some intellectuals greeted America's rise to world prominence as a boon. For instance, H. G. Wells's various rhapsodies to American progress as "the future" contrast British social hierarchy to American democratic ideals.[15] By the twenties, Ford Madox Ford identifies the United States as more important than Europe to Britain, claiming that "civilisation has become, quite integrally, a matter of what goes backwards and forwards across the Atlantic."[16] Not only did British writers such as Ford enjoy robust markets in the United States but, in the shadow of the Second World War, an increasing number of writers such as W. H. Auden emigrated to America, in some cases adopting American citizenship, further complicating their relationships to the United States.[17]

American Modernity, British Modernism, and the Entertainment Empire

The broader context for British reactions to Americanization, part of what lent them their weight and gravity, emerged through perceptions of an interwar shift in fortunes from Great Britain to the United States. Scholars of this shift tend to note its material markers: the dollar largely displaced the pound as the global currency of the moment, and the financial center began its migration from London to New York.[18] Whereas the United States had been in debt to Britain at the beginning of the century, the First World War effectively reversed the situation.[19] Britain suddenly found itself literally in debt to its former colony at the same time that the United States' military intervention at the war's end left Britain figuratively indebted as well. Historians have documented this interwar shift from British to American hegemony and sociologist Giovanni Arrighi has identified it as the defining phenomenon of the twentieth century.[20] Yet whereas Arrighi and others tend to discuss the shift as a material phenomenon, I am more interested in its imaginative dimensions. Along these lines, it is possible to frame the change in Anglo-American relations as a paradigm shift in the sense proposed by Thomas Kuhn.[21] The paradigm shift is a useful model here because it does not intimate a clean break or rupture but rather captures the accretion of change over time, generally accelerated by specific events, until a new world picture that once seemed impossible comes to seem inevitable. In the case of British reactions to the rise of the United States, the turning point can be roughly identified with the period following the First World War, a time when both material and psychic investments in the United States underwent considerable change.

Before the war, even those who anticipated a rise in American power generally imagined the United States would emulate British or European imperialism. Thus when the United States announced its imperial project via the Spanish-American War of 1898 and subsequent annexation of Cuba and the Philippines, many in Britain imagined the United States was following Britain's lead. In "The White Man's Burden" (1899), Kipling addresses a newly imperial United States with the assumption that the younger nation has much to learn from Great Britain. Yet increasingly in the years after the First World War, these earlier conceptions of American power were changing. Whereas Kipling's prewar model presents American power as a weaker but essentially similar variant of British power, later writers registered the shock of facing a new style of world power; one predicated more obviously on global commercialism and standardization than on occupation and colonial rule.

Parsings of such new styles of power emerged specifically in descriptions of the United States as an entertainment empire. More than one interwar British cultural critic noted that the United States seemed to be colonizing Britain and the world through its mass media. Even T. S. Eliot, the American who became a British citizen and held forth on the sanctity of Englishness, referred to American commodity culture as its special "imperialism."²² While the so-called imperialism of U.S. entertainment is distinct from the United States' territorial acquisitions, the two were often viewed collectively in the eyes of those in Britain who recognized the United States as a new kind of world power. Unlike the British Empire, which had historically expanded through occupation, the American Entertainment Empire seemed capable of spreading its influence far beyond its territorial borders and encroaching upon Britain and its colonies themselves.

Whether the rise of the United States was perceived as a boon or a menace, it persistently became a name for the condition of modernity itself. Books of the period such as *Americanism: A World Menace, The American Invaders,* and *This American World* variously proposed "America" as the name of the modern.²³ It is curious, then, that Americanization as it emerged in the interwar period has not drawn more attention from scholars of modernist studies. Modernist studies has long had an intuition, one grown stronger in the past decade or so, that its concerns were centrally with "modernity," an indistinct category capable of referring to the entire thickness of culture within which modernism came to be and of which it was a reflexive and constituent part. Without presupposing one to be prior to the other, it seemed that modernist writing was wrestling with all of the upheaval of its moment: electric streetlamps and motor cars, the birth of psychoanalysis, the aftermath of mechanical war, the movies, and the theory of relativity. For the field, this attention has been productive in much the way that the study of thick culture has informed earlier modernities—Victorian, Romantic, Medieval—and many specific parallels or interesting moments of collision have been traced between literary texts and their early twentieth-century context. Yet the construct, Americanization, is distinct from other aspects of modern culture insofar as it so fully stood for the very idea of modernity at the beginning of the twentieth century, often in its most negative guise. It is worth asking, then, what is the relationship of modernism to a construct that seemed to stand for the *idea* of the modern itself? And moreover, what specifically might this construct reveal about that category we call British modernism?

A surprising number of critics have suggested, in one fashion or another, that British modernism—or at least English modernism—is a misnomer and that the early twentieth century did not see the kind of experimental work from English writers as it did from other national traditions. As Peter Wollen persuasively puts it, "Modernism, in its pure form, appealed to very few in Britain, especially not in England."[24] Jed Esty likewise calls "English modernism relatively insular and traditionalist by comparison not only to the continental avant-gardes but also to the Irish and American elements of Anglophone modernism."[25] Of course, it is one of the special pleasures of scholars in the field of modernism more generally to debate—sometimes in deeply nuanced fashion—whether its primary subject can be said to exist at all. Such debate rests in part on the status of modernism as what Fredric Jameson has called "a belated construct," or the ideological project of critics after the Second World War.[26] Moreover, the claim for the great disappearing English modernism, or for its nonexistence, overlooks experimental work that has only lately entered the canon or that still maintains a marginal status (think of Edith Sitwell). It also discounts the more recognizably innovative work of writers such as Woolf or ties such work to Romanticism, as in the influential conceptions of Frank Kermode.[27]

At the same time, the persistent feeling we have that British modernism is a kind of oxymoron, or a ghost born of our critical longings for its existence, emerges out of more than post–World War II problems of canonization. It certainly seems true that those British writers who have been most fully canonized as modernists—Lawrence, Forster, even Woolf—express a more moderate or partial experimentalism than that of Joyce, Stein, or the Italian futurists. I suggest that this long-standing critical intuition that there is something incomplete or inconsistent about British modernism can be explained within a transatlantic framework. Unlike the work of the European avant-garde, British modernism has been written into literary history as a tug-of-war between the old and the new, tradition and the individual talent.[28] It is more than coincidence that Britain's uniquely ambivalent modernism emerged at a time when ownership of the modern seemed to be passing to America. While it would be going too far to suggest that American influence alone gave rise to the paradoxical qualities of British modernism, the unusual character of this writing reflects Britain's interwar struggle to define itself in relation to its former colony across the Atlantic. Thus while I do believe that there is such a thing as British modernism and that it is not a phantasm but rather a construct with a plausible set of literary objects, I also believe that the backward gaze of those British works we have most often called modernist—their ties to Romanticism, to English history and tradition—emerged in important part though the dramatic upheavals of the Anglo-American relationship and the pervasive fashion in which it changed the meaning of modernity.

A broad range of voices narrated these transatlantic upheavals, including those who are not ordinarily considered modernist. Writers such as Rudyard Kipling and H. G. Wells are not high modernists in the classical sense, yet their writing sheds light on the discourses that constitute modernism. The model that classifies writers as either modernist or not, I suggest, has limited utility for an inquiry centered on Americanization. I propose looking instead to what I call "modes of being modernist," not a name for the *writers* but rather for the *traits* that appear and cluster in works of the period. Such modes include all of the familiar features of modernist writing: formal experimentation, an interest in the materiality of language, a turn to subjectivity, and so forth. Rather than conceiving of modernism as an all or nothing proposition wherein writers are either in or out of the fold, this model allows us to focus on the modernist forms, tropes, and energies at play in a given work. Such modes can occur in some works by a given writer but not in other works, several modes can be engaged simultaneously or to varying degrees, and modes may concentrate at particular points in a writer's career. Under this rubric, it is possible to see how more conventional writers like Kipling and Wells engage some modes of modernism, to varying degrees, from time to time.

This model, in opening up a narrow canon, may seem to tend toward the universal embrace of calling all works of a given period modernist. Yet the "modes" model sidesteps this possibility in two ways. First, whether a given text engages one or more modes of being modernist can and should be a matter of debate. Critics who know texts well, from those of the canonical high modernists to those of the growing pool of "middlebrow" modernists, can identify the modes these texts engage. Second, this model suggests that the label modernist need not be a blanket term, precisely because there are multiple modes of being modernist. This approach lessens the danger of homogenizing the works of the period under an umbrella term, because the term itself, with the addition of "modes," has been outfitted for difference. My proposal that we append the term "modes" to the more familiar term "modernist," is not, of course, a call to do away with the broader term "modernism"—or as it has lately been configured "modernisms." Rather, it is to do away with the hard and fast division among writers of the period, a division that responses to Americanization complicate and undermine. It also serves to preclude what has sometimes been taken as the alternative: the practice of calling all early twentieth-century writers modernist; this practice lacks the nuance of explaining the different *ways* in which they are modernist, while threatening to make the term so inclusive as to render it meaningless.[29]

Given that literary modernism came of age at the beginning of what is often called the American Century, this model also begs the question of periodization. It may seem that a given mode could be found in literature of any time or place, and not only that of the early twentieth century. While it's true that formal innovation and interest in human interiority, to give just two examples, can be found in works from classical antiquity onward, it is in the early twentieth century that the modes concentrate sufficiently and spread contagiously enough to become a field worth identifying. Such an early twentieth-century concentration of modes is part of what I propose we take as a broader periodization, namely, the long twentieth century. The sociologist Giovanni Arrighi, in his book *The Long Twentieth Century* lays out a useful template. He identifies historical cycles of power and influence: dating the "the British cycle" from the second half of the eighteenth century through the early twentieth century and the "US cycle" from the late nineteenth century onward. Tellingly, Arrighi identifies the Edwardian era as "the high-point of Britain's free-trade imperialism"—the very point at which the U.S. cycle was just beginning.

Here is the key to Arrighi's relevance to modernism: his perceptive characterization of the early twentieth century as the period of *overlap* between the British and American cycles of power. This overlap takes place from the late nineteenth century through the early twentieth, the period of anglophone literary modernism. Even without Arrighi's framework, it is clear that the early twentieth century presented a unique historical moment in the history of Anglo-American relations. It is neither the mid-nineteenth century period when the thought of the United States superseding British power and influence was largely science fiction, nor the late Cold War moment when, with Britain sheltered under the American nuclear program, many believed a shift had already occurred. Rather, the early twentieth century—the period of literary modernism—was the uncertain period when the American threat to British dominance inspired both skepticism and fear; when the modern narrative of Americanization was being thought into existence. The long twentieth century foregrounds these shifts—or the stories of these shifts—and thus frames the modernist period as the key transitional moment of Anglo-American relations.

At the same time, periodization is a kind of storytelling. Almost any chronological division might be called a period, justified by narratives such as the developments in physics or the onset of European war. However, the American Age as a name for the twentieth century is compelling not only for economic and political reasons, but also because the early twentieth century itself narrated the American Age into being. In 1941, *Time* magazine publisher Henry Luce coined the term the "American Century" as a name for the twentieth.[30] Luce's unusual anointment—the naming of a century after a modern nation—embodies the fears of those in Britain who saw Osborne's "American Age" upon them.[31] And despite all that this name presumes and overlooks, its arrogance and its inadequacy, there is a way in which the twentieth century *was* the American Century, insofar as it was a century committed to telling stories, both celebratory and frightening, about the rise of the United States.

American Anxieties of English Influence

In the nineteenth century, Americans were also telling stories about the Anglo-American relationship but of a different type. Namely, American writers spilled considerable ink over their concerns about living up to Britain's literary heritage. These concerns might be parsed, with a nod to Harold Bloom, as American anxieties of English influence. In the years since *The Anxiety of Influence* (1973), critics have adapted Bloom's theories to the Anglo-American framework. For instance, in *Atlantic Double Cross*, Robert Weisbuch argues that American writers began from a "defensive position" against "the achievements of British literature and British national life."[32] Such a defensive position was embodied in the writings of Ralph Waldo Emerson, who in an 1856 account of an exchange with Joseph Carlyle called Britain "an old and exhausted island."[33] In order to build a national literature, many American writers of the nineteenth century, found it necessary to do rhetorical battle with the idea of British greatness.

Whereas Emerson's attitude exemplified nineteenth-century American defiance and individualism, Henry James—and later T. S. Eliot—offered subsequent counterexamples. Unlike Emerson, James was fascinated by England, becoming a student of English mannerisms and ultimately a British citizen. At once anglophile and cosmopolitan, James embodies the transmutation of what might seem feelings of American inferiority into a complex, ambivalent embrace of Britishness. James prefigured the American modernist expatriates, many of whom came into their own as writers while overseas. T. S. Eliot, perhaps the clearest inheritor of Jamesian anglophilia, not only adopted British citizenship but also took on those English mannerisms that James scrutinized in his fiction.

Not all American expatriate writers followed Eliot's lead. Pound, who introduced Eliot to the London literary scene, has long been known for his early anglophile leanings; he's also known for promoting Eliot's literary Englishness by editing the references to America out of *The Waste Land*. At the same time, Pound ultimately rejected both the United States and Great Britain. As early as 1913, he wrote of Britain, "I know that I am perched on the rotten shell of a crumbling empire, but it isn't my empire"; by 1929, he wrote that he saw "no present need to think of

England at all."[34] At the same time, as Alex Zwerdling points out, Pound decried American commercialism.[35] The author of "Make it New" was invested in the old, but neither America nor Britain held the answers for him. He was nonetheless an insightful participant in narratives of both British imperial decay and American capitalist degradation. Gertrude Stein, who chose Paris (as did Barnes, Fitzgerald, Hemingway, and others), claimed France offered freedom unavailable in England, where, as Gerald Kennedy puts it, "history, culture, and language seemed all too familiar."[36] For Stein, at least, Paris offered an escape from the Anglo-American world and a defamiliarization of the language that many writers understood Britain and the United States to hold in common.

Virginia Woolf inadvertently revealed much about the question of the shared English language through a controversial exchange in *The New Republic* in which she suggested that British and American writers do not in fact hold a language in common. Woolf's 1929 essay in *The New Republic*, "On Not Knowing French," set off a controversy by offering Henry James as an example of a writer working in a foreign language, namely, English. Innocent of her audience's likely reaction, Woolf wrote the fatal line in her very first paragraph: "Thus a foreigner with what is called a perfect command of English may write grammatical English and musical English—*he will, indeed, like Henry James, often write a more elaborate English than the native—but never such unconscious English that we feel the past of the word in it*, its associations, its attachments"[37] (italics added). Naturally, after this, no one was much interested in the rest of the essay, which was all about French. Rather, the American audience of *The New Republic* was up in arms about the apparent slur to James's English and, by extension, to that of Americans in general. In a letter to the editor, a dyspeptic American reader asked, "I am interested to know what she considers the native language of Henry James—Choctaw, perchance?—since he came from the wilds of Boston."[38] "Choctaw, perchance" perfectly sums up both the anxiety and the defiance of the American reader—the antiquated English of "perchance" attempting to foreclose the threat of "Choctaw." Fittingly enough, James had in 1905 argued in favor of preserving the English character of American speech against what he called, "the inferior quality of the colloquial vox Americana."[39]

While it may not be the case, as *The New Republic* reader indicated, that Woolf embodies the "condescension" of the British toward Americans, Woolf reveals an important line of interwar British thinking about language, England, and America.[40] Other British writers had identified "American" as its own language, including Ford Madox Ford, who boasted that he spoke "the languages of Germany, France, England and the United States almost equally well."[41] Some

American writers also identified the "American" language, most prominently H. L. Mencken.[42] Yet Woolf is especially revealing in her characterization of the linguistic dilemma. Specifically, by linking British English to the past and present-ing "American" as a new language, Woolf sounds much like a figure with whom she otherwise had very little in common, F.R. Leavis. Woolf and Leavis both take the English language—*England's* English language—as a storehouse of sensibility, as a lifeline to the associations of the national past. In contrast (and in self-defense), Woolf lauds the newness of the American language, with its "power to create new words and new phrases of the utmost vividness." In Woolf's estimation, therefore, to "make it new" would not be to make it English. In order to explain why British modernism does not feel as linguistically radical as that of the American expatri-ates, it is worth remembering that for many in Britain newness seemed to belong to the Americans—especially when it came to the chief medium of literary mod-ernism, language itself.

Moreover, it is revealing that *Woolf* is the writer to make these claims. In contrast to such writers as Forster and Lawrence, Woolf ranks among the most experimental British modernists; from her 1922 *Jacob's Room* onward, Woolf dem-onstrated her attraction to newness, formal innovation, and the possibilities of language. Feminist critics have long celebrated Woolf's "breaking the sentence and the sequence," which is an adaptation of Woolf's own comment in *A Room of One's Own*.[43] It is therefore interesting to hear Woolf of all people suggest that American English embodies the new, whereas British English embraces the old. The debate in *The New Republic* came to a close with Edmund Wilson critiquing Woolf for holding a view at once too simple and too separatist; the final respon-dent—a British professor relocated to the United States—furthered this critique with a brief genealogy of American idioms, suggesting that they were in fact older than Britain's modern tongue.[44] What all of this hullaballoo suggests is that feelings about language ran high, feelings that also found their way, in distinct fashion, into the British public sphere.

The tenor of British discussions of American English had begun to change just two years before Woolf's essay when the United States released the world's first talking film. Not everyone saw *The Jazz Singer* (1927), which didn't, after all, have much talking in it. Yet as cinemas around the world hastily outfitted for sound, debates began in Britain—in newspapers, elite circles, and Parliament—about the rise of American English.[45] Newspaper editorials expressed fears that American slang might infect England, transforming the speech and sensibilities of chil-dren and the working classes. Members of Parliament worried that American English might supplant British English abroad, becoming the new lingua franca of commerce and undermining British efforts to educate its colonial subjects through exposure to British literature.[46] As Dorothy Richardson points out, British audiences were learning to speak "American" from screen titles even before the rise of the talkies in 1927.[47] By the time of Woolf's exchange in *The New Republic*, British debates about American English were reaching their peak, spurred on by legislation around the import of talking cinema.

1927, the year of *The Jazz Singer*, represented a critical moment in British attitudes toward American English, at the same time that it marked the movement into late modernism. In the late years of the twenties and the beginning of the thirties, Britain was retrenching for a number of reasons, including the aftermath of the First World War and the build up to the Second World War, the economic crisis of 1929 and the global depression that followed, and the weakening of British imperial power and the ideologies that sustained it.[48] Such factors—war, economic crisis, and imperial disenchantment—heightened British reactions to the influx of American English. Moreover, American English spoke directly to the chief medium of literary modernism: language itself. While it would be going too far to say that 1927 explains late British modernism—or explains its relationship to language—it is a factor that should be added to the explanations of late modernism's shifting character. It is therefore interesting to note that the literary works that deal most overtly with Americanization, and that invoke Englishness in response, tend to fall in the post–1927 period of late modernism.[49] This is not a hard and fast turning point: the topic of American English worked its way fitfully into British public discourse in the years before and especially following 1927. Rather, the rise of talking cinema in 1927 is one among many conditions of the period—but one that is uniquely able to galvanize other factors, bringing British concerns with history and tradition together with those about ownership of the English language.

It is telling that the great linguistic experiment of literary modernism transpired during the era of Americanization and the consequent rise of American English. After all, it was the special project of the modernists to explore how language makes our worldview and thus makes our world. British modernists such as Woolf made it their life's work to demonstrate how the English language carries the weight of its cultural history, and how it contains and circumscribes what we are able to know. The old world—the world of British sea power, of patriarchy, the world that marched its boys to war—this is the world that the English language unconsciously wrote and dreamed. With the rise of American English, it seemed that in unprecedented fashion Britain might cease to be the linguistic center of its language and might lose its colonizing hold on English itself.[50]

In contrast to other varieties of world English proliferating in modern times, many believed American English was poised to become a universal language and a new frame for understanding and expressing experience. Michael North has persuasively argued that those early twentieth-century writers who imitated black American vernacular helped to produce the "dialect" or sounds of modernism.[51] To this insight, I would add that many British writers, including those who didn't sound especially American in their writing, nonetheless recognized how American English offered an alternative manner of inhabiting the world. In this sense, anglophone literary modernism was doing what American English was also doing: reclaiming the language, unshackling it from its years of British imperial service, and rendering it anew.

Yet if the disruption and decentering of British English by the rise of American English echoes the breaking of language that is modernism, in the work of many British writers, it is precisely not a pure or clean break. It is not the dizzying newness of the futurists or even the language-play of a Stein or a Stevens. It is knotted up with longing for the past and often for a specifically English heritage, as becomes clear in works such as *Howards End*. British literary modernism seems in many ways to echo and to understand what was happening to the English language, yet it only partially *embodies* what was happening to the language. This strange creature, British modernism, neither fish nor fowl, has caused critics to question it even as they codified and produced it. For these reasons, British modernism's emergence in the early twentieth century looks different when we view it in light of the threat or promise of Americanization. Its struggles with both tradition and the modern reveal a dialogue with the new styles of power, language, and culture associated with the specter of Americanization and the rise of the United States.

The Entertainment Empire: Popular and Mass

Attention to Americanization, and its chief vehicle, the Entertainment Empire, casts new light on the long-standing debate in modernist studies over "high" and "low" culture and the proposed "great divide" between them. Ever since Andreas Huyssen, in his 1982 *After the Great Divide*, suggested that literary modernism defined itself against mass culture, critics have gathered evidence to the contrary.[52] So much valuable work has pointed out the connections and confluences between and among popular culture, mass culture, and modernism that it is no longer possible to construe literary modernism as the virgin in the tower, sheltered from the bustling world below. Such a picture of isolation and elitism, if it ever quite existed, has been thoroughly debunked.

Nonetheless, a valuable subfield of modernist literary criticism has been shaped by the attempt to close the great divide. In general terms, the aims of this subfield have been achieved. In order to see where this line of inquiry might go next, it is necessary to be briefly reminded of where we have been. While there are many ways across the great divide, critical work tends to fall into one of a few types. One category of such work focuses on the authors, demonstrating how they hoped for broad audiences, how they appropriated or imitated mass culture, or how they enjoyed popular or mass culture in their private lives (for instance, T. S. Eliot liked to listen to jazz). Another category considers works that either formally resemble a type of entertainment or thematically treat it; Langston Hughes's "The Weary Blues," for instance, does both. A third category shows us how mass culture imitated modernism, or should itself be called modernism, as in Miriam Hansen's designation of Hollywood cinema as "vernacular modernism."[53] Such work has been rich and useful; moreover, it has largely succeeded in undermining the model of the divide, in changing our minds about modernism's relationship to mass culture.

Still, in the introduction to their landmark assault on the great divide, *Marketing Modernisms*, Kevin Dettmar and Stephen Watt allow, "this is not to say that the notion of a great divide misses the mark completely."[54] In this remark, Dettmar and Watt acknowledge that while they reject the idea of a "gulf" between modernism and mass culture, neither is it the case that modernism and mass culture always enjoyed fruitful and unfettered exchange.[55] Bridging the cultural divide does not fully account for the complex relations, identifications, and disidentifications between and among modernist culture and mass culture. I would thus suggest that at this point in our critical history, it's time to move away from the great divide debates in search of another model.

I propose that while there was no full-fledged *material* divide between modernism and mass culture, the early twentieth century saw the development of *ideologies of division*, as embodied, for instance, in the use of the terms highbrow and lowbrow. As Melba Cuddy-Keane puts it, "terms like highbrow were conspicuous sites of ideological debate."[56] Indeed the terms highbrow and lowbrow, which both apparently migrated from the United States to Britain, came into general circulation in the early twentieth century.[57] Lawrence Napper argues that the later term "middlebrow" emerged in Britain as the sign of a complex relationship to "more obvious commercial popular culture (epitomized by American mass communication forms)."[58] A transatlantic framework can help us to see how this discourse of the "brows" intersects with fears about the debasement of British culture through Americanization. At first glance, American culture seemed to embody the "low-brow." From Hollywood films to jazz dance tunes, from the best-seller list to sub-scription book clubs, the United States seemed the source of or inspiration to much lowbrow culture in Britain.

While it was certainly the case that public figures tended to identify American media culture as lowbrow, this category contained both mass and popular culture. Although the terms "mass" and "popular" were not mainstays of early twentieth-century discourse, the two are crucial for understanding the period. According to Michael Kammen, historians must take care not to conflate popular culture, which includes such discrete, live experiences as a music hall performance, with mass culture, which includes such technologically reproduced forms as a Hollywood film.[59] These categories remain permeable: jazz in London, for instance, could take the form of popular culture, such as a dance hall performance (often played by British musicians) or of mass culture, such as a gramophone recording or wireless concert. Moreover, a concert could be popular (live) for one audience and mass (recorded) for another.[60] But despite this overlap, the general distinction between live shows and mass-reproduced media, between folk songs in the corner pub and a Hollywood feature at the Odeon, remained significant. Whereas *popular* cul-ture in England was largely the provenance of English performers, *mass* culture increasingly seemed to come from America.[61] This distinction allowed guardians of English culture, such as Leavis and Eliot, to display nostalgia for English folk culture at the same time that they decried American movies. In other words, it is not necessarily a contradiction that, as critics have noted, Eliot celebrated the English music hall star Marie Lloyd but largely dismissed Hollywood films.

Even the discourse around that most British of mass cultural institutions, the BBC, participated in the invention of the American Entertainment Empire. According to Paddy Scannell and David Cardiff, "The BBC became perhaps *the* central agent of national culture," broadcasting the king's voice at Christmas and keeping its listeners on a schedule of national holidays.[62] A series of talks on the "National Character"—otherwise known as the National Programme—came under critique for collapsing British national and regional differences under the banner of a limited, London-based Englishness. But as Scannell and Cardiff sug-gest, "These differences were again collapsed when confronted with the inroads of foreign cultures, and above all that of the United States."[63] One social commentator of the day warned that the BBC's monopoly would not necessarily protect it from "the Transatlantic octopus," of American investment in British performers, writers, composers, plays, and copyrighted music. "It is even possible," this writer declared in 1929, that "the national outlook and with it, character, is gradually becoming Americanized."[64] A commentator for *Radio Times* took his estimations one step further: "the American invasion of the entertainment world is responsible...for changes of taste, for the blunting of dialect...for new manners of thinking, for higher pressures of living, for discontent among normally contented people."[65] While the material influence of American culture on the BBC was significant but limited, condemnation of it ran high.[66]

Such attitudes reflected broader fears of the erosion of class distinctions in Britain. While it might seem likely that British reactions to Americanization would follow existing class lines, this was only partly true. The working classes and the wealthy alike danced to jazz and often watched the same Hollywood films. When the Prince of Wales praised Duke Ellington's music, he was exercising what Matthew Arnold might have called his barbarian prerogatives, at least insofar as the prince was a jazz fan.[67] As Wyndham Lewis put it in his 1934 *Men without Art*, "Americanization—which is also for England, at least, proletarianization—is too far advanced to require underlining."[68] For Lewis and others, Americanization threatened the class hierarchy by subordinating difference to a uniform culture of mass entertainment. The fantasy of the United States as a classless society helped to sustain this particular sense that Americanization might flatten social difference. Consequently, the threat of Americanization led some educated elites in Britain to profess their desire to save the working classes from themselves. According to one school of thought, the working classes in particular needed protection from their predilections for jazz and Hollywood. This impulse fed into the period's reinvention of the working classes, both urban and rustic, as symbols of a national tradition under siege. Resistance to Americanization became a recognizably elite position, one increasingly marked by its nationalism. Those who would preserve English culture bore the burden of protecting it from American influence.

Americanization and English Studies

Given the growing emphasis on global perspectives in modernist criticism, and indeed in literary scholarship more generally, it is curious not so much that the story of England in the American Age hasn't been fully, expansively told but that it hasn't been told to death. Why hasn't this tale become a banal and familiar refrain among literary scholars, part of the globalizing tendency in the field? Why hasn't the growing influence of the United States become a central narrative in British literary studies and among scholars of modernism?

The reasons for our critical oversight largely emerge out of what we are trying to see. Despite literary studies' vast and varied genealogy, the modern English department can trace its heritage back to the period of the early twentieth century. Whereas classics had been the discipline at the heart of humanistic study, the interwar period saw a transition from the study of classics as the badge of learning and scholarship to the study of English. Prior to this time, English literary studies had been peripheral at major English universities; at Oxford and Cambridge, it was hardly respectable as a serious scholarly pursuit. Although Oxford appointed its first professor of English in 1904, many there shared the feelings of a theology professor who opined that English study was for "women" and the "second and third rate men who were to become schoolmasters."[69] English was for those without a classical education, that is, those who couldn't read Greek.

In part due to a growing desire to preserve Englishness through literary study, elite universities began to shift from the languages of ancient empires to English. The figure most fully responsible for this democratizing impulse was someone who might, in other contexts, seem old-fashioned and elitist: F. R. Leavis.[70] Best known for his reinvention of English literary studies at Cambridge, Leavis was also famous, among those who knew him, for his repudiation of what he called "Americanisation."[71] While these two stances aren't often viewed together, they were very much of a piece. As I will suggest in chapter 4, Leavis's project of elevating English to its current prominence emerged in important part out of his resistance to Americanization. Leavis's reading practices aimed to help his students connect through language to their English heritage in part to protect them from the influences of American culture.

Although Leavis was the most influential figure to feel this way, he was hardly alone. Rather, his deliberate reconstruction of an English tradition through the study of its literature represented a broader impulse in English education in the years following World War I. If the war sharpened and deepened feelings of national allegiance and English pride, then it also laid a foundation for resistance to that other style of invasion coming from across the Atlantic. The growth of English literary studies in primary and secondary schools around the nation was part of a broader feeling that literature could save and preserve that which was ineffable: namely, Englishness.

It is somewhat ironic that the effort to protect Englishness from American influence would make its way across the Atlantic to inform the development of literary studies in the United States. Leavis's and his colleagues' development of English studies fed the New Critical project that emerged in the United States in subsequent years. At the same time, it was this linguistic focus that led the New Critics into what seemed their abandonment of history and national identity; categories that for Leavis were contained within the language itself. It would be sufficiently ironic if the story stopped there. What we would be able to see is an intellectual trajectory that buried its own history in its evasion of history; one in which the English language in the United States became an orthodoxy seemingly purified of its connection to Englishness.

Yet even during the height of New Criticism, or in the poststructuralist linguistic turn that some believe to be its theoretical extension, English studies in the United States never truly abandoned national history. Rather, these categories were naturalized into the structure of the discipline: its division into British and American literature. When nation reemerged as an explicit object of inquiry with the flourishing of such perspectives as postcolonial studies in the 1990s, there was a nation-based epistemology already in place: one that reflected certain dominant historical trends at the expense of others. This is what allowed Joseph Roach to decry, as late as 1993, "the deeply ingrained division within English studies between American literature, on the one hand, and English or British literature, on the other."[72]

The example of postcolonial studies reveals the impact of this divide with particular clarity. While postcolonial studies was arguably the most important development in literary scholarship of its day, it too, especially in its early forms, entered English literary studies through the division between British and American literature. This division led away from the idea that American influence might help to explain Britain's relationship to the idea of empire. Even the controversial application of postcolonial theories to the United States was not primarily an attempt to bridge British and American studies. While one of the benefits of the postcolonial perspective has been to bring an increasingly global perspective to British studies, the United States has often been left out of accounts of the metropole-colony dyad of Britain and its latter-day empire.[73] The inclusion of the United States can complement, broaden, and deepen attempts to understand British imperialism by reorganizing existing knowledge within a distinct geographic frame.

Twentieth-century literature, and perhaps modernist writing in particular, might seem the obvious place to look for cross-fertilization between Britain and America. After all, anglophone modernism was written largely by expatriates; as Terry Eagleton put it in an influential early work, the modernist condition can be characterized as one of exile.[74] Moreover, for decades the field has been called "Anglo-American modernism," the hyphen bridging and binding the two nations in a phrase that affirms their unity. Yet this very formulation, the hybrid "Anglo-American," is not an account of Anglo-American relations so much as an occlusion of them, a remnant from the linguistic orthodoxy that grouped literary works by their aesthetic characteristics regardless of nation. Neither quite the property of British nor of American studies, Anglo-American modernism has long occupied the seemingly undifferentiated space between the division of the fields.

Roach's lament over the epistemological divide between British and American studies was part of a broader movement in the field: the growth of Atlantic studies. Other disciplines rediscovered the Atlantic before literary studies did; transatlantic perspectives on eighteenth-century literature, for example, largely followed the models of historians of the period.[75] At the same time, Atlantic studies came to popularity among anglophone literary scholars in part through the efforts of sociologist Paul Gilroy, who in turn reflected work done by anthropologists.[76] Two scholars who notably bring an Atlantic studies perspective to bear on early twentieth-century British literature are Paul Giles and Laura Doyle.[77] Whereas Giles compellingly attends to the influence of Atlantic revolutionary concepts on Anglo-American relations, Doyle persuasively demonstrates the importance of Atlantic racial ideologies to the development of modern literature. Yet neither of these works focus on what I find to be central to Britain's changing self-conceptions in the interwar period: the coming of American mass culture and its symbolic service to the emergent American empire. I bring the broad impulses of Atlantic studies to bear specifically on early-twentieth century British writing by demonstrating that many writers of the period reconceived England and empire in reaction to the threat or promise of Americanization.

My inquiry into the Americanization of Britain is divided in two parts. In my first three chapters, which treat American imperialism, jazz, and Hollywood, I consider both the emergence of Americanization in the British imagination as well as the range of British responses. In my concluding two chapters, on the writing of F. R. Leavis and T. S. Eliot, I look specifically at how certain styles of reaction against Americanization began to develop into an aesthetic and cultural philosophy and even a ground for English studies itself.

. . .

By the time of the Cold War, it was clear that the balance of power between Britain and the United States had shifted. Not long after the British Empire began to break apart in waves of decolonization, Britain found itself sheltered under the American nuclear program, dependent on its "special relationship" with its former colony. By this point, Kipling's 1899 vision of the United States as a naive adolescent with little hope of attaining world prominence had fully given way to America's neologistic anointment as a "superpower." The rhetoric of the "special relationship" that solidified in this period rested not only on diplomatic alliance but also on the circulation of mass entertainment in both directions across the Atlantic. While the British may not have awakened one morning to find themselves turned into Americans, Jimmy Porter's feeling that such an uneasy metamorphosis was on the horizon seemed increasingly plausible.

The pages that follow consider the prehistory of this Cold War moment—not the fait accompli of the perceived "shift in fortunes" but the tenuous, shaky period during which it was unclear what the respective roles of Britain and the United States would become. At the moment when the Anglo-American shift in fortunes seemed at once possible and incredible, those in Britain who would reinvent Englishness gathered strength from their reactions against the new and sometimes terrifying manner of being-in-the-world represented by the United States. The writing of the period, and not least literary modernism, records and reworks these tensions and in key ways functions as their linguistic symptom. That is to say, insofar as British modernism came of age within a turbulent early twentieth-century modernity, it also took part in Britain's diminishing self-identification with the modern during the era of Americanization.

The American Century is, by most accounts, over and done with. What we can see by looking back, then, is that the answers to our questions will be both intensely particular to early twentieth-century Britain and broadly illuminating. They will tell us how an age arises and how it passes, how the conflicts of modernity shape our most intimate narratives of belonging and renewal, and what the coming new age felt like to those who told the stories that conjured it into being.

1. Ameritopias

Transatlantic Fictions of England's Future

Our future is very much bound up in America's and in a sense dependent upon it.

—H. G. Wells, 1906

The future of America is the future of the world.

—Aldous Huxley, 1927

America is the most interesting thing in the world to-day... [the Americans] face the future, not the past.

—Virginia Woolf, 1939

America as a space of future possibilities, new social orders, as utopia or dystopia, has long appealed to the world's imagination. Indeed, the very word "utopia" entered the English language through Thomas More's invention of a land inspired by the travels of Amerigo Vespucci. Whereas the Americas may have stood for the outer reaches of possibility in an earlier period of European exploration and colonization, the newly founded United States came to represent British imperial loss even as it also presented a model of democratic self-governance and postcolonial defiance. After the United States' declaration of its own imperial project with the Spanish-American War of 1898 and subsequent annexation of the Philippines, it seemed to some in Britain that this former colony might become an imperial rival. Rudyard Kipling's 1899 poem "The White Man's Burden" responds to the birth of U.S. imperialism with the assumption that America might prove a lesser

Britain—an upstart empire in need of guidance from its wiser forebear. Yet by the interwar period, Kipling's imperial confidence was no longer the order of the day. Rather, British writers displayed growing concern that the United States might usurp British power and offer a distinct vision for the future.

I suggest the term "Ameritopia" as the name for texts that imagine the future *through* America and the term "Ameritopian impulse" as the general recognition of the importance of the idea of America to the great thought experiment of modern times: the attempt to rethink nation and empire. Under the rubric of the Ameritopia, I consider a series of mostly little-known texts by well-known British authors—Rudyard Kipling, H. G. Wells, Aldous Huxley, and Virginia Woolf—from both before and after the First World War. While these texts range from an anonymous work of science fiction to Virginia Woolf's essay for *Cosmopolitan* magazine, they work through a shared problematic, one that leads them to imagine the future of Britain and the world in reaction to American imperial, technological, and cultural developments. These texts, and the general cultural impulses that sustain them, reflect the ways in which the idea of America serves British attempts to imagine and define nation and empire. In other words, the concept of the "Ameritopia" embodies the use of America as the raw material with which to dream the future, even if that future is sometimes a nightmare.

In construing the "Ameritopia" as a concept, then, it may be helpful to recall Fredric Jameson's suggestion that utopias are never pure fantasies. As he put it, "even our wildest imaginings are all collages of experience, constructs made up of bits and pieces of the here and now."[1] Jameson's insight speaks to the double nature of the Ameritopia as simultaneously the grounds for dreams of the future and for the more pragmatic, even urgent, concerns about the impact of Americanization and American imperialism. In the first case, America serves as a symbol mobilized by the imagination in part because of what it represents: a new world democracy, a postcolonial empire, a unique entity in modern times. At the same time, Americanization threatens to undermine local practices, individual tastes, art, and high culture. In this second case, it feels as if the world might not only follow America, but actually become America. In such a case, America ceases to signify a nation and becomes the *name* for the condition of modern times, often in pessimistic and even catastrophic terms.

If "the future of America is the future of the world," as Huxley announced in a 1927 essay,[2] then America might be understood in imperial terms to have taken up the project of colonizing not only space but time. Texts of the period variously represent America as interrupting British imperial teleologies of progress and forcing redefinitions of Britain's place in the world. Some of these narratives imagine the world inexorably becoming American, turning into what H. G. Wells called a "United States of Everywhere."[3] Variously anxious and enthusiastic, the texts in this chapter chart the movement from the imaginative containment of the United States within the ideological framework of British imperialism to the fracturing of that framework. Yet ultimately, the Ameritopian impulse in modern Britain is not primarily about America, at least not in the most literal sense. Rather, the Ameritopian impulse charted here is finally about Britain and England, Britishness and Englishness, and their imaginative production through and against the idea of the United States. Ever since there have been cross-Atlantic fantasies of America, there have also been Ameritopias. In early twentieth-century Britain, these Ameritopias acknowledged the increasing reliance of understandings of British imperialism and English nationalism upon the model, threat, or promise of the United States.

Fables of Development: London's Transformation

Early twentieth-century Britain saw a flurry of oddly utopian and determinedly dystopian writing about America. Books and pamphlets with titles such as *The United States of the World: An Utopian Essay, Atlantis: America and the Future, The American Invaders*, and *The Triumphant Machine* used the United States as a vehicle for imagining Britain's future development.[4] Marshall Berman has identified development as the principal paradigm of modernity: the driving, often tragic, force informing works from Marx's *Capital* to Goethe's *Faust*.[5] One British work of the period, an anonymous short story called "London's Transformation," imagined modern development through Anglo-American relations, describing a prominent strain of pre–World War I British attitudes toward American influence. Published serially in a scientific journal and almost completely unknown today, this curious story illuminates the prewar attempt to contain American capitalism and modernization within a recognizably British imperial framework.

A tale of development gone awry, "London's Transformation" channels and reworks a host of pre–World War I British anxieties about the United States. In the story, an American businessman undertakes the radical project of paving over the Thames, transforming London into a blissful, modern utopia. Roads for automobiles replace dusty paths for horses, the interminable London fog lifts and clears, and Londoners find themselves more prosperous than ever before. Over the course of the brief narrative, this same businessman returns to the United States, becomes president, and invades London under the slogan, "America to rule the world!"[6] The story thus charts the easy slippage from capitalist incursion to military campaign, presenting the American development of London as a kind of protocolonization that threatens to tip the transatlantic balance of power in favor of the United States. "London's Transformation" wrestles with its desire to see Britain profit from American innovation while preserving an idealized picture of Britain at the vanguard of progress. In this fable of development, Britain is caught in the bind of either becoming too American and thus losing its ties to its heritage, or not becoming American enough and symbolically ceding its position of global leadership to its former colony across the Atlantic.

Ultimately, the story establishes the paving of the Thames as an act of colonization in line with Britain's imperial project. It presents this new site for banks, theaters, and hotels as "another addition to our Empire, of more importance perhaps than the settling of an extensive new Colony... since the population of the reclaimed area was sure to become very shortly equal to that of a large Colony."[7] Here development is not only assimilated into the British imperial project but becomes the name for a style of colonialism turned inward upon England itself. This is a boon for the British Empire insofar as it gains a "new" colony on the Thames, but it is also an example of development on American terms. Significantly, the story takes the Panama Canal as its imaginative antecedent, referring to the American usurpation of what had been a strategically and economically important project of *British* development. Both the romantic English associations with the Thames and the pragmatic operations of nineteenth-century British industry become relics of the past in this narrative of American development as colonization.

The story's chief surprise—the transformation of the United States into a self-declared American Empire bent on conquering Britain—emerges out of a recognizable pre–World War I British attitude toward global power as imperial after the British pattern. Power may shift to America, but only if America re-creates itself in Britain's image, effectively displacing and becoming its imperial forebear. After a fierce battle between the newly established American Empire and the plucky Londoners who defend their city, the story closes with a British triumph that safely contains the threat of the United States and allows Britain to take ownership of its own modernization. The American businessman's daughter, Libertia, marries the prince of England, thereby becoming an allegory for the subordination of American liberty to British imperial values. Whereas America had seemed a "thankless child" in the throes of adolescent rebellion, it can now serve as a devoted, submissive domestic partner, sharing its wealth without pretensions to imperial power.[8] In this way, the story imprisons the past within the future, gesturing back to the moment when America and Britain were conjoined as a means to

manage the modernization transforming the present. This odd temporal derangement emerges out of the attempt to resolve the seeming crisis of Anglo-American
comparison at the beginning of the twentieth century. The real project of the story,
"London's Transformation," is America's transformation, because it is the United
States that must change so that Britain may stay the same. That is to say, for a
nation that came in the nineteenth century to symbolize development, progress *is*
stasis. The utopian aim of the story is to dream of a geopolitics where British power
remains frozen in a static vision of unending progress; a vision only made possible
by the assimilation of the burgeoning world power across the Atlantic.

Kipling, Imperialism, and Democracy

While Kipling's "The White Man's Burden" has been canonized as the embodiment of British imperial sentiment, it actually shares a great deal with such meditations on American power as "London's Transformation"; although critics don't
always emphasize the poem's transatlantic dimension, Kipling addressed this work
to the Americans after they embarked on their own imperial project in the 1898
Spanish-American War. Kipling pictures the United States becoming an empire on
the British model, essentially following the path of its more seasoned forebear.[9] Yet
unlike "London's Transformation," Kipling's poem forecloses the possibility that
the United States could rival the British Empire. It imagines the United States not
as a threat but as a youthful imitator whose very mimicry serves to underscore
the value of the British imperial project. A decade later, in a piece of speculative
fiction entitled, "As Easy as A.B.C." (1910), Kipling would take such disenfranchise-
ment of America even further by imagining a future world-state predicated on its
erasure of the United States. Kipling, who married an American and lived for a
time in Vermont, had ample occasion to meditate on the concerns of the United
States. In his pre–World War I writing, such meditation leads him to proclaim the
superiority of the British Empire to American mass politics. Both in his 1899 poem
and in his lesser-known 1910 story, Kipling relies upon the idea of America in his
attempts to contain world power within the logic of British imperial rule and to
critique American pretensions to a new world order.

   "The White Man's Burden," framed as something of a how-to guide for naive
American imperialists, is also an imperial coming-of-age narrative, a Bildungspoem
that encourages the Americans to seek their "manhood" in their colonial efforts.[10]
This imperialism becomes an unnatural reproductive project, whereby the nation's
"sons" are sent into exile and sacrificed to the development of the colony.[11] As the

poem intones, America must make ports and roads and "mark them with [their] dead."[12] Thus the newly developed colony, which should be a hallmark of modernity, becomes a graveyard for the sacrificial sons of the mother empire. Through the poem's structure of address, which alternately counsels and commands, the American Empire is deferred indefinitely into the future. At the same time, however, because the speaker's advice stems from British experience, the poem ensures that the American future will be a reenactment of Britain's past. The American imperial project, according to the logic of the poem, will always be postponed, a shadow of Great Britain. This structure allows the poem to envision American imperialism without ever presenting the United States as a true rival. Rather, according to Kipling's poem, the American Empire remains frozen in potentiality, undeveloped even as it is charged with the task of development.

Kipling's disdain for American pretensions to power emerges with particular clarity in his response to Theodore Roosevelt's reading of "The White Man's Burden." Kipling had sent an advance copy of his poem to Roosevelt, who was then governor of New York, before its publication in the American *McClure's* magazine and the London *Times* in February 1899.[13] Roosevelt, who would become known for his imperial ambitions, privately called Kipling's ballad "rather poor poetry, but good sense from the expansionist viewpoint."[14] Yet Kipling was not entirely enthusiastic about Roosevelt's American expansionism. In his autobiography, Kipling recalls meeting Roosevelt "not long after his country had acquired the Philippines, and he [Roosevelt]—like an elderly lady with one babe—yearned to advise England on colonial administration … I assured him that the English would take anything from him, but were racially immune to advice."[15]

Whereas "The White Man's Burden" features the United States as a youthful upstart, Kipling's curious metaphor presents Roosevelt as aging, infertile, and finished with empire. In contrast to the fecund maturity of the British Empire, the United States seems developmentally out of joint—both a bewildered youngster and a feeble elder, simultaneously inexperienced and exhausted. Beginning an imperial project that is already at its end, the United States is unable to consummate the dream of becoming a vast empire on the model of imperial Britain. While some in Britain imagined the United States to represent the future, Kipling's biting response to Roosevelt denies the United States not only a glorious imperial future but also the possibility of power in the present. The Americans may be newly burdened white men, but as Kipling takes care to specify, they are not Englishmen: they are distinct from the British and unable to shoulder the weight of an imperial present that perpetually belongs to Britain.

Given the curious derangement of linear models of time that the Ameritopian impulse seems to produce, it is perhaps no surprise that Kipling would write his cleverest Ameritopia as a work of science fiction set far in the future. Called "the finest story of the future ever written," "As Easy as A.B.C." is largely set in a backward, violent Chicago that has survived the dissolution of the United States.[16] Kipling's decision to erase the United States from the future, rather than to inaugurate its imperialism, may rest in part on reactions against increasing American pretensions to power in the decade since Roosevelt waxed enthusiastic about his "expansionist viewpoint." While this story neither imagines a terrifyingly dystopian future nor a blissfully utopian one, it nonetheless depicts an authoritarian world-state whose power rests in part on its suppression of the world's remaining Americans. Although the United States may have disappeared from this fictional future, the story relies upon references to the American past to produce its concepts of world power and the persistence of empire.

Set among the airships of the year 2065, "As Easy as A.B.C." introduces a world governed by the Aerial Board of Control, a capitalist oligarchy dedicated to protecting air traffic and trade. As the story opens, trouble arises in Chicago in the form of a public demonstration, and international members of the Board fly in from England to subdue the crowd with blasts of light and noise, justified by the motto "Democracy is Disease."[17] The true misfits in this global future are the inhabitants of what was once the United States: a cluster of democratic throwbacks who insist on living in shared quarters and on voting on matters of communal interest. These American criminals are taken aboard the airship and ultimately donated to the owner of a popular Earl's Court music hall so that their voting and democratic practices might provide fresh entertainment for audiences in a wholly privatized, future London.

While it might seem that Kipling's aim in "As Easy as A.B.C." is dystopian, and the labeling of democracy as a "disease" an ironic twist, the conflicted antidemocratic impulses of the story exaggerate Kipling's professed skepticism toward American mass politics.[18] In a 1908 essay about the United States, "Newspapers and Democracy," Kipling calls democracy "any crowd on the move," underscoring its potential for "despotic tendencies."[19] By his 1930 memoir, American Notes, Kipling states his hesitations more boldly: "They say the Democratic Idea will keep things going...I found one man who told me that if anything ever went wrong in this huge congress of kings,—if there was a split or an upheaval or a smash,—the people in detail would be subject to the Idea of the sovereign people in mass."[20] Kipling's critique of American democracy rests on this belief in the easy slippage from mass politics to mob rule.

"As Easy as A.B.C." responds precisely to such a belief in the American exaltation of the masses. In Kipling's imagined future, crowds have become illegal and abhorrent, the individual's rights reign supreme, and privacy is an unassailable value. Through a range of historical allusions, Kipling's story stages a widespread critique of the idea of democracy in America. In reaction to the horrifying communal voting practices of the American criminals, the Chicagoans chant a song from the time of the revolution that overthrew the United States: "Once there was The People—Terror gave it birth; / Once there was The People and it made a Hell of Earth."[21] This invocation of the "people" at once echoes and critiques the declaration, "We the People," and invokes the subsequent reign of terror of the French Revolution. Furthermore, by setting the upheaval in Chicago, Kipling is able to allude to the Haymarket Riot of 1886, a violent clash between workers and the police that became an international symbol of mass agitation.[22] At the same time, the story contains an even more pointed historical allusion. In Chicago, the Board members discover a veiled statue of a burning black body in the town's center, a tribute to the "time of Crowds." Kipling, who lived in the United States when lynching was common, was horrified by the lawless, racist violence of American lynch mobs. The statue, which shocks and sickens the Board members who unveil it, is a palpable reminder of the worst mass behavior of the United States: the perversion of democracy into terror.

In contrast to the dangerous but defunct methods of American mass rule, the new world order in "As Easy as A.B.C." seems modeled on the ideals and principles of the British Empire. Although Kipling's story does not explicitly present the British Empire ruling the globe, it imagines the new world oligarchy in terms that recall the British imperial values expressed in "The White Man's Burden." At the end of the story, the Board's decision to dispose of the voters, not by punishing them but by putting them on the stage, gestures to the British tradition of colonial exhibition. The Greater British exhibition of 1899, the Franco-British exhibition of 1908, and the Coronation exhibition of 1911 all presented large groups of colonial subjects performing their daily lives for the entertainment of paying visitors.[23] When De Forest describes his American captives, the producer of the Earl's Court music hall responds with the hope that they will bring in a profit by performing the rituals of democracy: "Do you mean they know how to vote...can they act it?"[24] Such a performance satirically presents Americans as colonial subjects, recalling earlier colonial relations between Britain and the United States. In the end, the story manages Kipling's anxieties about crowds by transforming democracy into entertainment and Americans back into naive colonial subjects. Whereas American mass entertainment would become increasingly threatening to cultural conservatives in the period following the First World War, in Kipling's prewar story, entertainment is the benign and disabling counterpart of American mass politics.

Kipling, who won the Nobel Prize in Literature in 1907, has been widely recognized as Britain's most influential imperialist author of the early twentieth century. His popularity and importance as a writer emerged in part out of the way that he provided his British readers with a language to understand their relation to the empire, schooling them in the fundamentals of the white man's burden. Insofar as Kipling was invested in teaching Britain its imperial ABCs, it was necessary for him to invoke and manage burgeoning American imperialism. Kipling does so in ways that epitomize the pre–World War I Ameritopian impulse to view the United States as a lesser Britain. Subordinating the United States with a temporal sleight of hand that imagines the American Empire only to foreclose it, Kipling's 1899 poem and 1910 story both reveal the narratives of arrested development crucial to the imaginative containment of a growing American power. Kipling wrote many other works in and about America, but these two Ameritopian texts demonstrate with particular clarity how a modern education in what it means to be British rested upon the deft rhetorical management of the idea of the United States.

Interlude: Woodrow Wilson and the Global Dream

Some periods lend themselves to the writing of utopias more readily than others. Historical climate and mood, Fredric Jameson observed, may encourage or dampen utopian energies.[25] Whereas the first decade of the century was fertile ground for such fantasies as "London's Transformation" and "As Easy as A.B.C.," the writing of Ameritopias temporarily subsided following the First World War. This shift stems not only from the exhaustion of war's aftermath but also from the emergence of a real-world, political Ameritopia upon the global stage. Woodrow Wilson, hailed by thousands across Europe as a "savior" and a "messiah" in the period immediately following the war, offered the example of America as a model of nationhood to the world's imagination. Through his fourteen points, and most notably through his principle of "national self determination," Wilson based his philosophy upon a vision of a future world composed of nations *like* the United States.

Of course, for such beliefs, Wilson has been called idealistic, a failure, and, quite often, a utopian. Yet whereas history may variously pardon or condemn Wilson for his global vision, there was a brief period in and following 1919 during which, through the figure of Wilson, the United States became a catalyst for imagining the future of nationhood itself. The beginning of the interwar period is thus shot through with the Ameritopian impulse—the possibility that the United

States might represent the real political future of the world—even as the textual production of imaginative Ameritopias temporarily subsided. The height of this sentiment can be traced to Wilson's tour of the Allied nations before the Paris Peace Conference of 1918, when he was greeted by a fanatical audience of two million in Paris, by ovations in Rome and Milan hailing him as "the Moses from across the Atlantic," and by overflow crowds throughout England.[26] Popular sentiment in favor of Wilson was so high that the French Prime Minister Clemenceau was moved to put an official end to "any more demonstrations in favor of the President."[27]

This Ameritopian impulse traversed the globe, prompting nations only tangentially involved in the war, as well as enemies of the Allies, to send emissaries to Paris in hopes of realizing Wilson's promise of national self-determination. Japanese colonies, such as Korea, and British protectorates, such as Iraq, expressed hope that their freedoms would be written into the Treaty of Versailles, symbolically etched into the new world order. It was to be a brave new world of Americas, of independent and self-defined nations. Of course, Wilson's ideals were largely incompatible both with the goals of the peacemakers and with those of his own country; the hopes of most applicants to the peacemakers were brutally dashed.[28] Yet these hopes had been made possible in part by a radical belief in Wilson as representative of the new, as a figure outside of old Europe, independent from the imperial politics of the nineteenth century.

When Wilson is called a utopian, it is usually a term of censure critiquing Wilson's idealist dreams of a new world order. The casual betrayal of those constituencies whom Wilson inspired was written into history as the peacemakers scrambled to assemble a document so baggy, encyclopedic, and monstrous that no single person had read it in its entirety before it was signed into doctrine.[29] If modernist writing, in Franco Moretti's conception of the "modern epic," contains and subordinates historical energies through its all-inclusive form, then the Treaty of Versailles—coming as it did just before *Ulysses* and *The Waste Land*—might plausibly take its place among modernist attempts to manage the crises of history.

While Wilson generated much commentary in the years following the peace conference, including John Maynard Keynes's scathing critique of what he saw as Wilson's economic naïveté, perhaps the figure who was most imaginatively attuned to Wilson's utopian function was the British science fiction writer, H. G. Wells. Wells was himself well-known as a writer of utopian and dystopian narrative from his early *The Time Machine* (1895). More so than many of his contemporaries, Wells was favorably disposed to the idea that America might embody progress and the emancipation of man from the bourgeois constraints of nineteenth-century

Europe. Nevertheless, in one of his many representations of the future, *The Shape of Things to Come* (1933), Wells decided to locate the origins of the future world state in Wilson's failed peace experiment.

In *The Shape of Things to Come*, Wells reveals an uncanny and thorough understanding of Wilson as an Ameritopian figure capable of seizing the world's imagination and providing an American direction for its future. Like other Ameritopian texts before it, *The Shape of Things to Come* plays with linear chronology. In this case, Wells imagines a historian from the future narrating the history of the present:

> For a brief interval Wilson stood alone for mankind...So eager was the situation that all humanity leapt to accept and glorify Wilson—for a phrase, for a gesture. It seized upon him as its symbol. He was transfigured in the eyes of men. He ceased to be a common statesman; he became a Messiah.[30]

In the conception of Wells's future historian, Wilson serves as a symbolic link between the bleak, war-torn present and a future new world order. Wells's text recognizes the symbolic economy in which Wilson has become an idea, like the idea of America itself, around which a range of hopes and fears coalesced. Wells's use of the historian-narrator, who identifies Wilson's ultimately failed program as the moment when "the World-State had been conceived," and hence the basis for the entire fictional future that the work portrays, also speaks to the sense of temporal condensation that accompanied the "brief" moment of Wilson's glorification.[31] This was the sense that Wilson was producing or conjuring the future before the very eyes of his bedazzled admirers. As Wells's historian relates, "From its beginning the American republic was a break with history, a new thing, far newer, having regard to its period, than the Soviet Republic of Lenin, and from its beginning it was failing to go on with its newness."[32] Like Wilson, America is saturated with the promise of the new; a promise that it at once invokes and fails to fulfill. America, like Wilson, represents the dream of a new world order but fails to bring it about, making its betrayal of history possible through its irresistible appeal to the imagination.

H. G. Wells and the "United States of Everywhere"

Long before he wrote his wry tribute to Wilson in *The Shape of Things to Come*, Wells had registered and was working through a set of decisively Ameritopian concerns. Whereas Kipling went to considerable lengths to imagine a future

without the dangers of American democracy, Wells seemed positively in favor of
the growing power and influence of the United States. As early as 1906, Wells had
announced that "Our future is very much bound up in America's and in a sense
dependent upon it."[33] After the First World War, when Kipling's prewar fantasies
of American subordination could no longer be fully sustained, Wells's writing displays a largely favorable recognition of the American movement onto the global
stage. In contrast to many of his contemporaries in the world of English letters,
who increasingly resisted the rise of American influence, Wells continued to see
the fate of the United States as inexorably intertwined with that of Britain and the
world.

Whereas *The Shape of Things to Come* traces the origins of a futuristic new
world order back to Wilson and America, Wells's lesser-known thirties novel,
The Autocracy of Mr. Parham (1930), specifically turns to the idea of America
as a means to negotiate and critique conceptions of Englishness. It is in *Parham*
that Wells brings his utopian political vision to bear on what he views as elitist
English cultural ideals. While this novel is not well known today, it made a suf-
ficient impression at the time of its publication to arouse the ire of F. R. Leavis,
who singles out *Parham* for critique at the end of the influential essay, "Mass
Civilization and Minority Culture." After all, it is in *Parham* that Wells denounces
English cultural elitism, or the glorification of so-called high art, as protofascism.
Moreover, Wells portrays the greatest threat to England after the war as its own
reinvestment in "tradition" as a national ideology. In contrast to this retrogressive
Englishness, Wells imagines America as the land of the common man through its
mass entertainment and its political democracy. Wells's novel, even more clearly
than Kipling's early tribute to politics and performance, connects the burgeoning
ideologies of highbrow and lowbrow to broader issues of politics, nationalism,
and the global future. In the end, he proposes a diffusion of American values—a
"United States of Everywhere"—as a remedy for the English elitism that he locates
in the years between the wars.[34]

Wells manages his critique of English elitism and its far-reaching political con-
sequences by rendering his novel in two parts, realistic and fantastic. In the first,
realist section, we meet a cast of characters including the novel's chief antagonists:
an Oxford don committed to elite aesthetic ideals and an English capitalist who
pokes fun at the don's hierarchy of taste. In the second part, supernatural means
transform this petty don into a dictator of considerable political power. The novel
then engages in the thought experiment of translating the don's cultural ideals into
disastrous public policy. After a world war that pits England against the United
States, the Americans offer to lead the world in a new direction, to abolish the old

prejudices of British imperialism, and to realize something close to Wilson's vision of global peace. The novel, which treats the American proposition as a genuine possibility, allows the United States to stand for a benevolent capitalism in stark opposition to the tyranny of the old world order.

The novel opens, rather strategically, in London's National Gallery, where the don, Mr. Parham, has taken it upon himself to instruct the capitalist, Sir Bussy, on the importance of art and culture. In a scene that establishes the novel's standing on cultural matters, Bussy wonders at the difference between popular pornography and the nudes of Velasquez. For Bussy, it is not the paintings themselves but the estimation in which they are held that disturbs him. Bussy desires a world freed from stifling European traditionalism. In a novel that ultimately validates Bussy and criminalizes the ambitions of Parham, the insult that Parham mutters behind Bussy's back—"he has no tradition"—is transformed by the end of the novel into an indictment of Parham himself: "Mr. Parham was traditional."[35]

The irony of an immoderately well-to-do industrialist, whose career is simply described as that of buying and selling, standing up for the taste of the masses does not seem to concern Wells. For the purposes of the novel, Bussy is the patron of the popular. Bussy's lack of tradition not only takes the form of his equal disdain for art and aristocracy, but also manifests in his elaborate parties which showcase jazz music. As Parham expresses his shock at the sight of a black American jazz band, "What would the Virgin Queen, what would her dear and most faithful Burleigh have made of that bronze-faced conductor?"[36] Jazz had come to England with the black American bandleader James Reese Europe during World War I; by the twenties, as Eric Hobsbawm points out, much of London was dancing to jazz music.[37] Here Wells notes the extent to which England's enthrallment to jazz disturbed traditional cultural ideals, particularly along racial lines. In this, Wells's *Parham* is a parody of a nationalist reaction, one that marshals English history against the country's musical invasion by black America.

Such a style of juxtaposition finds its uncanny echo in Parham's musings on Anglo-American political relations. Parham considers the matter:

> The Americans, particularly since the war, seemed to have slipped away, mysteriously and unawares, from the commanding ideas of the world...Renegades! What on earth had they better? What in the names of Queen Elizabeth, Shakespeare, Raleigh, the Mayflower, Tennyson, Nelson, and Queen Victoria had these people better?[38]

Parham's litany attempts to animate British heritage into an enchantment against America. These names, which anchor Britain in the past, transform Shakespeare into ideological protection against American attempts at international coalition such as the League of Nations. Although Parham dismisses the collapsing League of Nations as "Poor Wilson's dying memorial," he is deeply disturbed at the prospect of an American role in the new world order.[39] In this first section of the novel, it becomes clear that Wells would pit British capitalism, as epitomized by Bussy, on the side of American internationalism and against the nationalist traditions writ large in Parham's list of British historic icons.

After the novel establishes its concerns with culture and the state of society, it undertakes a more direct political critique. Through the figure of Parham, Wells connects cultural elitism to political dictatorship, contrasting the values of the old European order with a new American globalism. He manages this rather ambitious set of connections through recourse to the supernaturalism for which he is famous. In the second section of the novel, Bussy and Parham begin to attend séances; at one Parham is suddenly possessed by an extra-worldly presence who turns him into the dictatorial Lord Paramount. As Paramount, Parham soon takes over Parliament, remilitarizes Britain, and in one of his first acts as dictator, bans jazz music. His florid rhapsodies on the state of Britain as "this crowned imperial jewel" capable of sustaining "the mightiest tradition that had ever been hewn from the crucibles of time" turn the beloved traditions of a fussy, cultured don into disastrous national policy.[40] Parham's extreme nationalism is recognizably fascistic and seems modeled in part on Mussolini, who had become prime minister of Italy in 1922 and whom Wells caricatures here as the Italian dictator, Paramuzzi. In short time, Parham has convinced other European nations to abandon democracy for dictatorships to aid in his vague plan of attacking Russia. This plan does not come to pass, however, as Parham finds himself confronted by America, the nation most resistant to his renewed militarism. Parham warns his navy against "America which might do anything, which might even go 'modern' and break with history— even her own brief and limited history. The fewer years she was given to think before the crisis came, the better for the traditions of our old world."[41]

America as a threat to British "traditions" is the refrain of the novel, both in its realistic and fantastic episodes. Parham's great fear is that the British public will be swayed by "American peace propaganda," a thinly veiled allusion to the U.S.-based antiwar Kellogg-Briand Pact (1928).[42] Parham's militant general Gerson perorates on the capitalist reluctance for global conflict: "And the business men and the bankers are rotten with pacifism. They get it out of the air. They get it from America… 'Does war pay?' they ask."[43] Gerson suggests that if this pacifism keeps up, "you'll have the United States of Everywhere, and fleets and armies will be on the scrap heap."[44] Such a fear follows from the way that globalization is, in this 1930

novel, imagined to be world-wide Americanization. After Parham sinks a U.S. ship and conflict with America becomes imminent, even the population of Britain and the Commonwealth seems to favor American ideology:

> He was to discover how extremely un-British, British peoples could be. That realization of the supreme significance of Empire, of which Seeley and Kipling had been the prophets, had reached only a limited section of the population...Not only the masses at home, but the Dominions had drifted out of touch...These larger, vaguer multitudes were following America in a widening estrangement from the essential conceptions of British history and British national conduct.[45]

Here Wells records the fear that Kipling dared not name: the possibility that the United States could turn the tide of history away from the British Empire. In contrast to the imperial confidence of much pre–World War I writing on America, Wells's 1930s novel mocks Kipling as a misguided "prophet" of British imperial supremacy, blind to the coming of the American age. Unlike "London's Transformation," which focused on the threat of American military power, Wells imagines the very example or idea of America to threaten the "essential conceptions" of what it means to be British both at home and throughout the Empire. His reference to the Dominions plays on the fear of imperial decline that had become palpable by the thirties, and especially the concern that other English-speaking colonies and nations might follow the example of Britain's most powerful former colony. When Wells's fictional "Battle of the North Atlantic" ends in a stalemate with the destruction of both the British and the American navies, it sets the stage for a denouement in which Wells fully displays his ideals of a new world order. In contrast to the warlike traditionalism of Parham, Bussy and his fellow capitalists appear at the end of the narrative to announce the possibility for the future. As one character explains to Parham, "We are the workers of a new dawn. Men of no nation. Men without traditions. Men who look forward and not back."[46] The Wellsian new world, as imagined in 1930, is one that followed what it deemed the capitalist, globalizing tendencies already in evidence in the United States. Here America no longer names an individual nation but the very condition of being modern. It is a vision of the "United States of Everywhere," at least insofar as such a name signifies a future world-state based on a pacifist, postnational capitalism and the end of English traditions.

   It is this attack on English traditionalism that guides Leavis's prominent denunciation of *Parham* in his cultural critique, *Mass Civilization and Minority Culture*; Leavis sums up Wells's project: "In his last book, *The Autocracy of Mr. Parham*, he makes his butt, a waxwork grotesquely labeled, 'Oxford Don,' representative not only of tribal nationalism, imperialism, and The Old Diplomacy, but also of culture."[47] Leavis, who may see himself caricatured in the waxwork don, condemns Wells's project of linking cultural elitism with imperialist, warmongering political tendencies. Wells's charges against elitism in art and culture, in the form of *The Autocracy of Mr. Parham*, spur Leavis to conflate Wells with an icon of American anticulture: " 'History is bunk!' said Mr. Henry Ford. Mr. Wells, who is an authority, endorses."[48] Wells's attack on tradition in *The Autocracy of Mr. Parham*, thus earns him what is possibly Leavis's most potent insult, a comparison to Henry Ford. Much as Wells turns to America to imagine a world free from British traditionalism, Leavis draws upon an icon of American capitalism in his rebuttal. This particular battle for English culture rests on both sides upon the example of America, either as a model to be emulated or as a fate to be avoided. The political slant of Wells's dismissal of English tradition reveals the extent to which he believes its values to be aligned with those of a retrogressive political nationalism. Here Wells, unlike most English writers of the period, embraces mass culture, industry, and Fordism specifically as a program for future world revolution. Wells suggests that this system—one that won't fight unless it is convinced that war "pays"—will safeguard the future of England and the world. In Wells's Ameritopian future, it is capitalism that brings the revolution.

The Brave New World of Americanization

Aldous Huxley recorded his skepticism toward what he saw as Wells's endorsement of progress, technology, and the superiority of the masses by dismissing him as "General Wells" in a 1929 piece in *Vanity Fair*. In this article, Huxley deems the "the dignified aspect, the world-wide reputation, the high intentions of General Wells" insufficient to sway "the Muse of History" to the side of Wells's project of advancing society through technological progress.[49] Huxley's disaffection with the ideology of progress underlies an antidemocratic political philosophy that at moments recalls that of Kipling. Casting aspersion on the Wellsian faith in a "preposterous theory of democracy" which presupposes that "you can educate any shepherd boy into a Newton, an Alexander, a Raphael," Huxley sardonically notes, "we have had universal education for about fifty years; the supply of Newtons, however, has not perceptibly increased."[50] In a statement that sounds as if it might have been uttered by Wells's elite Oxford don, Huxley dismisses attempts to transform society by elevating the masses: "Everybody can read—so the old traditions have died, the local peculiarities which gave a savor to life are being ironed out."[51] While Huxley exaggerates his critique of the reading public, he nonetheless sounds rather like Leavis in this nostalgia for the "old traditions" and "local pecularities" being lost to modernization.

Huxley knew Wells personally—Wells had studied under Huxley's grandfather, the biologist T. E. Huxley—and saw Wells's belief in democracy and mass culture as a dangerous outgrowth of his scientific rationalism. Yet whereas Huxley disagreed with Wells's faith in progress, he shared with Wells a sense that the future of such progress rested with the United States. In his 1927 essay, "The Outlook for American Culture: Some Reflections in a Machine Age," published in the American *Harper's* magazine, Huxley presents American culture as the template for world culture:

> The future of America is the future of the world. Material circumstances are driving all nations along the path in which America is going. Living in the contemporary environment, which is everywhere becoming more American, men feel a psychological compulsion to go that way. Fate acts within and without; there is no resisting. For good or for evil, it seems that the world must be Americanized.[52]

In Huxley's analysis, "there is no resisting" the coming Americanization of the world. America not only provides a model for an impending world culture—"the future of the world"—it also makes the very idea of a world culture possible. The heterogeneity of the world's regions and cultures, as embodied in the local and the traditional, will succumb to Americanization, the only type of globalization Huxley presents here as truly imminent. Whereas socialism had made inroads into English working-class culture since the nineteenth century, American mass culture, from jazz to the Hollywood film, was increasingly omnipresent across the classes in the twentieth. Moreover, American culture served both as the symbol and as the product of the eighteenth-century democratic ideals that Huxley treated with such skepticism in his essay on Wells. In "The Outlook for American Culture," America ceases to refer to the bounded entity of the United States but instead becomes the name for a radical homogenization of the world.

While Huxley briefly lauds aspects of American progress in "Outlook," he also undertakes a critique that lays the foundation for his concerns about the influence of American mass culture in England. Here Huxley critiques democracy through a discussion of mass production. The "machine age," for Huxley, is one marked not only by mass-produced goods but also by "mass-produced ideas and mass-produced art."[53] Huxley identifies the "the rotary press, the process block, the cinema, the radio, the phonograph" as instruments of "vulgarity"; his conclusions, he insists, "must be obvious to anyone who glances at a popular picture, looks at a popular film, listens to popular music on the radio or phonograph."[54] As Huxley explains, "machinery makes it possible for the capitalists who control it to impose whatever ideas and art forms they please on the mass of humanity. The higher the degree of standardization in popular literature and art, the greater the profit for the manufacturer."[55] This dismissal of mass culture lays the foundation for a further critique of what Huxley sees as its logical extension: mass politics.

Like Kipling, Huxley takes America to exemplify the worst characteristics of a political democracy. "To pay respect to a king or a duke may be preposterous," Huxley contends, "but is it much nobler to pay respect to a millionaire?... In America anyone with the luck or ability to make money can claim the respect due to a plutocrat and can take his share in the governing class's power and loot."[56] The trouble with such democracy, Huxley insists, is its susceptibility to market pressures and its commodification of power. Expressing his skepticism toward democracy in America, Huxley proposes turning to other models that have departed from the hegemonic political practices of the West:

> With regard to political democracy, its disadvantages are becoming daily more apparent in America as in all other countries which have adopted it as a system of government... The revolt against political democracy has already begun in Europe and is obviously destined to spread. There will be no return to autocracy, of course. Government will tend to be concentrated in the hands of intelligent and active oligarchies. The ideal state is one in which there is a material democracy controlled by an aristocracy of intellect... The active and intelligent oligarchies of the ideal state do not yet exist. But the Fascist party in Italy, the Communist party in Russia, the Kuomintang in China are their still inadequate predecessors.[57]

While the future of America may be the immediate future of the world, Huxley preserves the hope that democracy will be supplanted by a system of intellectual oligarchy. Here his postwar hope differs from Kipling's prewar ruminations: whereas Kipling seems comfortable with a capitalist oligarchy sustained by technological advance, Huxley disparages both mass opinion and the mechanical dissemination of culture that he imagines to produce such opinion. Of particular interest, however, is the way that both Huxley and Kipling connect American democracy to mass entertainment. Kipling imagines American voters as entertainers while Huxley more directly laments the confluence of mass culture and the populist machinations of the state. For Huxley, mass culture and democracy both feed the profitable standardization of the human mind. Huxley can rail against "universal education" in his essay on the American machine age because he believes democratic principles regarding education to be of the same faulty logic that structures the machine age itself.

Although Huxley wrote eleven novels and numerous essays over the course of his career, he is best known as the author of a particular work, his 1932 novel *Brave New World*. Most critics agree that *Brave New World*, a glib, dystopian picture of assembly-line human engineering—what Huxley has called "the standardisation of the human product"—draws heavily on tropes of the United States.[58] As Adorno puts it in a reading of *Brave New World*, "Americanism, the butt of parody, has taken over the world. And that world supposedly resembles the utopia... foreseeable in the light of technology. But, by extension, it becomes hell."[59] Adorno, who famously levied his own critiques of American mass culture, lauds *Brave New World*'s facility in exaggerating, and thereby making conspicuous, the hellish character of Americanization.

Critics are less quick to identify, however, the extent to which *Brave New World* not only indicts aspects of American culture, or of a world culture inexorably coming to resemble American culture, but also invents a version of Englishness in resistance. While *Brave New World,* as the title suggests, imagines a new world order, it is set only in the United States and England, with London standing as the prime example of modernized, Americanized society. Within this story of an American future for England, Huxley situates a second narrative that pits Shakespearean texts against the popular cinema and a system of values derived from such texts against the degeneracy of the future. Huxley's wry rewriting of *The Tempest*, from which his title is drawn, reinvents the relationship between England and the United States, imagining a values structure that has the potential to rescue the future from the horror of its impending Americanization.

In *Brave New World*'s largely Americanized London, the inhabitants spend in dollars and worship Henry Ford; members of the ruling class reverently intone Ford's maxims, such as "History is Bunk" while abbreviating the sign of the cross in gestural reference to his Model T. Workers not only toil on the assembly line but are literally created there through a system of biological engineering and social conditioning that produces rigid castes of manual laborers, elevator operators, and world controllers. The new society celebrates consumption and exists in a kind of self-consuming stasis in which scientific innovation, literature, history and the arts are all deemed dangers to social stability. In this new world, the arts have been replaced by mass entertainment, namely, the "feelies," a tactile cinema that recalls the "talkies," or talking cinema, that originated in the United States. Even the behaviorist social science used to condition the children of the new world draws upon theories considerably more popular in the United States than in England. While some of the names that have worked their way into the new society—Polly Trotsky, Bernard Marx, and Lenina Crowne—suggest a socialist heritage, private property and social hierarchy are very much the order of the day. In this early thirties work, Huxley captures the anxieties of anti-Americanization writers by developing a dystopian future for England in large part through a venomous satire of American capitalism and entertainment.

The sole social space at odds with Huxley's world-state is paradoxically located in America, on a Zuni reservation in New Mexico. This space not only harbors what D. H. Lawrence and other modernists saw as humanizing rituals, but it is also the repository for the novel's primary sign of English heritage, a copy of the complete works of William Shakespeare.[60] In the work's main plot twist, two of its protagonists, Lenina and Bernard, travel by rocket ship to New Mexico to visit the Zuni reservation where they are shocked to discover John, the white son of an abandoned Englishwoman. Born on the reservation, John is a study in socialization and particularly in the socialization that results from different literary and cultural forms. After John happens upon a copy of the complete works of Shakespeare during his childhood, he absorbs its idiom. Faced with a local man, Popé, who has taken to John's mother's bed, John becomes aware of his feelings through the filters of Shakespearean phrase:

> He hated Popé more and more. A man can smile and smile and be a villain. Remorseless, treacherous, lecherous, kindless, villain. What did the words exactly mean? He only half knew. But their magic was strong somehow and went on rumbling in his head, and somehow it was as though he had never really hated Popé before; never really hated him because he had never been able to say how much he hated him. But now he had these words.[61]

Here the Shakespearean text does not merely name John's hate for Popé, but actually produces it, in Lacanian fashion, by bringing it into the symbolic. Through this production and naming of his emotions, John is socialized into the Western cultural tradition. In a swift Oedipal transition from Popé to pater, John attacks the man in his mother's bed, is made to cry, and runs away in shame. Rather than suggesting that such behavior is natural, *Brave New World* marks it as utterly cultural, the product of socialization via Shakespeare. John becomes a walking repository of Elizabethan English: he arrives in the "brave new world" of Fordist London quoting *The Tempest*, he tries to woo Lenina after *Romeo and Juliet*, and he ends up hanging himself a day after muttering discontinuous lines from *Hamlet*.

When John meets with one of the World Controllers, Mustapha Mond, near the work's end, he stubbornly makes his statement of value: "All the same, *Othello*'s good, *Othello*'s better than those feelies."[62] Mond, one of the few moderns left who has read the prohibited plays, responds, "But that's the price we have to pay for stability. You've got to choose between happiness and what people used to call high art. We've sacrificed the high art. We have feelies and the scent organ instead."[63] In this imaginary future moment, Shakespeare becomes "what people used to call high art." The retroactive style of this naming recalls the musings of Leavis in the thirties, who noted that Shakespeare's plays were not "high" in Elizabethan times but became so in the movement toward modernity.[64] In a future of mass entertain-ment, Shakespeare's plays are not simply "high" but "what people used to call high art." Shakespeare thus stands as the name for the *practice* of according literary value. Moreover, literary value serves a particular socializing function that mirrors the new world's behaviorism. Whereas the inhabitants of the new world, condi-tioned in their behaviors and beliefs, are utterly the products of the machine, John, socialized in the ideals of freedom, individualism, and free will, is the product of *The Complete Works of William Shakespeare.*

It appears that while the machine takes away humanity, high culture superadds it. John is not a natural man, raised among Rousseauian savages, although he is referred to as "the Savage," or even "Mr. Savage," throughout. While the text takes care to distinguish high culture from the machine world of the future and literary sensibility from the "Ford mind" of the masses, John's socialization follows the form of the industrial production of humans. In fact, John behaves much like the inhabitants of England's brave new world but with a different script: while Lenina reiterates the conditioning rhymes played during her sleep as a child, John uses Shakespearean quotes to direct his decisions, produce his feelings, and place an interpretive framework upon the world. Much as Lenina turns to the rhymes in moments of perturbation or crisis, so John relates seeming inconsistencies back to the Shakespearean ur-text of his socialization. While it is clear that Huxley wished to present the dangers of a machine-based, behaviorist future, it is curious how deeply a conditioning model of behavior has saturated his work. It appears that *Brave New World* would suggest "high culture" as a cure for machine culture, not as a liberation from behaviorist conditioning, but as conditioning with alternative content. While the text has John rhapsodize on free will—"I want poetry, I want real danger, I want freedom, I want sin ... I'm claiming the right to be unhappy"—it simultaneously presents his desires as the effects of his reading.[65] When *Brave New World* makes the claim for "high culture" as protection against machine culture, it offers a behaviorist account of the value of high culture, suggesting not only that

Shakespeare is the name for the production of value, but also that such value lies in the ability to produce a particular kind of emotional and reasoning subject. In his famous dystopia, Huxley thus does not decry conditioning as much as he offers English tradition, embodied by Shakespeare, as its proper content.

Although British imperialism has long proceeded under the banner of progress, in *Brave New World* it tacitly becomes the nostalgic symbol of British history and tradition. Huxley's inversion of England and America—London deifies Ford and spends in "dollars" while New Mexico houses the complete works of Shakespeare— may well have mirrored the growing sense that Britain was ceding its place in the international vanguard to its former colony across the Atlantic. If "the future of America is the future of the world," as Huxley announced in his 1927 essay, then America can be understood in imperial terms to have taken up the project of colo- nizing not only space but time: the very future itself. In *Brave New World*, Huxley's creation of an Americanized future generates a vision of a defiantly English history, one that conflates high culture with a high imperial moment. Huxley's rejection of Wellsian progress thus stems from his vision of an Englishness that can no longer name the future and so has become the sign for the traditions of the past. In so doing, *Brave New World* reveals the extent to which, for Huxley, the idea of English tradition is produced in reaction to the threatening spread of Americanization.

Virginia Woolf's Cosmopolitan Nationalism

Near the end of the thirties, Virginia Woolf wrote a very different kind of Ameritopia, one that reflects and reworks much of the Ameritopian impulses of the earlier part of the century. Her 1938 essay in *Cosmopolitan* magazine, breath- lessly entitled "America Which I Have Never Seen Interests Me Most in This Cosmopolitan World of To-Day," is more than an intervention in the ongoing debates about America's importance to British self-conceptions. Rather, it is a largely self-reflexive narrative that builds the history of the British Ameritopia into its structure. Working through the Ameritopian discourses of the first half of the twentieth century, Woolf does not only accomplish her stated task of imag- ining America and her slyer project of thereby imagining England, rather, she contains these tasks within a broader, metadiscursive formulation of British anxi- eties *about* the United States. As a sophisticated reader of her cultural moment, Woolf is able simultaneously to ironize British tendencies to transatlantic contrast and to exploit them for their revelatory power in providing a new picture of what Britain may become.

While Woolf never visited the Americas, they represented an imaginative touchstone for her from her first novel, *The Voyage Out* (1915). In *The Voyage Out*, set in large part at a British tourist colony in Brazil, Woolf participates in a broader British history of viewing the New World as a blank canvas for exploring new social orders. While *The Voyage Out* is neither utopia nor dystopia, it uses the utopian technique of displacement, transferring its subjects to a famously inaccurate New World landscape to throw their idiosyncratic Britishness into relief. In her 1938 essay on the United States, Woolf again depicted an American space as a stark contrast to the Old World of England and the British Empire. By this late date, Woolf had become self-conscious about the act of imagining America in order to imagine Britain and was keenly aware of the Anglo-American lockstep whereby a vision of the first necessarily produces, shadows, or reveals the second.

In response to *Cosmopolitan*'s query, "What interests you most in this Cosmopolitan world of to-day"? Woolf answers, at the essay's outset, in decisively Anglo-American terms:

> That is an enormous question; the world is a very large object, buzzing and humming on every inch of its surface with interesting things. But if we compress and epitomize this essence and abstract of the world and its interesting things reduces itself undoubtedly to the United States of America. America is the most interesting thing in the world to-day. But what, if you have never been to America, does America mean to you? What does it look like, and the Americans themselves—what are they like? These are questions that the English marooned on their island are always asking of Imagination.[66]

Whereas Kipling invents a global future in which America has become a powerless backwater, Woolf, writing twenty-six years later, reduces the global to America itself. Rather than an expansive model of an empire upon which the sun never sets, Woolf compresses "this essence and abstract of the world" to the United States. Even more telling is Woolf's choice of the word, "epitomize." By one definition "to contain in a small compass," the word, "epitomize," signals the extent to which America is serving as synecdoche for the world.[67] It is no longer necessary to send one's ships to the farthest edges of the earth, but rather to accumulate the fascinating objects of technology and progress within one's national boundaries. England is not quite a sinking island, in Hugh Kenner's phrase, but one on which the English are "marooned," as if their ships have washed up for the last time on their own, inescapable shores.[68] The subtle shift in the rhetorical value of compression and expansion suggests that it may no longer be necessary to rule the waves as a ubiquitous imperial power to epitomize the interests of the world.

In her introductory remarks, Woolf also sets up her curious rhetorical strategy: she animates "Imagination" as the narrator of the larger portion of the essay set in the United States. In a description of her narrative methods, Woolf notes:

> And Imagination, unfortunately, is not an altogether accurate reporter; but she has her merits; she travels fast; she travels far. And she is obliging. When the question was put to her the other day, 'What is America like?' she gave her wings a shake and said, in her light-hearted way: 'Sit still on a rock on the coast of Cornwall; and I will fly to America and tell you what America is like.' So saying she was off.[69]

Woolf's use of Imagination as narrator is not only convenient, as it allows her to discuss a place she has never been, but also symptomatic of her broader reflections on Britain. Woolf's Imagination, while it purports to speak only for Woolf, serves also as the ironic counterpart of a particularly British cultural imaginary. In so doing, it variously absorbs, mocks, and extends British fantasies about the splendor and newness of the United States as well as the comparative retrogression of Britain. Woolf's use of this narrative "reporter" also recalls the earliest tropes of English utopian writing: the use, as in More's *Utopia*, of an English visitor whose accounts of the New World necessarily draw a contrast to the old.

After crossing the Atlantic, Imagination will begin to display her comparative function. Announcing that "the air here is about a thousand times clearer than the air in England" and "everything is a thousand times quicker yet more orderly than in England," the narrator waxes hyperbolic in her study in contrasts. Landing in "The City of New York," which "has no houses" and "is made of immensely high towers," the narrator offers a vision of the American city as a futuristic new world.[70] In contrast to England, the American atmosphere is one of dazzling size, speed, efficiency, and homogeneity.

The essay not only imagines America as a world of the future, but pictures it as one that renders the British class system, and its reliance upon imperial social codes, old-fashioned and obsolete. Turning to a domestic American scene, the narrator imagines a classless society, in which traditional English social relations are replaced by technology: "Nor, although it is dinner time, does a parlourmaid in cap and apron bring in a silver-covered dish. A spring is touched; a refrigerator opens; there is a whole meal ready to be eaten; clams on ice; ducks on ice; iced drinks in tall glasses."[71] In the manuscript of the essay, which contains slight but telling differences from the piece published in *Cosmopolitan*, Woolf playfully presents American society as utterly at odds with English social hierarchy:

The Americans have swallowed their dinner by the time it takes us to decide whether the widow of a general takes precedence of the wife of a knight commander of the Star of India. And the servant never says Sir or Ma'am; there are no servants. Everybody is equal. That saves time too.[72]

Woolf's last three sentences above, with their class-bound affirmation that in America "there are no servants," were excised from her original manuscript by the American periodical, perhaps because of their too blatant inaccuracy. Yet it is interesting to note that in the preceding reference to the "Star of India," Woolf presents the English class system as a traditional throwback to British colonialism. By 1938, it seems, Kipling's "White Man's Burden" can be fully and imaginatively reversed. The colonial project is not capable of representing newness and expansion but rather has become traditionalism. Thus the "wife of a Knight Commander of the Star of India" is an identifiable class position in Woolf's parodied England, although ambiguous enough in its precise social value to delay the settings for dinner. The fantasy that in America "there are no servants" overlooks American history and social relations, producing America as an *effect* of comparison to England.

Woolf's "America" essay disrupts a double script of British imperialism: the geographic model of expansion and the temporal model of linear progress. From cities and houses Imagination reaches the country, and here the essay begins its derangement of time. "We are in the country," Imagination avers, "but the country is not like England, or Italy, or France. It is a primeval country; a country before there were countries. The space is vast; mountains rise; plains spread."[73] The American countryside, Woolf's imaginative narrator explains, is not nationally a "country" like England, France, or Italy; it is a primeval space that exists concurrently with America's hypertechnologized city. Indeed, the ruins of this primeval plain are not, as the narrator points out, "Saxons burial grounds, Roman camps" but the "skeleton of an old motor car."[74] This is a country before countries, which even in its utter prehistoricism, represents the future. The technologized present is laid waste on the vast primeval countryside; the innovations that have made America so interesting are momentarily subordinated to the scale of the uncivilized, undeveloped land. The description of the countryside writes a vision of America as a wild, primeval land littered with the relics of technological advance into a national script about present, past, and futures. A technological advance, such as the automobile, can also be the relic or skeleton of what is already past, a primeval, prenational landscape. Here the ruin, the Benjaminian mark of allegory, is made decisively modern.[75] Time does not proceed in narrative sequence in Woolf's American landscape; rather, America itself is capable of postulating a new notion of time, one that inserts the present into ancient history.

The narrative moreover seems to view the confluence of England's past and America's future *as* the confluence of English literary heritage and American cultural practices. After crossing over the hill that represents the "future" and arriving in a modern city, Imagination recounts:

> But that immense building which might be a factory or a cathedral—what is that? It occupies a commanding position. In England it would be the King's palace. But here are no sentries; the doors stand open to all. The walls are made of stainless steel, the shelves of unbreakable glass. And there lie Shakespeare's folios, Ben Jonson's manuscripts, Keats' love letters blazing in the light of the American sun.[76]

As in Huxley's *Brave New World*, Shakespeare has been relocated to America. Yet in this case, the original documents of English letters—as represented by Shakespeare, Jonson, and Keats—appear in the modern, public space of the American library. This transference, in its way, represents the ultimate horror of the Americanization of English culture: here England's cherished literary heritage—in manuscripts and folios rather than copies—is turned over to the democratic archive. The blazing American sun both illuminates and destroys Britain's heritage as it becomes, like a film of *Romeo and Juliet*, the property of the masses. Melba Cuddy-Keane has called Woolf a "democratic highbrow," a self-conscious elitist who variously endorsed and spurned modern mass culture.[77] Here Woolf self-consciously reworks fears and anxieties about the fate of Britain's heritage in light of the rise of U.S. mass culture such as those visible from Kipling to Huxley. And like Kipling and Huxley, Woolf too situates this cultural effect within a political framework: the American library has replaced, not a private collection, but an Old World political entity, the king's palace. The library can replace the palace, in the article's momentary tribute to the future, because American cultural practice can so easily be imagined to merge with American democratic ideals.

Whereas Kipling would contain democratic impulses by converting them into popular performance, Woolf locates original documents of English literature not only in America, but within what are imagined to be egalitarian American cultural practices. The American library replaces the palace of the English king because American cultural practice is itself imagined as an assault on feudalistic political structures. The future of America is not only that of technological advance, but of a public culture that threatens to usurp England's literary heritage, detaching it from English soil, and displacing what Walter Benjamin refers to as the "aura" of the work of art.[78] In Benjamin's terms, mass cultural forms like the cinema are unable to generate the aura that he attributes to original, unreproduced works. This disappearance of the aura, according to Benjamin, is one sign of the movement toward a mass culture with revolutionary potential. While the documents housed in the archive of glass and steel are original, rather than mass produced, they participate in a mass cultural logic through their newfound availability to the American public. In the Americanized future, Woolf's essay calmly prophecies, English literary culture may no longer belong to England.

In ways that recall the nonlinear time of *Brave New World*, Woolf's essay further interweaves American and English history. As the narrator recounts: "This valley is like a cup into which time has dropped and stands clear and still. There is the England of Charles the First, still visible, still living in America. In her broad plains and deep valleys America has room for all ages, for all civilizations."[79] The invocation of Charles the First, who ruled England and Scotland in the early seventeenth century, briefly recalls America's past as a British colony. Although it invokes stereotypes of an American Indian wielding a "tomahawk" and wearing "eagle feathers"—an image picked up in the accompanying drawing provided by *Cosmopolitan*—the essay does not dwell upon the myths of England's colonization of the Americas, turning swiftly from the past to the future.[80] In America's landscape, time is geologically stratified. Not only is the primeval plain littered with the remains of America's technologized present, but it also keeps England's past "still living." America as the compression of the world's interesting things is also a compression of epochs into one synchronous body: "from this extraordinary combination and collaboration of all cultures, of all civilizations will spring the future."[81] Primeval newness and European heritage serve only as material, as if America were the laboratory for the development of the future as such. In the final word of Imagination's reporting, she explains, "That is what makes them the most interesting people in the world—they face the future, not the past."[82]

The newness of Americans, their future-facing capacity, stands in contrast to a simultaneous scene in England: "While she [Imagination] had been to America and back, one old woman had hobbled across a field and filled her basket full of dead sticks for her winter's firing."[83] Here Imagination has already nestled back into her Cornish rook; Woolf's own narrative voice offers this bleaker, more English vision. It is hardly a future-facing image: hobbling and filling a basket with a lifeless redundancy, "dead sticks." Moreover, this scene is rural and preindustrial. In contrast to America's machine age, it is retrogression itself. A caricature of English country life, the old woman behaves as an allegory for hoary England. England's past has been transferred to America's primeval forests, England's manuscripts to America's libraries, and the future waits for America's advance.

In this closing section, Woolf presents America not so much as place, but as a particular relationship to time. She does not simply equate America with the modern, or with "an up-to-date city," as her entanglements with cosmopolitanism might suggest.[84] Rather, while life in England proceeds apace, like an old woman gathering firewood, America appears to have been visited by the angel of history. America in Woolf's essay simultaneously contains "all ages" and "all civilizations" in a near Benjaminian vision of synchronous time.[85] Past and present are radically rearranged under the prophecy of the coming, global future. To view Woolf's chronos in Benjaminian terms, the messiah here *is* technological innovation and progress, the intended offspring of skyscrapers, perambulating rails, and a society turned classless not by revolution, but by refrigeration. Little England, allegorized as an elderly woman storing dead sticks for the long winter, has hardly a breath left in her.

Woolf catches the feeling of the modern compression we now associate with globalism in her treatment of America as the epitome of the world—in contrast to the altogether different feeling of the wide open seas upon which the British Empire rolled forth. In this way, Woolf's "America" essay fully revises the Atlantic journey of *The Voyage Out*. Whereas her earlier novel was very much situated within a British imperial framework, even as it challenged aspects of imperial conventions, the "America" essay recognizes and represents a new world order derived from the modernity of the United States. Britain's decline, Woolf's essay suggests, reflects its ties to a nineteenth-century expansionist colonial project and to the older modes of being in the world that such a project represents. While the protagonists of *The Voyage Out* cross an ocean and journey into the South American countryside, in Woolf's "America" essay, the English remain "marooned." Presenting England itself as a "desolate island" to which the English are condemned, Woolf reverses the literary—and indeed historical—trope of English sailors and prisoners marooned on distant, tropical isles. It is in the very language of high seas exploration and imperial adventure that England's inadequacies are ironically measured; the English are castaway on an island that has become primitive in contrast to the United States. As the term "marooned" implies, the English are stranded, lost, and exiled from the global future that is capable of proceeding without them.

Of course, this celebration of America's futurity was written for the largely American audience of *Cosmopolitan*. In its leading question, "What interests you most in this cosmopolitan world of to-day"? the magazine privileges the cosmo-politan—cities, technology, progress—at the same time that it exemplifies the

American mass media. Woolf was undoubtedly led in part to her playful metacommentary on American mass culture and the future by the very venue of her article's publication. Indeed, with her essay's publication in the American *Cosmopolitan*, Woolf brings English writing full circle from Kipling's meditations on America, both in her rhetorical undermining of empire and in her material participation in American mass culture. Whereas Kipling's Americans were imprisoned in a London music hall, here Woolf's oblique reflections on Britain's decline are distributed to the American masses.

What Woolf presents to these masses, in sly and elliptical fashion, is a repackaging of the concerns that prompted Kipling's tributes to endless British imperialism, Wells's transatlantic boosterism, and Huxley's anxious shepherding of Shakespeare. Whereas Kipling saw the United States as a weaker, younger Britain at the turn of the century, Woolf describes how by the end of the thirties, the United States has come to propose a new style of power. Registering a disturbance to the timeline that equates the United States with the future and maroons Britain in the past, Woolf offers an ironic performance of what modern British anxieties about America have become. Indeed, Woolf can write so cunningly about the United States without ever needing to visit because, as she well understands, by the late thirties Ameritopia exists nowhere as potently as in the British imagination.

2. Jazzing Britain
The Transatlantic Jazz Invasion and the Remaking of Englishness

Jazz tunes *are* our folk tunes.

—London *Times*, January 12, 1921

But jazzing in the Cotswolds!... Have these jazzing villagers no historical sense, no respect for the *genius loci*?

—London *Times*, September 5, 1923

When jazz arrived in England, the nation was on an imaginative precipice: both grasping after history and attempting to bury it, haunted by terrible loss and eager to forget it in a frenzy of music and dance. During the First World War, an all-black American army infantry band had introduced Europe to jazz; thereafter, jazz seemed to promise all the pleasures that had been stifled in wartime.[1] In this tenuous period of national redefinition, when it seemed unclear what England would become, jazz swept the nation in an unprecedented tide of popularity, becoming the music of the war-torn generation. Repeated references to jazz songs as the "folk tunes" of the English people reveal just how strange and singular this state of affairs was. A 1926 cartoon in *Punch* satirizes the uncanny role of jazz dance as the new favorite pastime of rustic England (see Figure 2.1). By 1927, the British writer R. W. Mendl did not hesitate to deem jazz "the folk music" of the nation.[2] While English folk culture in its very definition should come from the English people, the countryside, and the land itself, this new music came from

Figure 2.1 "Do You Have Any Folk-Dancing," *Punch*, August 25, 1926 (200). Folk-lore Enthusiast: "Do you have any folk-dancing down here?" Villager: "Lor bless 'ee, yes, sir. Lots on' em jazzes every night up at the Blue Bull."

America and, even more shockingly to some, was largely the product of black Americans. For the first time in modern memory, England's folk music was no longer quite English.[3]

For this reason, jazz provoked enormous resistance on the part of those who saw in the music an end to England's distinctive national character, to the organicism of its pleasures, leisures, and pastimes, and to the urgent interwar desire for a national culture. A 1923 lament in the *Times* of London—"Have these jazzing villagers no historical sense"—reflects the feeling that English heritage was under siege.[4] Part of the trouble with jazz, for those who watched with horror as its popularity spread, was that jazz could modernize England out of itself, rendering its pastimes identical to those enjoyed in America as well as France, Italy, and even Germany. Europeans too had a range of reactions to jazz, from the delighted swoon of the French surrealists to the universal ban on jazz in Nazi Germany. In Britain, varying reactions to jazz reflected the broader history of Americanization, developing into a conflicted love-hate relationship with American jazz. The British musician's union agitated long and hard for a ban on American jazz performance—a ban finally put into place in 1935[5]—but this was not because they disliked jazz. Rather, they wished to play the jazz exclusively themselves, to make it British, to make a new home for themselves in the music. Yet the more jazz's aficionados pledged their faith to this new folk culture, the more anti-jazz elites determined that jazz could destroy British culture. As one British periodical summarized the debate as early as 1919, "The world these days seems to be dividing itself into two camps—the pro-jazzers and the anti-jazzers. To Jazz or not to Jazz—that is the question."[6]

Jazz rapidly—even shockingly—transformed British culture by creating what Eric Hobsbawm called, "a new epidemic of mass social dancing."[7] Spanning a range of overlapping styles, from foxtrot to blues, "hot" and "dirty" jazz to swing, the music moved the bodies of its listeners, who most often were also dancers.[8] Public dance proliferated throughout Britain as if overnight; according to one account, almost eleven thousand dance halls and nightclubs opened in the first half of the 1920s.[9] Even at home, young Britons planned dance parties around wireless broadcasts and gramophone recordings.[10] Jazz shook their hips and led their feet in quick, intricate patterns. It fed the new, minimalist fashions for women—including the shorter, flimsier dresses that lent greater intimacy to couples dance. Moreover, jazz dance crossed class lines. Whereas prior to 1918 "public dancing" was a mark of the well-to-do, it soon became an obsessive pursuit of all the classes, most notably the working and lower-middle classes.[11] At the same time, the sexualized fervor of some jazz dance motivated racial fantasies, such as those that characterized Josephine Baker's performances in Paris in her infamous banana skirt. Jazz often seemed dangerous, foreign, sexualized, and racialized—the *Times* variously called it "noise," "the plague," and "madness"[12]—at the same time that it was a pervasive aspect of interwar British culture.

As the contest over the jazz invasion raged in English newspapers and periodicals, in drawing rooms and public houses, the debate turned jazz into a metaphor for the modernization of England. Literary texts of the period thus not only take sides in the debate but register jazz's figurative nature, turning to it time and again as a means to work through a series of conflicting discourses about the fate of national identity. While it may seem surprising for writers to turn to American jazz music to explore the interwar crisis of Englishness, it was precisely because jazz invoked so many competing discourses—art and entertainment, whiteness and blackness, England and America—that it served this end so well. Endlessly mobile and transgressive, crossing the boundaries of race, class, and nation, jazz fed England's burgeoning crisis of national insularity by failing to be insular. At the same time, the equally transgressive character of jazz as high art and lowly entertainment prompted the reorganization of thinking about art and culture. As Bloomsbury writer Clive Bell lamented in a 1921 essay, jazz music might spell the end of high cultural "traditions" and the discriminating taste

American. "Do I like dancing the Charleston? B'lieve me, Hostess, St. Vitus is my patron saint."

Figure 2.2 "Do I Like Dancing," *Punch*, July 7, 1926 (27). By 1926, Americans were famous for their dance antics.

APPRECIATION.

Important Lady (doing her best, to distinguished pianist who has been discoursing Chopin for the last hour). "CHARMING—DELIGHT-
FUL—SO RESTFUL! SUCH A PLEASANT CHANGE FROM JAZZ—FOR ONCE IN A WAY."

Figure 2.3 "Charming," *Punch*, February 24, 1926. The music of Chopin proves "a pleasant change from Jazz—for once in a way."

that sustains them.[13] Other writers, such as Elizabeth Bowen, W. H. Auden, and Virginia Woolf, turned to jazz to explore the decline of British imperialism and the consequent rise of little Englandism. Nancy Cunard embraced jazz's transatlantic character while the postwar writers, Philip Larkin and Kingsley Amis, tried to understand what it would mean for jazz to become truly British. Much more than the background music of modernity, jazz in these various writers' conceptions provides a means to explore what is happening to England and a language to name the crisis that overtakes the nation in the years after the First World War.

Jazz and Nationalism: W. H. Auden, Virginia Woolf, Elizabeth Bowen

In his 1936 poem "Letter to Lord Byron," W. H. Auden looks back on the twenties and early thirties, summarizing in a few lines the way that jazz has come to symbolize the disruption of traditional ties to Englishness. According to its central conceit, the poem acquaints Byron, its ghostly poet-tourist, with the new world of modern England. Opening with a comparison between Byron and the American movie star, Gary Cooper, Auden goes on to insist that "John Bull of the good old days" has been replaced by Disney's iconic, "Mickey."[14] As he wryly apostrophizes the poet, "Which is the better, I leave you to judge."[15] This question of judgment remains crucial to Auden's description of modern England and the new transatlantic culture that is becoming its heritage. In a stanza in which he readily conflates Britain's political decline with the rise of American entertainment, Auden proclaims:

> Byron, thou should'st be living at this hour!
> > What would you do, I wonder, if you were?
> Britannia's lost prestige and cash and power,
> > Her middle classes show some wear and tear,
> > We've learned to bomb each other from the air;
> I can't imagine what the Duke of Wellington
> Would say about the music of Duke Ellington.[16]

In rhythmic understatement, Auden offers one of the thirties' starkest summaries of British national decline: "Britannia's lost prestige and cash and power." On the heels of this announcement, Auden presents a seemingly incongruous couplet on the state of culture, "I can't imagine what the Duke of Wellington / Would say about the music of Duke Ellington." This couplet, with its reference to the early nineteenth-century prime minister who ruled Britannia before its latter-day decline, brings the political energies of the stanza into juxtaposition with jazz. Here jazz signifies a break from the intertwined regimens of national power and nineteenth-century taste that the Duke of Wellington represents. While the references to bombs and lost prestige are blunt and unmistakable signs of the changes coming to England, the poem presents "the music of Duke Ellington" as the point at which its thought experiment breaks down and the speaker "can't imagine" the reconciliation of newness with tradition. Ellington's jazz, now inexorably part of the changed English landscape, thus becomes reliable figurative shorthand for the nation's decline from the time of Byron to the present day.

. . .

In a work published after "Letter to Lord Byron," Virginia Woolf's final novel, *Between the Acts* (1941), jazz again serves as the disruptor of Englishness in ways that seem more symptomatically modernist than Auden's glib tribute to changing times.[17] Nonetheless, Woolf is not the modernist who immediately comes to mind when one thinks of jazz. Whereas T. S. Eliot was well known as a jazz fan and Langston Hughes wrote his own version of the blues, Woolf has not inspired much critical reflection on what Alfred Appel calls "jazz modernism."[18] Moreover, her last novel, *Between the Acts*, with its pastoral, English setting, seems largely at odds with the kinds of cosmopolitan literary experiments influenced by jazz. Although *Between the Acts* may seem an unlikely source for the consideration of jazz, it is in this novel that Woolf reveals jazz's unique value to a critique of ideological Englishness. By the time she wrote *Between the Acts*, Woolf had absorbed and reworked the discourses about jazz circulating in interwar England. Jazz is useful to her exploration of English country life precisely because it seems so anomalous. At once foreign and local, exotic and ubiquitous, jazz threatens to transform the meaning of Englishness by *becoming* English.

A stylistic experiment of a new sort, *Between the Acts* presents the history of England as a pageant play put on by villagers on a country-house lawn, while also detailing those moments before and "between the acts" when the audience plays out other, more personal dramas. As one character notes, the pageant's "scenes from English history" are specifically those calculated to produce that nostalgic construct, "Merry England."[19] Yet the emphasis in *Between the Acts* on the interstitial and the fragmentary—the pageant is often interrupted, misheard, or unheard—belies the pageant's ideological consolidation of Englishness. While *Between the Acts* is precisely not, like some works of the period, saturated with jazz, it brings jazz into the pageant in a key moment that signals the disruption of a nationalist telos. At the moment that the program announces the historical pageant will enter "The Present Time. Ourselves" the gramophone switches to jazz.[20] While the audience rejects this jazz as "cacophony," the novel allows it to stand for the fragmentation of the nationalist discourses that the pageant otherwise represents. Although Woolf rarely makes reference to jazz in her writing—the single use of the word "jazz" in her fiction occurs in *Between the Acts*—her last novel relies on jazz in the formulation of what seems the metastatement of an experimental narrative, suggesting the potential for the modern music to interrupt a coherent mythos of patriotic Englishness.[21]

The pageant's gently comic tributes to England's past, from bumbling Canterbury pilgrims to a forgetful, stammering Queen Elizabeth, fill the stage to the sounds of that most modern commodity: the gramophone. Hidden offstage with the pageant's director, Miss La Trobe, the gramophone cues audience emotion with snatches of familiar recordings that change as quickly as the scenes. In a nineteenth-century scene, for instance, the strains of "Home Sweet Home" provoke the wistful ruminations, via interior monologue, of a Mrs. Lynn Jones, an otherwise unidentified character. Between records, the gramophone envelops the entire pageant with the blank sound of its machinations: "chuff, chuff, chuff, went the machine."[22] One character muses that the chuffing gramophone is "marking time," while another insists that time "doesn't exist for us... we've only the present."[23] The position of the gramophone as the sign of the present places it at odds with a pageant that is modern in its very nostalgia for an imagined past. The machine encodes the modernity of the moment, even as it masks it with archaic songs and patriotic hymns. The gramophone thus both musically accompanies "merry" English history and provides a machine-age reminder of the incommensurability of the present moment with mythic narratives of the past.

When the pageant finally reaches what the program calls "Present Time," the gramophone shifts to a music that shocks and dismays the previously complacent audience: jazz.[24] After setting a brief, improbable tribute to the League of Nations to the strains of a waltz,[25] the music suddenly becomes less comforting:

> The tune changed; snapped; broke; jagged. Foxtrot, was it? Jazz? Anyhow the rhythm kicked, reared, snapped short. What a jangle and a jingle! Well, with the means at her disposal, you can't ask too much. What a cackle, a cacophony! Nothing ended. So abrupt. And corrupt. Such an outrage; such an insult; And not plain. Very up to date, all the same. What is her game? To disrupt? Jog and trot? Jerk and smirk? Put the finger to the nose? Squint and pry? Peek and spy? O the irreverence of the generation which is only momentarily—thanks be—the young.[26]

In the rampant, free, indirect discourse that is the stylistic hallmark of *Between the Acts*, Woolf's audience professes a recognizably anti-jazz position. With its sharp, rhythmic breaks, Woolf's description of the "up to date" music mimics the very formal qualities that the passage decries in jazz. The surfeit of questions in the passage, including those that interrogate the music itself—"Foxtrot, was it? Jazz?"—emphasize jazz's unsettling newness, as opposed to the reassuring familiarity of such tunes as "Home Sweet Home." In other words, Woolf subversively writes this anti-jazz position in an echo of the very formal style that it critiques. In *Between the Acts*, the abrupt, irreverent music reflects more than the passage that it describes; it also provides an aesthetic template for the novel as a whole. Like jazz, *Between the Acts* is marked by breaks, fragments, and the impulse "to disrupt"; even the sense of its ending follows a fragmentary form. It is not that Woolf has learned her style from jazz—antiformalism was already her own—but that she recognizes a stylistic ally in the mass-reproduced music that has taken Britain by storm. Here Woolf harnesses the energies of jazz to make her fragmentary aesthetic more palpable, meaningful, and modern. The antinarrative structure of the jazz music, as dismissed by the audience, uniquely echoes *Between the Acts'* own inconclusive ending. In this way, the tension between the conventional structure of the pageant of English history and the fragmentary aesthetic of *Between the Acts* finds its counterpart in the sudden movement from familiar European music to jazz.

This new, disruptive music opens the final and most cryptic scene of the pageant; a scene that plays upon the mimetic representational functions it had long been Woolf's project to challenge. With the sounds of jazz in the background, the players come forth holding fragments of mirrors and other reflective objects:

> Anything that's bright enough to reflect, presumably, ourselves?
> Ourselves! Ourselves!
> Out they lept, jerked, skipped. Now old Bart... He was caught. Now Manresa. Here a nose... There a skirt... Then trousers only... Now perhaps a face... Ourselves? But that's cruel. To snap us before we've had time to assume... And only, too, in parts... That's what's so distorting and upsetting and utterly unfair.[27]

In the movement of the pageant into the "present time," Woolf's montage of aborted utterance reflects the fragmented bodies of the audience seen "in parts" in the mirrors. From behind the mirrors, the players declaim lines from earlier scenes simultaneously, as if English history itself had been transmuted into synchronic time. After identifying the embarrassed audience as "scraps, orts, and fragments," the formidable Miss La Trobe reassures her listeners by directing their attention to the gramophone: "A hitch occurred. The records had been mixed. Fox-trot, Sweet Lavender, Home Sweet Home, Rule Britannia—sweating profusely, Jimmy, who had charge of the music, threw them aside and fitted the right one—was it Bach, Handel, Beethoven, Mozart, or nobody famous, but merely a traditional tune."[28] Unlike the jazz in which "nothing ended," the "traditional" European music soothes the jittery audience, reaching a recognizable finale that "crashed, solved, united."[29] It is significant that this European music is recognizable without the identification of its composer: rather than having to choose among "Bach, Handel, Beethoven, or Mozart," the audience accepts what may be "merely a traditional tune" that, like traditional literary narrative, follows a familiar structure and proceeds to a recognizable end.[30]

Jazz thus does not have the final word in a pageant that brings its audience from medieval times to the present day. Rather, the strains of classical music, the oratory of the local pastor, and the familiar anthem of "God Save the King" safely recontain the pageant within its tribute to Englishness. Yet jazz marks the disorienting moment when the pageant shifts to portray the present. Such movement into the present emerges specifically through the fragmentation that Woolf's novel attributes to jazz. Woolf's formal project had long expressed a commitment to the new literary endeavors that her 1924 essay, "Mr. Bennett and Mrs. Brown," suggests may take the initial form of "the spasmodic, the obscure, the fragmentary, the failure."[31] In this essay, Woolf famously declared that the narratives forms of the past are inadequate to capture the turbulent energies of the present; jazz offers a particularly useful aesthetic template for such modernist endeavors. Whereas in her 1938 essay in *Cosmopolitan* Woolf revealed herself to be an astute reader of the impact of Americanization on the British imaginary, in *Between the Acts*, she displays the reverberations of this impact upon her literary form. By the writing of her final novel, jazz is singularly available as both an experimental aesthetic and a widely perceived threat to nativist Englishness. In a stunning reading of her cultural moment, Woolf translates jazz's *cultural* disruption of a coherent mythos of Englishness into a *formal* disruption of nationalist pageantry, of the telos of a "traditional" narrative. Woolf, in some ways at her most quintessentially English in *Between the Acts*, is therefore also at her most American. That is to say, by echoing jazz, Woolf acknowledges the ways in which a form of American mass entertainment can also *be* English modernism, insofar as this modernism ironizes and interrupts older aesthetic forms lodged and reprised in the national memory.

In an essay on the use of the gramophone in *Between the Acts*, Bonnie Kime Scott notes that Woolf may have been introduced to jazz in the form of records by T. S. Eliot, whose wife, Vivien, liked to dance to jazz. Scott surmises, "these records became social and cultural glue, bonding not just Eliot and Woolf but a multicultural Atlantic modernism as well."[32] Whereas Scott identifies the use of music in *Between the Acts* as its participation in multicultural modernism, Jed Esty focuses on Woolf's embrace of the folk art of the pageant play as a departure from the dominant modernist aesthetics of the teens and twenties. Attention to jazz reveals the interdependence of these two viewpoints by demonstrating how *Between the Acts* registers the conflict between an older, communal form tied to English nationalism and the transatlantic mass culture capable of disrupting this older discourse. Woolf's final novel, by remarking on its own formal innovations, unmistakably displays its modernist impulses. In *Between the Acts*, it is the formal experimentation of the novel as a whole, embodied and echoed by jazz, that quite literally has the final word.

Over a decade before Woolf wrote *Between the Acts*, an editorial appeared in the *Times*, "Tithe Barn: Jazz in the Cotswolds," that displays just the sort of reaction to jazz's invasion of the English countryside that Woolf mocks in *Between the Acts*.[33] The editorial, written by the *Times*'s anonymous "dramatic critic," recalls his shock, when peering into a Cotswold barn, at the sight of a piano and an item pinned to the wall reading, "Fox-trot." With more earnestness than irony, he laments, "Oh, profanation! Oh, sacrilege!"[34] In the critic's words:

> Obviously, the simple fact is, the barn had been used for a dance by the villagers. It offers an immense area of smooth floor, which seems nowadays inevitably to tempt all and sundry, villagers as well as burgesses, to jazzing. But jazzing in the Cotswolds! And worse, jazzing in a venerable edifice that must have been standing when they fought at Hastings, and still looks more like a cathedral than a barn!...Have these jazzing villagers no historical sense, no respect for the *genius loci*?[35]

For the *Times*'s drama critic, "jazzing in the Cotswolds" is the abrogation of English history. It is the loss of the "historical sense," the sacrilegious disturbance of the Cotswold barn with its radiant English aura. Like the audience of Woolf's nationalist pageant, the critic cannot help but recoil at jazz's disruption of the continuous historical time embodied in the English countryside. In this conception, jazz threatens to sever the connection between (historical) time and (the English) place. For the *Times*'s critic, much as for Woolf's audience, jazz undermines the very idea of the rustic English place as the embodiment of national history.

. . .

The belief in jazz's ability to upset the links between a nation and its history appears even more directly in a work of Anglo-Irish, rather than English, origin. Elizabeth Bowen's *The Last September* (1928), introduces jazz as a powerful, modernizing force that destabilizes the institution of the Anglo-Irish manor house and ultimately harbingers the violent end of the landlording class. Set during the unrest among the Irish, the Anglo-Irish, and the British shortly before the establishment of the Republic of Ireland, *The Last September* meditates on national identity from an imperial outpost shaken by the struggle for Irish independence. The child of an Anglo-Irish landlording household, Bowen grew up in the years before the establishment of the Irish state and escaped to Oxford where she wrote *The Last September* ten years after that particular historical moment had passed. Calling the novel "fiction torn from the texture of history," Bowen evokes the finality that attends the title, *The Last September*, through an accretion of signs that the old Anglo-Irish way of life was coming to an end.[36] As the most metaphorically pervasive of such signs, jazz music and dancing insinuate a threatening modernity into the traditions of Anglo-Irish manor life. First introduced into the narrative as a "disgusting noise" that nonetheless thrills the young protagonist, jazz stands for the longings of stultified youth even as it dangerously effaces class markers and blurs national boundaries.[37] The music brought over with the British troops signals the disruption and foreclosure of Anglo-Irish identity even as it presents an altered Englishness, turned modern and almost illegible by its embrace of jazz.

In the most obvious outline of its plot, *The Last September* is the tale of romance and misunderstanding between Lois, the niece of Anglo-Irish landlords at Danielstown, and Gerald Lesworth, a young English officer come to put down Irish revolutionary violence. Whereas Bowen in her preface characterizes the climate as one of "ambushes, arrests, captures and burnings, reprisals and counter-reprisals," the novel insists that Lois is only "half-awake" to such events.[38] Indeed, *The Last September* indulges something of the air of a Bildungsroman, in that its true focus is not the doomed romance between Lois and Gerald, but Lois's struggles with her burgeoning adulthood and her restlessness as a young woman of the leisure class who needs neither to work nor to marry. Such feelings find their figurative counterweight in the solidity of the Anglo-Irish manor house, as well as in the polite rituals that its occupants perform. By the end of the novel, with Gerald killed and the house at Danielstown burned to the ground, the ideals and traditions of Anglo-Irish landlording life finally succumb to earlier intimations of a disruptive modernity.

In its entry into the narrative, jazz persistently encroaches upon the spatially symbolic boundaries of the manor house. From the first, jazz assaults the house-guests Hugo and Francie Montmorency in their room with the abrasive sounds of "someone playing the gramophone."[39] In a later scene, the jazz music playing on Lois's gramophone seems to rearrange the interior space of the manor house itself:

> Below, through the floor, a light drawling scrape climbed into stuttering melody; syncopated dance music, ghostly with the wagging of hips and horrid in darkness. Lois, child of that unwise marriage, was playing the gramophone. Laurence listened, paralysed with indignation, then reached out and banged a chair on the floor. She attended; the music broke off with a shock, there was a tingling calm as after an amputation.[40]

In a passage riddled with run-on sentences, jazz's syncopation makes its way unbidden into the room of Lois's cousin, Laurence; it rises through the floor much as it trespassed the private space of the Montmorencys' room. Here the music is capable of conjuring spectral dancers, or at least their metonymic body parts: "ghostly with the wagging of hips." These ghostly body parts, while they perform the pleasures of dance, also mirror a landscape that will increasingly be littered with the bodies of soldiers and revolutionaries. The figurative "amputation" that accompanies the end of the music further encodes the bodily associations of jazz with the language of violence. Thus long before the fire travels through the ceilings and walls of the house at Danielstown, Lois's jazz stages an invasion, thick with ghostly limbs. The music, which penetrates the house in a disturbing, horrid, but immaterial fashion, figuratively brings the conflict inside this ostensibly safe space, presaging the moment when the house and what it stands for succumb to political unrest.

The jazz-playing gramophone not only sets ghosts loose upon the house but also maps the relationship between the house and its exterior. When Lois's uncle, Sir Richard Naylor, tells his guests that there has been no violence at his property, he anecdotally assures them, "We never have yet, not even with soldiers here and Lois dancing with officers up and down the avenue."⁴¹ To the guests' consternation, Lois explains she danced up the avenue, "Only once, for a bet. I and a man called Lesworth danced to the white gate, and the man that we had the bet with walked after us carrying the gramophone."⁴² Notably, the travels of the hand-cranked gramophone describe the potentially dangerous space beyond the house. Although the whimsical image of Lois dancing on the avenue does not match the intensity of the ghostly jazz seeping into Laurence's room at night, it presents jazz as eminently transgressive, capable of altering the meaning of the property's exterior spaces, and providing multiple and conflicting indices of their safety.

Whereas Lois persistently wreaks social havoc by playing jazz on her gramophone, the young officer Gerald Lesworth, the object of her affection, more trenchantly brings jazz into the narrative. In an early scene, Lois's first thought of Gerald and "the perfectness of their being together" is not interrupted by the image of his military service but by his role in a jazz band: "But he was very musical, he conducted a jazz band they had at the barracks, and while reaching out in her thoughts she remembered the band would be practising now...To a line of tune the thought flung her, she danced on the avenue."⁴³ Although Ireland is in a state of insurrection, what Lois can most easily imagine at the military barracks is a jazz rehearsal. Much like the gramophone that trailed Lois and Gerald up and down the avenue, here jazz is psychically mobile, the tunes "flung" into her mind as she dances.

Jazz persistently delineates and trespasses private spaces in this novel, whether a bedroom or the boundaries of the house; Gerald, the soldier and jazz musician, threatens mobility of a different sort in his desire to marry Lois. In this endeavor, his class status and his "musical" inclinations to head a jazz band count against him. Lois's aunt, Lady Naylor, stringently opposes a marriage between Lois and Gerald. Her reasoning rests at the intersection of nationality, class, and mobility: "I think all English people very difficult to trace. They are so pleasant and civil, but I do often wonder if they are not a little shallow: for no reason at all they will pack up everything and move across six counties."[44] Gerald is illegible, Lady Naylor suggests, in part because he is English. As opposed to the Anglo-Irish rooted in their manor houses, the English have a propensity to move about, effacing readable traces of their class positions in the process. Such movement, like the fluidity of jazz itself, is that which the Anglo-Irish landlording class most resists. The American military brought jazz to Europe; here English soldiers bring it to Ireland. The arrival of jazz in the Irish countryside signals new forms of cultural movement and transnational exchange while foreclosing fantasies of national and class-based purity. The circulation of jazz in *The Last September* thus characterizes the Anglo-Irish in their futile attempts to resist its modernizing call as well as the English soldiers, whom the novel presents as mobile, uprooted, and strangely *like* the music that they brought into the country.

In a further ironic turn, it seems that insofar as Gerald is English, his Englishness reflects his participation in modern American culture. When he takes Lois outside the dance at the barracks, he offers her a cigarette, "American, extra mild," and she asks him, "How is your jazz band?"[45] This, then, is Bowen's scene: the English soldier and the Irish girl smoking American cigarettes and talking of jazz, while the world is poised to crumble around them. Such signs of American culture offer to Ireland the transnational pleasures that have already overtaken England. In the late twenties, English youth culture derived from American culture to such an extent that American cigarettes and jazz become signs of Gerald's Englishness and his difference from Anglo-Ireland. In her longing to leave Ireland, late in the novel, Lois briefly considers and then dismisses traveling to America: "there was America, but one…would get a crick in one's neck from just always looking up at things."[46] What she wants, rather, is London, which she imagines as "somewhere nonchalant where politics bored them, where bands played out of doors in the hot nights and nobody wished to sleep."[47] Lois's ruminations on escape reveal that while she rejects America, she embraces an Americanized England.

In contrast to Lois's metropolitan fantasy of late-night jazz without the interruption of politics, it is political strife that puts an end to Gerald and his jazz band. In a climactic scene at a barracks dance, enthusiastic revelers break the gramophone. Gerald intends to fetch a new one from Cork, but he is killed in an ambush west of Clonmore. Gerald's death ends the fantasy of insularity for the inhabitants of Danielstown, evoking the sense of finality that attends the title. At the same time, the novel ties his death to the broken gramophone and the end of the jazz band. After receiving news of his death, Lois wonders "what would become of the jazz band"; a military orderly sent to handle Gerald's affairs is shocked to find "in Gerald's room some new music for the jazz band, caught in a draught, flopping over and over."[48] The jazz music, flopping in the breeze, is out of place, unruly, disorderly. Like the jazz seeping through ceilings and walls of the house at Danielstown, here the sheet music itself manifests a syncopated restlessness, a final sign of what has been lost.

The many instances of jazz in *The Last September*—the sheet music, the band, the jazz dance, the gramophone records—seem almost oversaturated with meaning. In a novel torn between its nostalgia for a time and place destroyed by history, and its fascination with the sounds and dancing that signal modernity, jazz both foreshadows and accelerates the end of Anglo-Irish traditions.[49] The fire at the novel's end that destroys the house at Danielstown moves transgressively through ceilings and walls in a figurative echo of the jazz played on Lois's gramophone. The very mobility of jazz, and its class impurities, erodes the readable links to location upon which Lady Naylor's interpretative powers depend. There is no place for this new music, jazz, in old Anglo-Ireland. By the end of the novel, the flopping pages suggest it is the restless music, rather than the landlord's eponymous ties to the land, that will have the final word. *The Last September* thus not only channels its anxieties about the changes coming to Ireland through its figurative recourse to jazz, it also brings an Americanized Englishness into the conflicts of Irish modernity.

. . .

In a poem published three years after his rhyming couplet on Duke Ellington, Auden joins Woolf and Bowen in turning to jazz to capture the transnational mobility of modern times. The poem "Refugee Blues" (1939) follows several other "blues" poems that Auden wrote in the thirties. Auden's blues are a funny hybrid: they transpose the rhythms of the blues into an undeniably British idiom. In one poem, for instance, Auden inserts a fussy tribute to a policeman's white gloves into the structure of his lament. In all their incongruity, Auden's blues beg several questions. If the blues, according to Houston Baker, produce "the expressive site where American experience is named" what are the blues *outside* of America?[50] And while the blues can create a space for identification, through what Baker calls "an invitation to energizing intersubjectivity," what about blues that begin not as a personal lament but by telling the story of *other people's* troubles?[51] This, apparently, is what happens to the blues when it is written by a white, Oxford-educated English poet, even one who would ultimately go on to take American citizenship. Auden's late-thirties poem opens with a tribute to displaced German Jews: "Say this city has ten million souls, / Some are living in mansions, some are living in holes: / Yet there's no place for us, my dear, yet there's no place for us."[52] While the blues is an entirely different music than the frenetic dance tunes of *The Last September*, here it serves a surprisingly consonant function.[53] Insofar as Auden's "blues" poem tells the tale of a wide-scale uprooting, the expulsion of a people from the body of a nation, it also serves to trace the fault lines in nationalist discourse. For Auden, this tale of modern homelessness finds its best expressive counterpart in the music of America.

Auden may have been driven to write a blues song about Jewish migrants because of both the transgressive associations of the music as well as the associations of jazz with Jewish composers and performers. Whereas the British most often associated jazz with black Americans, in Germany and the United States it was also associated with Jews. Reporting on new legislation toward the ban in 1935, the *Times* surmised that "hitherto Nazi antagonism to jazz music was based on the allegation that expressed the primitive culture of an inferior race, the negroes, but [the Reich Broadcasting Organization director], for reasons not given, regards it as Jewish."[54] This director is recorded in the *Times* as insisting, "We will no longer hear Jewish-like speech (Mauscheln) on the wireless...not even when rendered with music."[55] Without any apparent awareness of inconsistency, this same broadcasting director also reportedly declared that jazz should "Get back to Africa."[56] In a rigorous attempt to censor any racially degenerate sounds, the director added that "even 'disguised jazz' would be prohibited."[57] By the thirties, of course, Jewish American songwriters and musicians, such as Ira and George Gershwin, were known overseas, at least for the pieces they wrote for Hollywood films.[58] Yet the German association of jazz with Africa and with Jews, and in neither case directly with black Americans, reveals the tenacious complexity of jazz's racial associations at the time that Auden was crafting his blues poems.

Auden's choice of the blues for his poem about German Jewish refugees offers a poignant tribute to the transnational fluidity of the form. By the time Auden wrote "Refugee Blues," jazz and blues were available as forms that even at their most "disguised," could be understood as an affront to Nazi ideology. Indeed, the history of jazz's mobility; its transnationality; and its ability to produce audiences across racial, national, and class lines stands in opposition to the Nazi project of consolidating and purifying the Heimat. Auden's decision to produce a set of poems under the name of the blues—poems that treat the massive uprooting that would mark Europe in the coming decade—signals his growing desire to reject rigid ideologies of nation. Whereas Woolf was alert to the possibility that jazz could interrupt a triumphant narrative of Englishness, Auden, by the end of the thirties, takes jazz's political edge even further by using the formal energies of the blues to denounce the rise of fascist nationalisms.

Jazz, Race, and Cultural Value

British works such as those of Woolf and Auden offer jazz as the sign, either acclaimed or abhorred, of the disruption of nationalist discourses. In a number of other cases, this disruption reaches its peak around questions of race. In Clive Bell's and Wyndham Lewis's interwar discussions of jazz, for instance, the rhetoric of high and low culture frequently leads to racial analogy and racist discourse. With greater irony, Evelyn Waugh's exemplary 1928 *Decline and Fall* explores inter-war conceptions of race and cultural value *through* discussions of jazz. Whereas jazz fans often responded with primitivist fervor to trends such as Josephine Baker's transformation from a comic player in New York's *Shuffle Along* into an "African" exotic dancer in Europe, one British fan in particular, the writer Nancy Cunard, took jazz as the starting point for a leftist political program of racial jus-tice.[59] Although varied in nature, texts of the period reveal the racial assumptions, ideologies, and conflicts that jazz brought to the foreground of British culture.

In 1921, at the beginning of the decade that Fitzgerald named the "Jazz Age," Clive Bell announced the end of jazz.[60] Bell, a Bloomsbury art critic, was not alone in hoping for the swift demise of what seemed a faddish obsession; an article that same year in the London *Times* gleefully proclaimed, " 'Jazz' is in its death agonies."[61] Yet in his essay, "Plus de Jazz" (1921), Bell revealed that the stakes of such disenchantment with jazz were much greater than mere exhaustion with the latest craze. Bell's wishful thinking arose because he, as an art critic, feared that jazz rep-resented an assault upon art and especially upon the critical judgments that were his stock and trade. Characterizing the anti-jazz movement among intellectuals, Bell explained:

> What, I believe, has turned so many intelligent and sensitive people against Jazz is the encouragement it has given to thousands of the stupid and vulgar to fancy that they can understand art and to hundreds of the conceited to imagine that they can create it. All the girls in the 'dancings' and sportsmen

at the bar who like a fox-trot or a maxixe have been given to believe by
people who ought to know better that they are more sensitive to music than
those who prefer Beethoven.[62]

The identification of jazz as "art," Bell submits, is what has given rise to the violent
reaction of "sensitive people" against it. Bell numbers himself among the sensitive
souls whose outrage at jazz follows not from the music itself but from what he sees
as its transformation from lowbrow to highbrow, and the consequent weakening
of the distinction between the two. For Bell, this is a problem of cultural capital,
in Pierre Bourdieu's sense of the term.[63] Jazz aficionados suffer from the misapprehension that they have as much or more cultural capital than those who listen to
music of the European Romantics. The primary aim of "Plus de Jazz," is to correct
this misapprehension, preserving a cultural hierarchy that safely subordinates the
populist pleasures of dance music to the enjoyment of Beethoven.

Although Bell parades his disdain for jazz fans, he preserves his keenest dis-
taste for the jazz musicians. With ominous hyperbole, Bell prophecies the end of
Western civilization if jazz continues to hold sway: "No more classical concerts
and music lessons; no more getting Lycidas by heart; no more Baedeker; no more
cricking one's neck in the Sistine Chapel: unless the colored gentleman who leads
the band at the Savoy has a natural leaning toward these things."[64] Here Bell invests
jazz with the power to institute a new system of value that nullifies Milton and the
Sistine Chapel. In this scenario, jazz threatens the icons of European culture from
its newly hegemonic position, the Savoy, at the center of London. Specifically, the
"colored gentleman who leads the band" at the Savoy has become a tastemaker
capable of negating such icons. In Bell's view, the bandleader has taken the place of
the critic, the place that Bell believes to be his own.

Bell's dismissal of jazz significantly rests on his observation that the bandleader
who supersedes Bell's critical judgments, and thereby threatens Western civilization, is "colored." As his other essays reveal, Bell is not categorically opposed to art
produced by peoples outside of Europe. In an essay entitled "Negro Sculpture," Bell
lauds African art, suggesting that it has gained such favor in Europe in part because
of its amenability to European interpretation and criticism.[65] Yet while Bell imaginatively transforms the art objects of the African continent into blank sites for the
interpretive work of critics like himself, jazz music arrives with its own black bandleaders who threaten to set the new standards of taste. With unmistakable racism, Bell insists that black musicians "can be admired artists without any gift more
singular than high spirits: so why drag in the intellect."[66] Such references to race,
scattered throughout the essay, are central to his ideology. If the problem with jazz

is that it does not merely allow English critics to cast an admiring, primitivist gaze on a set of art objects but rather transfers the role of critical judgment to the "colored gentleman...at the Savoy," then it seems that the agency of the black musician poses the ultimate threat.[67] The very word *jazz* here serves as code for this disruptive agency. When Bell insists that "Jazz cannot away with intellect or culture," he rhetorically invests the form with the potential for agency that, as he explained, follows from the dangerous influence of jazz's bandleaders and musicians.[68]

In a later version of Bell's essay, his opposition to the agency of black musicians in setting new standards of taste, rather than to the musical form of jazz itself, becomes clearer. Here Bell moves away from jazz music itself to treat what he calls, "the Jazz movement."[69] Bell explains that "during the last ten years Jazz had dominated music and coloured literature: on painting, as I have said, its effect has been negligible."[70] With surprising approval, Bell describes the influence of jazz upon Stravinsky—"He has composed ragtimes"—while circumscribing its influence on painting to the Italian futurists.[71] Even more intriguingly, Bell assesses a series of modern writers as what he calls "Jazz writers."[72] Chief among them is the American, T. S. Eliot. As Bell describes this movement:

> It may claim Mr. T.S. Eliot—a poet of uncommon merit and unmistakably in the great line—whose agonizing labours seem to have been eased somewhat by the comfortable ministrations of a black and grinning muse. Midwifery, to be sure, seems an odd occupation for a lady whom one pictures rather in the role of a flapper: but a midwife was what the poet needed, and in that capacity she has served him.[73]

This minstrel image, drawn directly from racist stereotype, converts Mammy into muse in its strange tribute to the influence of jazz. While black jazz musicians "cannot away with intellect and culture," T. S. Eliot can use the influence of jazz to become "about the best of our living poets."[74] Not only does Eliot remain sufficiently elite to maintain the hierarchy of taste, but he also remains sufficiently *white*, bolstered by an unseen, grinning midwife. Bell's double evaluation of jazz, as simultaneously the dangerous populist form that will force the end of Milton and the servile muse behind Eliot's experimentalism, rests on the racial ideologies that separate Eliot from the bandleader at the Savoy. Much like the European critics who interpret African art objects, Eliot is the interpreter of jazz: his poetry arises from his own agency. In this strange identification of the genre of jazz writer, Bell further reveals his reliance on racial ideologies in his analysis of the cultural impact of jazz.

While Bell goes on to identify other "jazz writers," including Jean Cocteau, Blaise Cendras, and James Joyce, he reserves his strongest acclaim for a modern author whom he largely exempts from the classification, Virginia Woolf. By the time he wrote "Plus de Jazz," Bell knew Woolf well, not least because he was married to her sister.[75] In what Bell seems to imagine as the highest praise, he disassociates Woolf from jazz:

> She is not imbued with that spirit which inspires the authentic Jazz writers…In her writings I find no implicit, and often well-merited, jeer at accepted ideas of what prose and verse should be and what they should be about; no nervous dislike of traditional valuations, of scholarship, culture, and intellectualism; above all, no note of protest against the notion that one idea or emotion can be more important or significant than another. Assuredly, Mrs. Woolf is not of the company on whose banner is inscribed, 'No discrimination!' 'No culture!' 'Not much thought!'[76]

Because of her commitment to "traditional valuations," Bell insists, Woolf proves herself the opposite of a "Jazz writer." Rather than imagining art in blindly democratic terms, Woolf is an exemplar of discrimination. While it is ironic that Woolf in *Between the Acts* would come to use jazz as a symbol to disturb these hierarchies of taste, tradition, and nationalism, becoming the style of jazz writer that Bell decried, it is perhaps not entirely surprising. After all, both Bell's diatribe against jazz and Woolf's subversive use of it draw on the shared symbolism of jazz's disruption of entrenched ideas of national tradition.

Whereas jazz left Bell fearful for the aesthetic underpinnings of Western civilization, there were others who believed jazz might threaten the stature of the British Empire itself. A 1927 *Times* article reported on the address of Sir H. Coward to the Sheffield Rotary Club, in which he reportedly announced that if Britain "wished to avoid the fate of the great empires which had dominated and declined, including Egypt, Babylon, Greece, and Rome" it would do well to put an end to jazz.[77] Calling jazz "a low type of primitive music," Coward explained, "the popularization of 'jazz,' and the attendant immodest dances, had led to a lowering of the prestige of the white races. To prevent further loss of prestige we must ban 'jazz.' "[78] Without reservation, Coward in his address held forth on the need for transatlantic separatism and the end of jazz: "Let Americans embrace 'jazz' if they chose, but as it was neither lovely nor of good report we must taboo it in every shape and form until its baneful influence was gone."[79]

Coward was content to quarantine jazz's "baneful influence" to America; the British modernist, Wyndham Lewis, even more strikingly came to imagine the value of English culture, and white English skin, to hang in the balance of the attitudes developed in the United States. In so doing, Lewis, perhaps the writer in England most vehemently opposed to Bell and Bloomsbury, shares and even intensifies some of the terms of Bell's jazz critique. In his massive treatise on race in America, *Paleface: The Philosophy of the 'Melting-Pot'* (1929), Lewis announces, "the cultural 'present' that the Negro has made to White America, and through America to the whole White World, can be summed up in the word, 'jazz.'"[80] For Lewis, jazz summarizes the insidious cultural influences that threaten nativist ideologies of whiteness in England as well as in America. As Lewis warns his English reader at the opening of *Paleface*, "For what our white skin is worth, symbolically or otherwise, it is in America that its destinies are most clearly foreshadowed."[81] With alarmist urgency, Lewis insists that America and especially the cultural products of black Americans have the power to determine the meaning of whiteness in England and the world.

To express this interwar anxiety, Lewis tellingly substitutes a transatlantic paradigm of race relations for an older, imperial one. Invoking Kipling's "The White Man's Burden," Lewis explains that "though there is no White Man's Burden in Europe at present," such a burden exists in America and its effects can spread contagiously across the Atlantic.[82] Whereas Kipling presents his poem as an imperialist lesson for the Americans, Lewis finds the United States to have altogether too much control over the meaning of race. Paying little heed to the racism of a segregated America, Lewis focuses on the cultural products, such as jazz and black American fiction, that have made their way to England and threaten to produce white "inferiority-complexes."[83] Lewis's overriding concern in *Paleface* is that black American cultural products could produce a psychological sea change among whites in Europe, redefining what it means to be European *by* redefining what it means to be white.

Like Bell, Lewis understands jazz to participate in the construction of cultural value. Yet, much more pointedly than Bell, Lewis presents this construction of cultural value within narratives of *human* value. Meditating on the cultural tendencies of the twenties, Lewis heuristically proposes the future state of affairs that could follow upon the current one:

> The sort of situation you would have eventually to anticipate is this. In such towns as New York and Johannesburg you will get a Black quarter, where there will be large dance-halls where nothing but waltzes and mazurkahs and possibly minuets will be danced, by stately Negroes; and there will be a Paleface quarter, where there will be a dance-hall with nothing but

jazz... The plays in the Black quarter will be such plays as *Hamlet*: the plays in the White will be *All God's Chillun*.[84]

Lewis's segregated future scenario is one in which, as he sees it, the greatest irony comes from a chiasmic crossing of race and culture. For whites to dance to jazz while blacks put on *Hamlet*, Lewis avers, is to sever culture from what he sees as its racial origins in a fashion symptomatic of the modern moment. Curiously, Lewis presents this chiasmus within a set of assumptions that translate artistic values into the relative merits of a race. In so doing, Lewis stages a debate of sorts between the races:

> But the Black will say fiercely that he is a better man than the White because he is more dignified in his amusements (pointing to his waltzes, his Shakespeare Repertory Theatre, etc.) The White will insist that he is the better man, because he is not so emotional and jazzy as the Black, and because he is responsible for Shakespeare, Molière, and so on.[85]

Although Lewis imagines Shakespeare to be the contested signifier of value for both groups, the conflicted arguments about jazz split into something like the Freudian distinction between wanting to have and wanting to be. While the whites may have jazz, in the sense of taking pleasure in the music, the blacks are accused of *being* jazz-like, that is to say, of being "jazzy." The slide into identification presupposed by the adjective presents jazz as inextricable from racial identity. Despite *Hamlet* and waltzes, Lewis's scenario insists to be black is to be "jazzy," a term the *Oxford English Dictionary* dates from only 1919, defining it primarily as "pertaining to or resembling jazz" but also as "spirited, lively, vivid, gaudy."[86] While jazziness is here presented as the ultimate condemnation of a group attempting to assert its cultural worth, Lewis seems more concerned with disparaging jazz itself than with a commitment to biological essentialism. That is to say, his racism is surprisingly relativist. As Lewis glosses his own scene, "long before such a state of affairs as that came to pass, the races would, in practice, have intermarried and that their habits would have become identical."[87] For Lewis in *Paleface*, black and white may mingle and racial distinctions disappear, but jazz shall never mix with *Hamlet*, and their values will remain fixed through time.[88]

Lewis's interest in jazz as a signifier of cultural value and human worth follows from an argument he stages in *Paleface* with the well-known Harlem Renaissance intellectual, Alain Locke. Relating a published debate between Locke and the white supremacist Lothrop Stoddard, Lewis interprets Locke on culture: "But Mr. Locke...insists that the White Man cannot dance every night to negro music, and throng to *Porgies* and *Emperor Joneses*, and continue to be haughty where the Negro is concerned."[89] The style of argument taken up by Locke, in which he refers to the "tragic irony and imminent social farce" of America's simultaneous racism and thrall to jazz, is one that other supporters of racial justice will echo, including the British writer Nancy Cunard.[90] Yet Lewis responds to Locke that social justice cannot possibly be sought through an inferior vehicle such as jazz. In 1929, Lewis would base such a claim foremost upon jazz's rampant popularity: "White people everywhere have tumbled over each other to pick it up, and it had almost superseded every other form of activity."[91] The widespread desire for jazz is then interwoven into Lewis's dismissal of jazz as nothing more than "a barbarous, melancholy, epileptic folk music."[92] Lewis's presentation of jazz as a music at once like earlier forms of European folk music and so utterly widespread as to have "almost superseded every other form of activity" reveals the extent to which his objections to jazz arise from its mass influence and appeal. "White people everywhere," and not only in America, are at risk of succumbing to jazz precisely because jazz has already established itself as omnipresent by the end of the twenties. At moments, Lewis almost sounds as if he imagines jazz to perform a socialist function: "all that the 'Afroamerican' has succeeded in supplying is the aesthetic medium of a sort of frantic proletarian subconscious."[93] For Lewis, much more pointedly than for his anti-jazz contemporaries, jazz is the conspicuous bearer of racial ideology and is already at work around the world changing the meaning of race and nation. Whereas Bell feared primarily for the status of art and the role of the critic, Lewis reveals his concern for the effects of an influential folk music upon the impressionable minds of the proletariat.

In Lewis's conception, the transatlantic cultural attack, from America through jazz and fiction, threatens Englishness and whiteness in one fell blow. Although Lewis revealed his nationalist impulses in the first issue of his avant-garde journal, *Blast*, in which he chose to "bless" England, he also identifies strongly through England with the European continent.[94] Implicit in Lewis's outcry against America's role in determining interwar racial ideology is a fear that Europeans will cease to be European and become simply white. The extension of this state of affairs, Lewis conjectures, is that the Americans, and not the Europeans or the English, are producing the new meanings of whiteness. The "Borzoi big-guns" that are trained on England from America are precisely those of a publishing house with a line of Harlem Renaissance literature. The omnipresent cultural form that has nearly subsumed experience and that has "almost superseded every other form of activity," is none other than jazz.

The cultural products of black America, Lewis ultimately insists in melodramatic prose, suggest "that the White World is 'finished,' that it is a culture or political organism that is going to pieces under assaults from without and from within, quite on the traditional, historical, *Decline and Fall* pattern."⁹⁵ Whereas Bell at the beginning of the twenties primarily considered the threat that jazz posed to art, and implicitly to English culture as such, Lewis at the end of the decade makes a serious plea for the threat of black American cultural products to the stability of the West. Although Lewis, an avant-garde writer who would turn increasingly to fascism by the thirties, is recognized for his extreme and racist viewpoints, it is important to note that he bases *Paleface*'s dire political predictions on the transatlantic circulation of cultural products such as jazz. In his meditation on the dangers of the music and fiction of black America, Lewis reveals the extent to which American entertainment could be imagined to have lasting, transformative effects on the West.

. . .

Just one year before Lewis's announcement that cultural products like jazz were throwing the world into a "*Decline and Fall* pattern," Evelyn Waugh saw fit to parody such beliefs in his irreverent 1928 novel *Decline and Fall*. By the aftermath of the First World War, Gibbon's history of the decline of the Roman Empire was beginning to seem a story about England's future as much as about Europe's past.⁹⁶ In Waugh's eponymous tale, an encounter between a black American jazz musician and the staff of an English public school reveals the latter's underlying belief in the power of Englishness to resist all that jazz represents: modernity, change, and the nexus of race and nation. Whereas Bell and Lewis both seriously urged the dismissal of jazz for the sake of culture, Waugh parodies this anti-jazz stance, at moments with uncanny precision. Yet Waugh's treatment of jazz can also be seen as the moment when his parody breaks down, doubling back on itself and revealing the novel's investment in emblems of Englishness capable of resisting jazz's new systems of value.

Midway through the series of outrageous episodes that make up *Decline and Fall*, the public school, Llanabba, which has been identified as exclusively "English" despite its location in Wales, stages a series of footraces as a day's entertainment for the wealthy parents of their pupils.⁹⁷ In the central event of the gathering, Mrs. Beste-Chetwynde, the mother of a spoiled young fellow, shocks the occupants of the refreshment tent by entering with a black American jazz musician. The musician, Chokey, appears from the first as a kind of fashionable accessory that bespeaks Mrs. Beste-Chetwynde's ostentatious wealth: like the "enormous limousine of dove-grey and silver" that announces her arrival, Chokey steps out of the car impeccably dressed in "a clinging dove-grey overcoat."[98] Swaddled in the matching apparel of man and machine, Mrs. Beste-Chetwynde needs little more to announce her status. Chokey in particular functions as a sign of wealth in a manner that recalls the patronage system of interwar New York. The narrative itself negatively acknowledges Chokey's symbolic role in its estimation of Mrs. Beste-Chetwynde's social status: "With or without her negro, Mrs. Beste-Chetwynde was a woman of vital importance."[99]

Waugh's narrative quickly draws Chokey further into the very crises of value upon which English cultural decline and fall appear to rest. Introducing Chokey to the school's headmaster, Dr. Fagan, Mrs. Beste-Chetwynde announces the musician's symbolic disruption, and ironic reinforcement, of English systems of value:

> "You can't move Chokey once he's seen an old church. He's just crazy about culture, aren't you, darling?"
> "I sure am that," said Chokey.
> "Are you interested in music?" said the Doctor tactfully.
> "Well, just you hear that, Baby," said Chokey; "am *I* interested in music? I should say I am."
> "He plays just too divinely," said Mrs. Beste-Chetwynde.
> "Has he heard my new records, would you say?"
> "No, darling, I don't expect he has."
> "Well, just you hear *them*, sir, and then you'll know—am I interested in music."[100]

The culture about which Chokey is "just crazy" is none other than English culture, as exemplified here by the "old church." In fact, as Mrs. Beste-Chetwynde will explain in a moment, "He's just crazy about England, too."[101] Here culture is equivalent with English culture, or indeed with England itself. Doctor Fagan's ignorance of Chokey's music signifies the Doctor's cultured status as defined by the insularity of the public school from popular musical forms. Mrs. Beste-Chetwynde's casual assumption that Doctor Fagan wouldn't have heard Chokey's new records only reinforces the separation between those with organic ownership of English culture and those who come merely to gawk at it. This particular distinction reaches its satirical height in the discussion Chokey and the Doctor have about higher education. Chokey lists the schools he has visited—"Oxford and Cambridge and Eton and Harrow. That's me all over"—in what seems an attempt to absorb their cultural capital through tourism.[102] Doctor Fagan trumps Chokey's litany of English cultural institutions when in response to Chokey's query, "Have you ever seen Oxford," Fagan calmly replies, "Yes; in fact, I was educated there."[103]

While all of the characters in *Decline and Fall* are subject to humorous critique, the invention of the jazz musician who fawns upon English culture is exceptional. It certainly might seem the characters most subject to Waugh's satirical racism are the musicians in the Welsh "silver" band, which the narrative describes as "revolting," "crafty," and "ape-like."[104] Presented utterly as animals, "growling and yapping" like the denizens "of the jungle at moonrise," the Welsh band inspires Dr. Fagan's diatribe against all Welsh as "the only nation in the world that has produced no graphic or plastic art, no architecture, no drama."[105] Yet the extreme description of the Welsh band—"low of brow…and crooked of limb," slavering at the mouth and loping like wolves—marks the passage as an unmistakable attempt at comedy, whereas the presentation of Chokey and Mrs. Beste-Chetwynde provoked in at least one American reviewer of *Decline and Fall* the "joy of recognition."[106] Still, what is most interesting about the description of the Welsh band in this episode is how forcefully it links traditional British folk music to British ideologies of race and nation. It seems that whether a new script of race and entertainment will come to supplant the old, both Welsh folk music and jazz leave the high status of English culture intact, producing English culture as high through scripts of ethnicity, race, and nation.

In describing Chokey's attachment to English culture, Waugh proposes an inversion of cultural value similar to Lewis's imaginary scenario in *Paleface*. Chokey describes his emotional response to his tour of England: "When I saw the cathedrals my heart just rose up and sang within me. I sure am crazy about culture. You folk think because we're coloured we don't care about nothing but jazz. Why, I'd give all the jazz in the world for just one little stone from one of your cathedrals."[107] Here Waugh provides a statement of cultural value in the market language of exchange: one English cathedral stone for all the jazz in the world. This statement of value is ironic in that it comes from the jazz musician himself, who takes care to explain that he cares not only for jazz but participates in the humanizing dialogues symbolized by the English cathedral. Moreover, Chokey assures his listeners that the sight of the cathedral makes figurative music—"my heart just rose up and sang"—thus functionally replacing jazz as well. Both Lewis's and Waugh's scenes suggest that, by the late twenties, markers of cultural value are commonly taken to stand for racial value. Though Waugh's comedic impulses lead him to present Chokey as a pretender to English culture, such a scenario follows from the chiasmic crossing of cultural values that appears to be a favorite trompe l'oeil of the decade. The utility of the figure, chiasmus, to both Lewis and Waugh rests in the manner in which it lays bare its own improbability. Whereas Lewis uses chiasmus to threaten his readers with a future in which the links between race and culture have been crisscrossed, Waugh seizes the comic potential in what he presents as the startling reassignment of cultural interest between the races. If whites can thrall to jazz, he seems to say, why not imagine black American devotion to English culture. The stark use of chiasmus thus underscores the extent to which the scrambling of race and culture is seen as unnatural, as improbable, and, according to Waugh and Lewis respectively, as the stuff of comedy and danger.

Through Chokey's tributes to English literature and culture, Waugh suggests the extent to which the jazz-riddled interwar years saw the reactionary production of English culture as highbrow. In anticipation of Lewis's chiasmic predictions, Chokey disparages jazz and lauds Shakespeare: "*I* appreciate art. There's plenty coloured people come over here and don't see nothing but a few night clubs. I read Shakespeare... *Hamlet, Macbeth, King Lear*. Ever read them?"[108] As a symptom of Chokey's obsession with English literature, one character tells another, "He asked me whether I had ever heard of a writer called Thomas Hardy."[109] The comedy accorded to Chokey's claims upon Oxford, the Salisbury Cathedral, Shakespeare, and Hardy stems from the manner in which it implies the organic and unshakeable claim to English culture of his interlocutors. Doctor Fagan, who has attended Oxford and read Shakespeare, Lady Circumference, who grew up near Salisbury Cathedral, and the others, who have assuredly heard of Thomas Hardy, are reassured of their indisputable claims to English cultural capital by Chokey's doomed attempts to prove his worth.

Lady Circumference and Doctor Fagan both implicitly assert that they have the kind of organic, lived-experience connection to places that Chokey can only tour and to authors Chokey seems inclined merely to name. Chokey's identification of Hardy particularly suits his project of anglicization in part because of the intimate ties in Hardy's work to an English sense of place. Such an emphasis on place may be seen as an effective counterweight to jazz, a mobile cultural form capable of crossing the Atlantic and spreading throughout England. As a form of resistance to the transatlantic circulation of jazz, the litany of English places—Salisbury, Oxford, Eton—reveals the desire to ground English high-cultural resistance in the land itself. The very trade that Chokey would make, all of jazz for a single cathedral stone, pits a fluid, transnational cultural form against the weight and groundedness of Gothic architecture. The joke that is on Chokey, the idea that a black American jazz musician could become closer to English culture than the English themselves are, participates in the mutually constitutive production of high culture and English culture. It is thus worth noting that while Waugh could have imagined a similar scene of Oxford haves and have-nots within the English class system, the effect could not have been more different. Through the character of Chokey, high culture is rendered synonymous with white, English culture; it is that to which a black American jazz musician can aspire only in vain.

Two years after the publication of *Decline and Fall*, Waugh returned to the topic of jazz in his novel of "massed humanity" and interwar decadence, *Vile Bodies*.[110] Where *Decline and Fall* demonstrates the importance of race and Englishness to jazz's ideological impact, *Vile Bodies* extends these insights into a broader geographic field that includes the British colonies. When the novel's hapless protagonist, Adam, joins "a man named Ginger" who is lately returned from Ceylon at London's Café de la Paix, jazz places pressure on Ginger's systems of value as soon as it enters the narrative: "A coloured singer appeared, paddling his black suède shoes in a pool of limelight, who excited Ginger's disapproval."[111] As Ginger puts it, "one doesn't come all the way from Colombo to London" to see "a coloured singer."[112] Here Ginger laments the way in which imperial ideologies of race and value fail to apply in the London club. Tellingly, the appearance of the singer motivates Ginger to more pervasive, gloomy ruminations on modern England: "Ginger became a little moody, saying that London wasn't home to him anymore and that things had changed."[113] In a scene that seems wryly to echo Wyndham Lewis's fear of black American culture, the appearance of the black singer alienates Ginger from London, which suddenly seems under the sway of a new and disturbing modernity: "things had changed." In order to palliate the symptoms of his brush with modernity in the form of a jazz singer, "Ginger had a drink, and then he and an American sang the Eton Boating song several times. At the end of the evening, he admitted that there was some life left in the jolly old capital of Empire."[114] A performative therapy, the "Eton Boating song" effectively counters the disruptive spectacle of the jazz singer through its musical ties to English place and tradition. For Ginger, singing the Eton Boating song transforms London from a disturbingly modern metropole in which colonial racial distinctions do not seem to hold back into "the jolly old capital of Empire." The old counters the new, the Eton Boating song drowns out the jazz singer, and the anglophile American plays backup chorus to the resurrection of Englishness through song.

· · ·

Waugh's depictions, satirical as they may be, had their real-life counterparts. For instance, liaisons such as the one Waugh depicts in *Decline and Fall* between a wealthy white Englishwoman and a black American jazz musician find their counterpart in the story of Nancy Cunard, the British writer, publisher, and heiress who celebrated black American art and culture. Shortly after the publication of Waugh's

1928 novel, Cunard met the American jazz pianist Henry Crowder in Venice. Their longstanding relationship may have predisposed the British press to fabricate stories about Cunard and another black American, Paul Robeson, with whom she spent time in 1932.[115] Cunard responded to these stories with a successful libel suit, putting her settlement funds toward the most ambitious project of her lifetime, a massive anthology entitled *Negro* (1934). Motivated by the Scottsboro trial and the cause of racial justice, Cunard collected commentary on black struggle and achievement from more than 150 contributors, including W. E. B. Du Bois, Zora Neale Hurston, Theodore Dreiser, William Carlos Williams, André Breton, and Samuel Beckett, along with hundreds of illustrations. The anthology's tributes to jazz, which includes photographs of Armstrong and Ellington as well as a range of articles, take part in a general attempt to celebrate the cultural accomplishments of black Africans and Americans around the globe. While *Negro* discusses jazz as one of the great achievements of an oppressed people in part because of its wide-ranging, international influence, the anthology ultimately reveals how jazz vexes and transforms the notion of an emergent, modern transatlantic culture of dance and sound. As the essays in *Negro* display, jazz disrupts national and racial boundaries even as it calls attention to them, reinforces and remakes them.

The articles on jazz in *Negro* share the premise that jazz is marked by its mobility. One piece in particular discusses that international dance phenomenon, the Lindy Hop, which owes its name to Charles Lindbergh's pioneering transatlantic flight from New York to Paris. In its reference to the Lindy Hop, the *Negro* anthology thus takes part in the assumption that jazz too was capable of bridging old divides, rendering distance, language, and ethnicity as no barriers for the infectious rhythms of modern times. Yet *Negro* seems unable to avoid the question of what it means for jazz to be American if it is performed, reproduced, and enjoyed outside of America. The question of what jazz does to national identity—whether it transcends or consolidates it—lingers in a series of pieces that variously meditate on the movement of the music back and forth across the Atlantic.

In three essays in particular, an Englishman, a Frenchman, and an American discuss their respective positions on jazz and America. The Englishman, John Banting, insists that while jazz may have crossed the Atlantic, it remains staunchly American, so much so that the best jazz dancing can only be found in the States. It is a case of "wine being best in its own country," Banting declares.[116] Such a metaphor—even in cliché—ties jazz to the soil of its national origins, a local product best sampled in Harlem clubs; jazz is foreign and literally out-of-place in England. In an essay translated from the French by Samuel Beckett, Robert Goffin offers a distinct view insofar as he ranks jazz as America's greatest cultural achievement—"surely of more importance than sky-scrapers and Fordism"—but one which most Americans fail to appreciate.[117] In Goffin's view, it takes a European cultural critic, namely himself, to celebrate the art form that Americans callously take for granted. The American, George Antheil, provides a third perspective, one that most closely matches the fears of anti-jazzers outside of the United States. The question of where jazz properly belongs, Antheil suggests, is moot because jazz transforms the places it touches, "leaving everywhere gigantic mulatto patches," racializing and Americanizing audiences and musicians alike.[118] Despite all of the reactionary "papal decrees" leveled against jazz, Antheil insists that it is too late for Britain or Europe to escape it.[119] Using Stravinsky as an example, he argues that no music written after jazz can be wholly free of its influence. In his conception, Europe has become Americanized in precisely the way that Clive Bell fearfully predicted. What Antheil argues, and what Banting the Englishman wants to resist, is the way in which jazz leaves its mark, its sounds, its stain on the nations whose populace embrace it, producing a transnational, consumable "American" identity that will not stay put in America.

Conclusion: From Jazz in Britain to British Jazz

In his memoir, Kingsley Amis, one of the best-known young British writers of the fifties, describes his relationship to jazz as a stark departure from that of his predecessors: "Born in 1922, I suppose I was one of the first British generation to whom jazz was a completely natural thing, not new, not a fad, not exotic, and certainly not in any way unrespectable, or suspect because 'negroid.' Older people were against it then, an added recommendation."[120] According to Amis, for the generation born in and after the *annus mirabilis* of modernism, jazz was "a completely natural thing," an organic part of their culture rather than a foreign invasion of it. Moreover, the appeal of jazz was only strengthened by its ability to offend the highbrow, nationalist ideals of those born before the First World War. In Amis's *Lucky Jim* (1954), jazz serves the purposes of youthful rebellion, an effect that draws directly on the discourses developed during the interwar years. In an exemplary moment, the novel's antihero, Jim Dixon lets loose a "long trombone-blast of anarchistic laughter" while plotting the downfall of his Oxbridge professor, whom Jim despises for his devotion to "the English tradition" and nostalgia for "Merrie England."[121] Even more striking than Amis's gleeful recruitment of jazz for anti-establishment metaphor is the extent to which Amis understood jazz to *belong* to his generation of British youth. By Amis's day, jazz remained capable of offending elitist sensibilities, but it was neither new nor shocking. Rather, it had become the "natural" property of Amis's generation.

Amis's good friend, the poet Philip Larkin, also displayed a lifelong devotion to jazz. Larkin, who doubled as a jazz commentator for ten years for the *Daily Telegraph*, commented in 1961 on the place of American jazz performers in England: "an American musician can no more play with British ones than an American docker can give a hand down at Tilbury."[122] Referring to the protectionist legislation that dates back to the thirties, Larkin explains that American jazz musicians were barred from performing in England. After similar legislation on the part of the American Federation of Musicians in the forties, British bands found it harder to play in New York, though admittedly there was less demand in America for British jazz. Although Larkin insists that jazz "remains solidly American" and that "it is the American musicians who matter," he also goes out of his way to chart the movement from jazz in Britain to British jazz.[123] In the forties, Larkin insists, British audiences out-danced American ones and "jazz records were more sought after in Britain than in America."[124] By the time of his writing for the *Daily Telegraph*, as Larkin records in an article entitled "Cool, Britannia," British jazz had come into its own. Larkin notes:

> Not so long ago, the unlikelihood of the Briton as a jazzman would have been perfectly expressed by thinking of him in a bowler hat. Result: complete incongruity, like Mrs. Grundy dancing the can-can. Yet today the bowler hat is worn with jolly unselfconsciousness by some of this country's most popular groups as part of their stand uniform. Nobody laughs. In fact, they cheer. British jazz has arrived, in Britain at any rate.[125]

With a pun on "Rule, Britannia," Larkin explains that Britain's new "cool" has emerged with its jolly, bowler-hatted jazz bands.[126] While Larkin's pun is almost as precious as Mrs. Grundy's incongruous can-can, it accurately summarizes the cultural transition embodied in newly British jazz. By the time of Larkin's writing in the early sixties, Britain's struggle over its identity as a declining world power has subsided into earnest attempts to be cool. Since the interwar years, British culture had become so thoroughly Americanized that American culture can now, finally, become British. After the beginning of the Cold War, a call-to-arms-and-Englishness such as Clive Bell's "Plus de Jazz," had become unthinkable, not so much in its content, but in its utter faith in its own ability to announce the end of jazz. By this late date, American culture had permeated British culture: Nancy Cunard's transatlantic field of exchange had become the new state of the nation, and the Beatles, whose early work displayed jazz influences, were launching their own style of transatlantic invasion. Jazz's British legacy is Larkin's crooning in his 1964 poem "For Sidney Bechet": "On me your voice falls like they say love should."[127] The British affection for jazz in the postwar period relies in part upon a nostalgia for the end of nostalgia, or at least for the nostalgic protection of an idealized lost Englishness. If jazz continues to represent the transatlantic assault on traditionalism even after the wars, then it does so in service of the rebellious art of the next British generation.

3. The Entertainment Empire
Britain's Hollywood between the Wars

England keeps her colonies, but she does not keep them entertained.

—American filmmaker, 1926

So far as films go we are now a colonial people.

—British filmmaker, 1937

Let every part of Merry England be merry in its own way. Death to Hollywood.

—John Maynard Keynes, 1945

Near the end of the Second World War, John Maynard Keynes, the well-known economist and Bloomsbury intellectual, gave a rousing BBC speech on the founding of the British Arts Council. At this strained moment in Britain's history, it is not surprising that Keynes would frame his tribute to the British arts as a battle against a formidable enemy. It is surprising that this enemy was not a military opponent but rather the source of a well-loved leisure pastime: Hollywood. When Keynes proclaimed "Death to Hollywood" as the means to resurrect "merry England," his tongue-in-cheek battle cry rested its wit upon the symbolic significance of Hollywood in Britain in the twenties and thirties.[1] To some, Hollywood cinema seemed to be invading England, transforming local practices to such an extent that a new British Arts Council could only hope to repair the damage. At the same time, Hollywood's sphere of influence had global implications. In Britain in particular, some saw the potential for a new kind of world power emerging out of the mass cinema from across the Atlantic.

The historian A. J. P. Taylor has called film-going the "essential social habit" of the modern era, Lenin referred to cinema as the "most important" of the arts, and Mussolini called it the era's "strangest weapon."[2] It is no wonder that as Hollywood films became increasingly popular, it sparked defensive anxieties among elites in Britain. Unlike jazz, whose early international influence focused mainly on Britain and Europe, Hollywood held global appeal. By the mid-1920s, most of the films seen around the world were American: according to some estimates, 80 percent of cinema worldwide and 85 percent of that in Britain came out of Hollywood.[3] While British films regained a share of the domestic market under a set of protectionist film acts in the twenties and thirties, the perception of Hollywood as colonizer remained.[4] From one British filmmaker's assessment of the English as "a colonial people" under Hollywood's rule, to the "colonies" of European talent clustered in Los Angeles, descriptions of Hollywood persistently translated the industry's influence into imperial rhetoric.[5] Such phrasing registered the feeling that Britain might play the colony to Hollywood's empire, rendering Britain colonized at home and superseded abroad by the films themselves. Although the so-called imperialism of U.S. entertainment was distinct from the United States' territorial acquisitions, the two were readily conflated in the eyes of those in Britain who recognized the United States as an emerging world power. For whereas the British Empire operated most blatantly through occupation and governance, the American Entertainment Empire easily trespassed territorial borders. Through its mass reproduction of leisure and commodification of the everyday, the Entertainment Empire served as the ambassador of a broad system of Fordist capitalism. Moreover, in contrast to the violence and bureaucracy of much British imperialism, Hollywood was seductive. From the viewpoint of its British detractors, Hollywood had managed to construct a strange and largely unprecedented worldwide scenario in which consumers eagerly clamored and even paid to become subject to their new imperial master.

Like Britain, Europe spent the years just after World War I in thrall to Hollywood. Moreover, as in the British case, cultural elites and conservative politicians alike denounced Hollywood as a rapacious monster, a corrupting influence, and, indeed, as an empire. Nonetheless, Britain's narrative of the Entertainment Empire was unique for two reasons. First, Britain found itself particularly susceptible to the influence of American English, initially encountered in the captions of silent films and later on the soundtracks of the talking cinema. Second, America's status as a former British colony turned rival empire intensified the assault on Britain's imperial self-image. Indeed, reactions against Hollywood drew strength from assessments of growing American military and economic power

on the world stage. Even more tellingly, accounts of American cinematic prowess implicated racial ideology, suggesting that the Americans might take control
of the meaning of whiteness. As early as the twenties, Hollywood's film presence
throughout Britain and its empire prompted grim announcements of colonization
in reverse, long before the post–World War II period with which such images are
most often associated.

Most broadly, Hollywood appeared as an arbiter of national identity, the author
and merchant of an idea of America. In a 1927 debate in the House of Commons,
one representative quoted a film column in the *Daily Express* that announced, "The
bulk of our picturegoers are Americanized to an extent that makes them regard
a British film as a foreign film... They talk America, think America, and dream
America. We have several million people, mostly women, who, to all intent and
purpose, are temporary American citizens."[6] According to British elites, certain
populations were especially vulnerable to the consumption of American ideals:
women, children, the working classes, and beyond England's borders those colonial subjects who learned about the West through the moving pictures. At the same
time, the dangers of this imaginative citizenship were economic. Some believed
that Hollywood films offered free and compelling advertising for American commodities, thus paving the way for the further Americanization of the globe. As
Lord Nelson put it in a 1925 debate in the House of Lords, "the Americans realized
almost instantaneously that the cinema was a heaven-sent method for advertising
themselves, their country, their methods, their wares, their ideas, and even their
language, and they have seized upon it as a method of persuading the whole world,
civilized and uncivilized, into the belief that America is really the only country
which counts."[7] While both Lord Nelson and the *Daily Times* somewhat overstated
Hollywood's actual influence, they each reveal how film was beginning to unsettle
scripts of place and nation in their suggestions that the British could be naturalized as Americans in front of the screen.

Through my concept of the "American Entertainment Empire," the work of
film historians can be profitably brought together with scholarship on American
imperialism. Film historians such as Sarah Street, Jeffrey Richards, and Christine
Gledhill have amply recorded Hollywood's ascendancy in Britain, Europe, and
around the world.[8] Whereas Hollywood was one among many burgeoning national
cinemas at the turn of the century, it grew exponentially during the First World
War, a time when European cinematic innovation was put on hold.[9] Because of
the American launch of the talking cinema or "talkies" in 1927, Hollywood posed
a new type of threat, particularly in English-speaking regions. While British films
regained some of the home market under the protectionist film act of 1927, public

critique of Hollywood persisted. Work on American imperialism occasionally nods to Hollywood, yet studies such as Giovanni Arrighi's treatment of American hegemony in *The Long Twentieth Century* tend to focus on economic and political dominance rather than cultural influence.[10] Historian Victoria de Grazia begins to bridge the gap in her account of continental European conceptions of the United States as a "Market Empire" whose dominance grew from its range of desirable commodities.[11] My concept of the Entertainment Empire builds on such observations by foregrounding the ideological scripts and messages—the semiotic invasion that Hollywood in particular seemed to propose. Indeed, the Entertainment Empire concept rests less on the actual global impact of Hollywood and more on British perceptions of that impact. Rather than recounting a history of Hollywood's rise and spread, I consider how British elites told the story of the Entertainment Empire as a means to make sense of their own place in the world.

Perhaps the most significant aspect of the Entertainment Empire, from the interwar British perspective, can be traced to anxiety about language. British citizens and colonial subjects alike learned to speak American English from Hollywood pictures—first from the intertitles and later from recorded dialogue. One British commentator noted with dismay that the East London youth who pumped his petrol affected an American accent: "He is only one among millions whose entire lives are being influenced by the American Cinema. What good can all this do to England? Will it create patriotism? Will it create a desire to keep our great Empire together?"[12] The film acts of 1927 and 1934 protected the economic interests of British production companies, but they also, in the rhetoric used by many politicians, aimed to return the English language to the nation.[13] Even the advertisement for Hitchcock's *Blackmail*, Britain's first talking film, tellingly read, "Hear English as it should be spoken."[14] Part of the resistance to the American talkies emerged out of a sense that American slang was more than an abrasive dialect; it was a threat to the moral authority and habits of mind housed in the English language. As the language of the people of England slowly and pervasively Americanized, some in Britain imagined so too would their national character change, leaving "merry England" in desperate need of renewal. At the same time, as American English began to rival British English around the world, it threatened to undermine the schooling in the mother tongue that was such a fundamental aspect of the later British imperial project.

This promise of linguistic revolution on a global scale caught the attention of modernists writing in English. Early film critics had already envisioned silent cinema as a universal language of images with the potential to bring together disparate peoples without the divisive babel of distinct tongues. Proponents of this theory included the members of the avant-garde film collective known as POOL, namely, the American poet H. D., the English writer and heiress Bryher, and the Scottish director Kenneth Macpherson. With the dream of a universal language of silent cinema violently disrupted by the rise of the American talkie, the POOL collective condemned Hollywood in the pages of their film journal, *Close Up*. Although the journal itself had European inclinations—spending considerable time on French and Russian films—the core group of POOL sounded increasingly British in their reactions against Hollywood. Through such condemnation, the members of POOL drew on broader cultural discourses to produce a modernist narrative of the Entertainment Empire in the pages of *Close Up*, presenting Hollywood as a double threat to art and to Englishness.

As a case study in the discursive production of the Entertainment Empire, *Close Up* reveals how a British modernist view of cinematic art depends upon narratives of Americanization. Attention to *Close Up* further reveals how an ideology of modernism, as distinct from the actual diversity of modernist literary production, came into being through a series of dialectical oppositions: highbrow and lowbrow, art and entertainment, Britain and America. Of course, this is not to reproduce those critical views that imagine modernism to be completely at odds with American mass culture. Rather, film criticism gives us a different account of the invention of modernist aesthetic modes. Miriam Hansen has argued that classic Hollywood films were what she calls a "vernacular modernism," persuasively suggesting that the films were more visually savvy than earlier critics had assumed. Moreover, critics have amply discussed how Hollywood films and modernist writing influenced or spoke to each other. Susan McCabe, for instance, argues that modernist writers such as Stein and Moore drew upon cinematic techniques of montage and superimposition in their poems; David Trotter suggests that cinema and modernist writing followed "parallel histories" of development.[15] Moreover, Hollywood, although strategically supported by the U.S. government, was hardly homegrown American—the town was populated with European and British directors and stars, from Louis Gasnier to Hitchcock to Chaplin.[16] Furthermore, as Priya Jaikumar points out, Hollywood films were often censored, edited, and adapted in foreign markets, such as those in India; Miriam Hansen notes that in Russia, cheerful Hollywood films were often given tragic endings.[17] All of this heterogeneity and diversity fed rather than foreclosed the narrative of the Entertainment Empire. In a world of blurred boundaries and trespassed divisions, the idea of a division between art and entertainment, such as that expressed in *Close Up*, seemed all the more necessary.

The range of texts taken up in this chapter, from a travel diary to news editorials, from film criticism to satirical novels, all participate in the construction of the

Entertainment Empire. Because the Entertainment Empire was itself a narrative, the new genre of film criticism, with its central, modernist project of distinguishing art from entertainment, serves this chapter's inquiries more fully than analyses of individual films could. Moreover, although the burgeoning field of audience studies, reflected in the important work of Richard Maltby, Melvyn Stokes, and others, has given us detailed pictures of ordinary filmgoers, *Close Up* shows us something different.[18] Specifically, attention to *Close Up*, which called itself the first English-language journal of film criticism, can help us to see how the narrative of the Entertainment Empire was not at odds with the central concerns of modernism but rather produced in concert with them.

In its concluding section, this chapter looks at two novels published after the end of *Close Up*'s run, as well as a Hollywood film co-authored by Aldous Huxley. Taken together, these texts help to establish another important thread, the reinvention of British literary tradition to counter the imagined influence of Hollywood. From images of Britain's imperial decline to the call for the resurrection of Englishness, certain British redefinitions of nation and empire emerged through a discursive battle against the foe they had themselves created. While the British may be the primary authors of the narrative of the Entertainment Empire, it is this narrative that reflexively puts pressure on conceptions of Britain and its modernism, at least insofar as American entertainment seemed to propose a new and competing style of imperialism poised to reshape global culture in modern times.

"We are now a colonial people": Hollywood and the Reversals of Empire

In his 1926 travel memoir, *Jesting Pilate*, Aldous Huxley makes the observation, in all earnestness, that Hollywood threatens to undermine the British Empire. Huxley recalls a trip to Java during which he and a few other Englishmen found themselves watching a Hollywood comedy—he doesn't specify which—among a group of Javanese. The slapstick antics of cops and robbers, so benign at home in England, give Huxley pause when viewed abroad. In Huxley's words:

> To the subject races of the East and South, Hollywood proclaims us a people of criminals and mental defectives. It was better, surely, in the old days before the cinema was invented, when the white men's subjects were totally ignorant of the world in which their masters lived. It was possible for them,

then, to believe that the white men's civilisation was something great and marvelous—something greater, perhaps, and more extraordinary than it really was. Hollywood has changed all that.[19]

According to Huxley, when Hollywood films portray whites as crooks and bumbling fools, they threaten to dilute the ideological power of whiteness in the non-Western world. In this conception, Hollywood's comic trifles quite unwittingly put pressure on the edifice of prestige and superiority that undergirds Britain's modern imperialism. While Huxley may seem extreme in holding such beliefs, he was hardly alone. As a government official put it in 1927, "Today films are shown to millions of people throughout the Empire and must unconsciously influence the ideas and outlook of British people of all races."[20] In 1932, the British Commission on Film issued a report that insisted in all seriousness that "the conception of white civilisation which [colonized peoples] are receiving from third-rate melodrama is an international menace."[21] While the commission also suggested, on a brighter note, that film could be a force for "social education," one member, echoing Huxley, warned that "The success of our government of subject races depends almost entirely on the degree of respect which we can inspire. Incalculable is the damage that has already been done to the prestige of Europeans in India and the Far East through the widespread exhibition of ultra-sensational and disreputable pictures."[22] In strikingly similar language, the editors of *Close Up* evince such an opinion, noting that in the contemporary films of the day, "European (or pseudo-European via America) civilization very often does not appear to advantage and might easily do very great harm to European prestige."[23] A contributor to *Close Up*, in reference to cinema's increasing global power and importance, even proposed funding a British film school out of the budget of the national defense.[24]

Although these reactions against Hollywood reflect a disparate range of sources—Aldous Huxley writing in the twenties, a government-sponsored commission, and an avant-garde film journal—the sentiment is much the same: Hollywood threatens European civilization and British prestige through its undignified images of white people. Whereas jazz transgressed racial boundaries and invoked images of blackness, Hollywood put pressure on the meaning of whiteness. Moreover, Hollywood had a fuller claim than jazz to visual representation and thus a faster route to the global masses. From the point of view of some in Britain, such a widespread attack on racial purity might be expected from a film industry that was already a haven for Jews and other Eastern European immigrants. At the same time, such fears for the fate of whiteness are particularly ironic given the racist legacy of American cinema, as embodied in D. W. Griffith's influential 1915 celebration of the Ku Klux Klan *Birth of a Nation*. Yet the threat that Hollywood seemed to pose to European and especially to British imperialism goes well beyond the content of individual films. The perceived assault upon whiteness was part of a broader sense that Britain was losing control over the story of the West. The Entertainment Empire had its own stories—cops-and-robber stories, melodramas, and Westerns—apparently capable of disrupting the British imperial narrative. Hollywood's implicit and largely unintended insult to the British Empire was therefore not to critique it but rather to imply its obsolescence. Increasingly since the end of the First World War, Hollywood proposed a new style of world power that made British imperialism, conventionally lauded as an engine of progress, seem fusty and traditional. As a former American film producer wrote in a 1926 letter to the London *Times*, "England keeps her colonies, but she does not keep them entertained."[25] Entertainment, the letter writer proposes, is the new globalism that keeps us "all tied fast together." By the 1920s, such sentiments explain why it was already beginning to feel so crucial to rout the spread of American entertainment in order to preserve the ideological underpinnings of the British Empire.[26]

Sounding American: Hollywood English and the Talkies

Fears such as those of Aldous Huxley for the fate of European imperialism emerged in the early twenties during Hollywood's first ascendency. Yet the end of the twenties brought a new kind of threat: the launch of the talking cinema or "talkies," with the 1927 American film *The Jazz Singer*. It seems almost overdetermined that the first talkie was also a film that simultaneously invoked jazz music, racial transgression, and Jewish American immigrants—a film, therefore, that embodied much of what was already threatening about American culture even as it took the form of a new and potentially dominant technology.[27] As this new technology spread around the world in fits and starts, cinema houses struggled to outfit themselves for sound. Writing about the film industry in England, Christopher Isherwood called the scramble to keep up with Hollywood talkies "the time of the Panic."[28] Due to the enormous expense of a talking production, smaller, avant-garde filmmakers were hard pressed to make the transition to sound. And at least initially, it seemed that the world might devour an English-language cinema as eagerly as it had consumed Hollywood's silent fare. Nonetheless Britain, unlike Europe, rightly saw itself and its colonies as particularly vulnerable to Hollywood productions by virtue of their shared language. Indeed, Hollywood viewed Britain as a major overseas market and the British Empire and dominions as prime territory for its profits.[29] British grumblings against the Hollywood film thus took on something of a new tone with the rise of the talkies, amplifying earlier fears for English culture into a protectionist attitude toward the English language itself. In the House of Commons in 1929, Sir Alfred Knox voiced a widespread concern when he asked "whether the import of the American talkies could not be limited in order to protect the language of the people of England."[30] Such parliamentary debate evinced particular concern that children and the working classes would absorb American slang and the true English idiom would be lost.

This assault on English seemed at once an allegory and a driving force for the Anglo-American shift in fortunes. As an American writer put it, "the language of the British Isles may, in time, become a set of quaint and curious dialects on the American periphery."[31] For perhaps the first time in modern history, it seemed that the imperial center might cease to be the linguistic center, that an ex-colony might control what was becoming the new international language, and that not only England but the world might start to sound American. Of course, looking back, these fears may seem extreme: everyone in Britain and its former empire doesn't really sound like an American or like a Hollywood film. But the early twentieth-century spread of American media through film and the wireless promoted the rise of global English, and, even more important, sparked fantasies about the future of national and imperial identity by presenting an alternative to British linguistic hegemony.

To be sure, there was a fair amount of resistance to American English and the Hollywood talkies across the British Commonwealth and parts of the empire. Canada and Australia, for instance, saw an increased desire for linguistic purity to protect their versions of British English from American influence. The director of education in New South Wales, Australia, accused the American talkies of a "sickly sentimental English in an objectionable nasal twang, full of slang," and called for "drastic steps...to preserve the purity of the English tongue."[32] At the same time, there were those who saw American English as the herald of a new internationalism. An article in the *Melbourne Sun* suggests that even non-English speaking countries would learn English in order to enjoy their favorite films:

> To keep up their acquaintance with Mary Pickford and company, it will be necessary for even staid and old-established European countries to get busy with grammars and dictionaries, and learn enough English to follow the spirited conversations of the screen...It may seem unlikely that people will take their pleasures seriously enough to go to the trouble of learning a complete new language...but love of amusement is a fairly general tendency,

and there are many picture-goers who, apparently, would rather go without their dinners than miss their regular nights at the local theatre.[33]

A 1929 editorial in the *Times of India* builds on such assumptions in its vision of a new world order heralded by the talkies:

> Suppose American becomes the universal language. It is America's greatest creation, and there is every likelihood that it will one day find the world guessing. The 'talkies' will penetrate every quarter of the habitable world, and an Ambassador can greet the President of the Chinese Republic with a 'Say boy' and yet run no risk of being misunderstood.[34]

This positive slant on the global adaptability of American English suggests that the language of the talkies could become that of international politics, brokering a new era of global communication through the felicity of shared slang. In Britain, too, American English had its champions, perhaps none greater than the linguist C. K. Ogden, who along with literary critic I. A. Richards, saw American English as a precursor to an age without linguistic barriers, an age of what they called "debabelization."[35]

Both its champions and detractors shared a sense that Hollywood's American English had the potential to become a new world language. Yet there were some who had particular fears for the fate of those in England. In his 1934 treatise, *Men without Art*, British writer and artist Wyndham Lewis connects such fears about the English language and Britain's place in the world with cognate concerns over Hollywood's impact on class structures at home. Lewis notes wistfully, "while England was a uniquely powerful empire-state, ruled by an aristocratic caste, its influence upon the speech as upon the psychology of the American ex-colonies was overwhelming."[36] According to Lewis, Britain once ruled and shaped America; now "the tables have effectively turned," putting England in the role of colony to America's new media empire.[37] Lewis laments that Hollywood has thus undermined Britain's empire, aristocracy, and language in one fell swoop: "But today that ascendancy has almost entirely vanished. The aristocratic caste is nothing but a shadow of itself, the cinema has brought the American scene and the American dialect nightly into the heart of England, and the 'Americanizing' process is far advanced."[38] For Lewis, the trouble with Hollywood English was the erosion of class hierarchy that followed in its wake.

Even before the advent of sound, Hollywood films seemed poised to undermine the British class system by debasing its higher and lower elements alike. What seemed the bad democracy of the cinema became even more threatening with the rise of the talkie. Diction and accent, which had long been indicators of social rank, were becoming even starker signs of class difference in an age of increasing social mobility. The popularity of George Bernard Shaw's *Pygmalion* (1913, 1916), in which the cockney flower girl Eliza Doolittle becomes a lady primarily through the transformation of her speech, was a tribute to the tenacious bond between language and social class. By outfitting moviegoers from across the class spectrum with a homogenized vocabulary of American slang, the talkies threatened to erode the role of speech as an indicator of class position. As Lewis puts it, " 'Done gones,' 'good guys' and 'buddies' sprout from the lips of cockney children as readily as upon those to the manner born."[39] While it might seem that a handful of slang terms would be insufficient to erode a class system entrenched by centuries of power and privilege, Lewis explains that it is precisely this power and privilege that are vulnerable to Americanization. In his words, "there is no politically powerful literate class any longer now, in our British 'Banker's Olympus,' to confer prestige upon an exact and intelligent selective speech. Americanization—which is also for England, at least, proletarianization—is too far advanced to require underlining."[40]

It is significant that Lewis considers Americanization to be a synonym for the proletarianization of England. In Lewis's conception, there is a social algebra at work by which members of the various classes are morphing into Americans, and, in so doing, forming a vast undifferentiated mass rather than occupying distinct niches in a social hierarchy. Lewis's fear, although deeply elitist, is not mere snobbism. Even those who were committed to the elevation of the working classes through education and to a less stratified England, did not tend to favor the democracy instigated by Hollywood. Unlike education, Americanization seemed capable of spreading equality only through debasement. According to writers such as Lewis, English literature refined the sensibilities whereas the Hollywood talking film dragged the working classes and much of the rest of society down to new depths of crass feeling, bald consumerism, and, of course, bad slang.

Close Up and the Talking Cinema

It is one of the ironies of film history that *Close Up*, the avant-garde film journal devoted to the artistic potential of the silent cinema, should publish its inaugural issue in 1927, the same year in which America launched the first mainstream talking film. Whereas Wyndham Lewis directly lambasts the Hollywood talkie, key contributors to *Close Up* become increasingly condemnatory over time, constructing a narrative of the Entertainment Empire in tandem with their call for British cinematic modernism. *Close Up*'s relatively short run from 1927–1934 coincided with the heyday of American talking cinema. *Close Up* resembled a work of literary modernism more than a mass publication—its modest circulation of only five hundred copies per issue (printed monthly until 1931 and quarterly thereafter) were distributed in bookshops in Paris, London, New York, and Geneva.[41] Indeed, as Anne Friedberg notes, even "the journal's appearance resembled that of the literary masterpieces of the decade."[42] Moreover, its financial supporter, Bryher, also directly or indirectly a patron of writers such as Dorothy Richardson and James Joyce, allowed the editors to represent their views "free from the constraints of commercial publication."[43] Such literary sensibilities would lead *Close Up* to define itself against what it increasingly framed as the antithesis of cinematic modernism: Hollywood's talking cinema.

Before they fully understood the impact of the talking film, *Close Up*'s editors embraced Hollywood as one among many national cinemas. Because it took some time for *The Jazz Singer* to cross the Atlantic to Britain and Europe, the editors paid it less attention than one might imagine in hindsight. More important, in these early years some of *Close Up*'s contributors were skeptical that the talking cinema would endure; others held out hope that it might be a novelty that would peacefully coexist with the grander world of the silent film.[44] Once it became clear that the talkies were no novelty but would in fact supplant silent cinema, *Close Up*'s attitude toward them grew hostile, leading the editor of *Close Up*, Kenneth Macpherson, to denounce the talking film as a "monstrosity" and Bryher to lament that the Americans "forced the talking picture on the silent screens of the world."[45]

Close Up did not only experience what its critics called a crisis of speech but, more specifically, a crisis of American speech.[46] Scrutiny of *Close Up* from a transatlantic perspective reveals that this "international" journal was international on an older, British model during a time when Hollywood was putting pressure on the very meaning of the international. While Michael North rightly notes that the talkies heralded the return of "cultural specificity" through the use of national languages, it is also the case that for many in *Close Up*, Hollywood talkies represented the loss of national and local specificity.[47] For key contributors to *Close Up*, Hollywood seemed to preclude the return of what might be called cinematic regionalism to England. In contrast to *Close Up*'s vision of unique national film traditions, Hollywood seemed to propose a flattening of national specificity and to encourage a global embrace of American accents and Hollywood endings. Moreover, Hollywood spoke to a vast audience. Whereas *Close Up*'s universal language of silent cinema would have mainly reached the avant-garde, Hollywood addressed the masses.[48]

In their efforts on behalf of *Close Up*, the avant-garde film collective of H. D., Bryher, and Kenneth Macpherson illuminate the story of the Entertainment

Empire in a particularly revealing manner. First, because *Close Up* imagined itself as the first English-language journal of film criticism, its stated purpose was to distinguish art from entertainment, or the diamonds from the dross. This critical endeavor kept entertainment, which Macpherson dismissed as "eyewash and bunk," at the center of the group's aesthetic project.[49] Such reactions against entertainment were also in large part reactions against a particular idea of America. Indeed, the long-standing critical contention that modernism variously defines itself through and against mass culture is, in this context, incomplete without attention to national identity and its discontents. In the writings of the POOL collective, the ideas of entertainment, Hollywood, and America are deeply entangled and interdependent. Such interdependence drives *Close Up*, despite its international scope and mission, to turn surprisingly and forcefully British in its attempts to chart the future of cinema. Particularly the core group of three, the Scottish Macpherson, the English Bryher, and the American expatriate and British citizen, H. D., establish the British dimension of *Close Up*'s reactions against Hollywood.[50] In their unique blend of aesthetic criticism and social commentary, these members of the POOL collective present Britishness and specifically the idea of a British tradition as the necessary antidote to the influence of the Entertainment Empire.

In the pages of *Close Up*, Macpherson boldly frames the talking film as a new imperialism, based in American English, taking over the territory that once seemed to belong to the universal language of silent pictures. Calling the talkie a "parricide" and "the militant imperialism of the screen," Macpherson explains that it "is, indeed, to his parent what all Rome's clap-trap was to intellectual Greece."[51] These references to the talkie's Oedipal capacity resonate with tacit reference to the Anglo-American relationship. While images of the United States as an imperial upstart were common by the interwar years, Macpherson translates this image into an indictment of Hollywood as empire. It is interesting to note that while the British Empire had long been analogized to ancient Rome, here it is the United States, or at least its new talking film, that stands for a militant assault on intellect and tradition. Moreover, the very creation of the talkies was sometimes imagined as an act of violence. As a contributor to *Close Up* slyly suggested, it seemed as if, in response to the British quota restricting Hollywood films, "the Americans... invented the talkie by way of revenge."[52]

Bryher takes up Macpherson's critique and extends it into a full-blown assault in her *Close Up* articles "Danger in the Cinema" and two-part series "The Hollywood Code." Even more clearly than Macpherson, Bryher, patron of literary modernism, presents Hollywood as a national threat. Notably, Bryher explains that by going to the movies, the British public have become "children" and "idiots" devoted to little more than the on-screen antics of Mickey Mouse.[53] Whereas Bryher previously defended Hollywood against its many detractors, with the entrenchment of the talkie, she flatly announces that "Hollywood...cannot produce art."[54] Rather, she avers, Hollywood numbs the intellect of the English viewer, rendering his "critical perception...blunted through a continuous diet of Hollywood patent foods."[55] In Bryher's revealing analogy, Hollywood cooks up a perniciously bland foodstuff capable of transforming the consumer. Insofar as Hollywood fare is ingested, metabolized, and made flesh, it is capable of remaking the modern subject in its image. At the same time, Bryher's analogy offers an easy transition from the gusta-tory to the critical: after all, it is the interwar commitment to the stratification of taste that provides a framework for Bryher's distinctions.

Bryher's fears for the individual filmgoer translate into even broader concerns for England and Englishness. Insisting that Hollywood rings the death knell for art in cinema, Bryher explains that "so dangerous has the position become that it is possible that the film as an art-form will die out, for the way is made infinitely easier for Hollywood to impose its standards on the English market."[56] Because of the economic crisis at the end of the twenties, England is particularly vulnerable to Hollywood: "owing to the crash of the pound, Americans can pay the duties at comparatively little cost" and thus invade England all the more readily.[57] In con-sequence, Bryher asserts, "there will be few foreign films and the Hollywood code will dominate British pictures."[58] Bryher predicts that the Americans themselves will be driven away from Hollywood by "its low quality and merit," forcing the stu-dios to look to "England as their only profitable market."[59] Bryher's unrealistically grim musings lead her to a revealingly dystopian vision of English audiences, alone in all the world, thronging to the latest Hollywood film. Her depiction of a future ruled by a Hollywood more horrible than any Nosferatu warns her English readers away from the leisurely film-going that would drive the nation to such a fate.

Bryher's fears for England and its people also harbor a particular class dimen-sion: a fear for the fate of the middle classes. Whereas many in England professed their concern for working-class audiences, the middle classes were also increas-ingly consumers of cinematic spectacle. In her denunciation of Hollywood, Bryher attempts to dissuade middle-class moviegoers from attending the cinema by appealing to class superiority. Insisting that middle-class Americans do not go to the movies, Bryher asks, "How many of our readers know that the middle classes in the States neither go to films nor do they discuss them, any more than we should in England, discuss an amusement park or swings at a fair."[60] Bryher further admon-ishes her British audience with the contrasting example of the American middle classes: "They go to the theatre...and leave the cinemas for the children or the unskilled, whose parents probably couldn't talk English."[61] The force of Bryher's claim not only rests on the idea that British filmgoers might turn into Americans but that they might also turn into the *worst* Americans: the unwashed, uneducated masses. With its visceral appeal to ideals of ethnic and linguistic purity, Bryher's warning reflects the related anxiety that Hollywood itself was being run by Eastern European immigrants who had further eroded the faint traces of Englishness lingering in America. By going to the movies, Bryher ultimately suggests, the British middle classes are degenerating and speeding the dissolution of the class system. In an uncanny echo of the sentiments of Wyndham Lewis, a writer with whom Bryher would otherwise have very little in common, Bryher builds a picture of Hollywood as a threat to the British class system into *Close Up*'s call for home-grown cinematic art.

Although Bryher, Macpherson, and others in *Close Up* excoriated the American talkie, they celebrated the release of the film advertised as the first British talkie, Alfred Hitchcock's *Blackmail* (1929).[62] According to his own accounts, Hitchcock shot both silent and sound versions of the film nearly simultaneously.[63] Great lengths were taken to assure that the characters would sound British. Anny Ondra, the lovely Polish-born star of *Blackmail*, did not lend her voice to the film; instead, British actress Joan Barry provided the crisp, proper dialogue that Ondra pantomimes on screen. Whereas Macpherson had lately called the talkie a "monstrosity" and a "parricide," he refers to *Blackmail* with considerable national pride: "I was touched and amazed to find it thus in a British film, far and away the best talkie we have seen."[64] Macpherson reserves special praise for the film's "superb" British sound in the form of "Joan Barry's ghosting for Miss Ondra's voice."[65] In Britain at large, film reviewers were ecstatic upon the opening of the newly dubbed *Blackmail*. One article in the *Times* of London calls *Blackmail* "completely successful" and something of which the production company, British International Pictures, "might be proud."[66] Another highlights the manner in which Hitchcock, "sweeping aside American traditions of speed and glamour, has given us a piece of uncompromising 'cinema.' "[67] Focusing on the film's use of British places—scenes at Scotland Yard and an extended chase through the British Museum—the review sums up the way in which many hope that *Blackmail* "should appreciably raise the stock of our fluctuating British film industry."[68] Yet while Macpherson and others identified *Blackmail* as the film capable of sweeping aside American ascendancy and clearing a path for a British talking cinema, one film was not enough. More pervasively, *Blackmail* sparked the desire in Britain not only for well-liked individual films but also for a national film tradition capable of supplanting American talkies by successfully sounding British.

The Case of the Missing Cinema:
The British Film Tradition

Despite the success of *Blackmail* and the legacy of Hitchcock, the French new wave film director, François Truffaut, famously quipped that the terms "British" and "cinema" are incompatible.[69] In response to such an undeserved reputation, contemporary film critics have taken pains to point out the myriad ways in which interwar British cinema, particularly under the protection of the film acts, served the needs of the British public. Lawrence Napper argues that interwar British cinema constituted a "middlebrow" art that spoke to the British public in ways that Hollywood never could. Sarah Street, likewise, points out the relative popularity of the so-called quota quickies: British films that were produced rapidly and often cheaply in partnership with American companies attempting to circumvent the film quotas.[70] Nonetheless, during the twenties and thirties, *Close Up* prefigured Truffaut's dismissal, obsessing over what it saw as the dearth of compelling British cinema. In *Close Up*, H. D. warned her British audience that "in time foreign nations will cease to judge England by a past and vanished Trafalgar, and will expect nothing of a people who...present so comparatively little on the screen."[71] According to H. D.'s image, cinema is the new Trafalgar. It represents the battle the British must win to keep up in the world. Whereas the British government, with its quotas and various film boards was motivated in part by the need for national pride, many in *Close Up* felt little more than despair at the British films that had made it to the screen.[72] Most of these films failed to win widespread popular support while at the same time disappointing the elite circles of film buffs. Elizabeth Madox Roberts summed up a common sentiment in the first volume of *Close Up*: "Oh dear, oh dear, these Brrrrrrr-itish Films."[73] And Bryher, with characteristic restraint, noted that her "experience of English films had not been encouraging."[74]

H. D.'s invocation of Trafalgar and Britain's glorious military past reveals a precise knowledge of the state of anxieties in *Close Up* about the British film. Throughout *Close Up*, contributors link their desire for the British film to the past through invocations of "tradition," suggesting the extent to which they wish to imagine this new art form as continuous with Britain's past greatness. According to frequent contributor Robert Herring, if the British could only develop their cinema, they would be able to offer unique national attributes: "Restraint, for instance, reason, taste possibly and tradition."[75] From a slightly different perspective, *Close Up*'s American correspondent, Clifford Howard, suggests that the American talkie in Britain "presents truly a most serious situation for those who feel themselves entrusted with the guardianship of traditions and proprieties."[76] While Howard takes a skeptical view of British fears of "the influence of the 'American' language upon our classic English," he insightfully diagnoses the guardianship of tradition as the increasingly familiar recourse against the encroachment of American cinema.[77] It seems a bit of a paradox that this call for Britain to participate more fully in a radically new art form should be wedded to traditions and the past. Yet in the nationalist logic that H. D. so astutely recorded for *Close Up*, it is precisely this notion of tradition that is necessary to preserve Britain's past greatness in the age of Hollywood.

Such reactionary grasping at tradition as the missing element in the development of British cinema is the symptom of a painful ideological shift from conceptions of Britain as advanced and modern to traditional and steeped in heritage. Film prompts this shift because it offers such a sharp shock to the system: while Britain retains a late nineteenth-century sense of itself as the one of the most powerful empires in the world, it can't reliably dominate the new medium of cinema in its home market. Not only does British film woefully lag European productions in most accounts of artistic value, but it has also left control of imperial propaganda, and even the English language, to the Americans. This failure produces a kind of identity crisis whereby one aspect of English national character, its venerable ties to tradition and the past, shift to the foreground in contrast to America's seeming ownership of the new, modern, and progressive. As the influence of T. S. Eliot's writings on tradition attest, part of the modernist project that took root in England grew out of a desire to reconnect with the past. Ironically enough, Hollywood itself would embrace the associations of Britishness with tradition, propriety, and a glorious past in the 1930s when its string of anglophile pictures began to emphasize the British traditionalism and propriety that emerged in part through reactions against Hollywood.[78] While there had long been a subset of the British population that valued tradition and the past over progress and new technologies, it is poignant to see this emphasis on tradition suddenly applied to the new technology of film. By threatening British prestige, American cinematic ascendency helped to bolster that central ideology of British modernism: the desire for new works of art to remain firmly grounded in the past.

Art, Modernism, and the Idea of the Minority

Close Up's desire to see the British film take its place on the world stage emerged in part out of a fervent belief in the status of film as the new art form of the century. In his opening editorial in *Close Up*, Macpherson announces his conviction that film will "turn into THE art" of modern times.[79] In his attempts to distinguish

this art from entertainment, Macpherson borrows and extends an idea from the culture at large, that of the minority audience. Early in *Close Up*, Macpherson explains the journal's project of cultivating an audience capable of seeing cinema as an art form: "our concern is not with the masses, but with the minority—again, I repeat, a minority of millions,—whose tastes are disregarded, and whose tastes matter supremely and *must* be studied."[80] Here Macpherson's telling "minority of millions" gives him away. If there is a minority among cinemagoers, then it is a somewhat embarrassingly *big* minority, one that will begin to reveal the pressures of American entertainment on such stratification of taste.

Macpherson's desire to cling to the notion of a minority, even when faced with audiences of staggering proportions, depends on his investment in the mass-minority distinction. In a show of magnanimity, Macpherson does not begrudge the masses their bad cinema as long as the minority remains to appreciate cinematic art. Through this mock graciousness, Macpherson distinguishes himself from that other big minority, the "great many" cultivated skeptics who look to Hollywood as an excuse to condemn all cinema.[81] While Macpherson confidently wields the vocabulary of mass and minority, his ungainly "minority of millions," as well as his minority of a "great many" film skeptics, bulge at their categorical seams. These uneven measures of scale speak to the ways in which the minority and masses are not fully distinct and coherent groups but rather variously permeable and overlapping ones. For instance, while Macpherson seems to count himself a member of the artistic minority, he occasionally endorses films such as *Blackmail* that have widespread popular appeal. It is precisely because the distinctions between film as art and as entertainment are so murky, contaminated, and blurred, that the rallying idea of the minority film audience comes to seem so necessary. In an almost perverse departure from what Walter Benjamin would later identify as film's inherent potential to reach the masses, Macpherson's modernist response to Hollywood is ultimately to invent the dividing line between the films of the masses and the films of the tasteful minority.

More broadly, *Close Up*'s investment in the concepts of the "mass" and "minority" is itself a response to how the arrival of cinema both intensified and undermined the stratification of taste in the early twentieth century. Film managed to create a new mass audience whose sheer size and global scale outstripped that of readerships within a given language. Yet *Close Up*'s contributors often present cinema as another art form similar to literature.[82] In Bryher's words, "It is always the intelligent minority who will make and discard an author just as it will be the intelligent minority who will eventually make or discard films."[83] Like Macpherson, Bryher believes in the necessity of a cultural elite to assign value to individual films. Given that *Close Up* advertised itself as the first English-language journal "to approach films from the angles of art," it presents *itself* as a minority capable of determining aesthetic merit.[84] By extension, *Close Up*'s necessarily small readership could also count themselves among the elect. Whereas Macpherson may have wished to reach his "minority of millions," *Close Up*'s minority audience nonetheless stands in structural opposition to the mass audiences attending Hollywood films.

Roughly midway through *Close Up*'s run, the journal experienced a shock that would bring its concerns about the status of cinematic art violently together with those about film and nationality. This shock was the largely negative English reception of Macpherson's prized film project *Borderline* (1930). A silent film written and directed by Macpherson, *Borderline* showcased the black American singer and activist Paul Robeson, as well as Robeson's wife Eslanda, H. D., Bryher, and the British actor Gavin Arthur.[85] While there were pragmatic and financial reasons to produce *Borderline* without sound, it is nonetheless ironic that Macpherson chose such a well-known and formidable vocal presence as Robeson to star in a silent film. It is also particularly fitting, given Macpherson's resistance to the American talkies, that *Borderline* should silence a well-known *American* singer. In its transgressive treatment of interracial relations as well as its nonlinear and abstract formal experiments, *Borderline* defies the conventions of Hollywood cinema. Thus what was to be Macpherson's cinematic masterpiece and the next step in the evolution of the British film tradition, contained from its beginnings a desire to define itself against the mass entertainment of the day.

Set in a village in Switzerland, *Borderline* depicts a tumultuous interracial love triangle that inspires violent jealousy and leads to a tragic end. Both in its theme and its experimental cinematography, *Borderline* seemed poised to appeal to Macpherson's imagined "minority" of film connoisseurs. Yet the real connoisseurs, at least in England, were not impressed. After its debut screening in London on October 13, 1930, *Borderline* was dismissed by critics, by intellectuals, and even, according to Macpherson, by his friends. While *Borderline* was somewhat better received in Europe and denied a screening in the United States, most likely due to its interracial content, it was the negative reception in England that inspired Bryher and H. D. to rally to Macpherson's defense.[86] The rejection of *Borderline*, they argued, suggested the extent to which the English were becoming Americanized and ruined by Hollywood cinema. For this national malady, the proper remedy was not only the birth of an English film tradition but of a self-consciously modernist one.

In response to *Borderline*'s negative reception in England, H. D. published a lengthy pamphlet defending both Macpherson and the film by contrasting it to the reigning mass cinema of the day. Citing Macpherson's virtuosity behind the camera, H. D. notes that "the camera has for the most part been the property of monsters, like those three Gorgons in the waste-land, holding a precious legacy, one human EYE between them."[87] Coyly she asks, "Would it be altogether inept to say that Mr Macpherson and his young colleagues are just the least bit like Perseus who snatched the EYE from the clutch of the slobbering and malign Monsters."[88] This clutch of "slobbering" one-eyed monsters, unable to perceive the richness and complexity that appeal to Macpherson, are none other than the huge production companies, mainly or exclusively born of Hollywood, that run most of the cinema in England. H. D., who regrets the sight of these monsters wielding the camera, unabashedly drives her mythological analogy to its immodest conclusion: Macpherson and his "young colleagues," including H. D. herself, are heroes to Hollywood's Gorgons, blessed with an artistic vision that far outstrips that of the film industry. Of course, H. D. scrambles the myth slightly: it was the Graeae, sisters of the Gorgons, whose single, shared eye was snatched by Perseus. Yet in her piecemeal mythology, H. D. manages a double assault on mass cinema. First, in her emphatic, capitalized allusion to the Graeae's single "EYE," H. D. accuses the production companies of sharing a single, standardized point of view, and of harboring the monstrous commitment to sameness often associated with Hollywood's growing hegemony. Moreover, by invoking the Gorgons, H. D. playfully hints that those who gaze upon this mass cinema will be metaphorically turned to stone, their sensibilities coarsened, and their critical faculties blunted and immobilized.

H. D.'s analogy draws its strength not only from the mythological subtext but also through allusions to well-known literary achievements of the day. Her view of the cinematic landscape as a "waste-land" evokes Eliot's treatment of modern life, and her tribute to the single eye recalls the monstrous Cyclops of *Ulysses*. Of course, like Joyce and Eliot, H. D. is well known for bringing mythology into her treatment of modern life. Yet here she allows the contemporary works of the day to provide their own mythology, turning their commentary on modern life into her critique of mass cinema. In so doing, H. D. implicitly situates Macpherson's heroic incarnation as Perseus—his resistance to mass cinema—within a particularly modernist tradition. Throughout the pamphlet, H. D. associates Macpherson and his film with modernism through references to his "intensive Leonardo-esque modernism"[89] as well as to *Borderline*'s "concise modernistic abstraction."[90] While the term, "modernism," held a range of meanings in the interwar years, here H. D. uses it to refer to an avant-garde aesthetic at once new and tied to classical art.[91] In aligning Macpherson with modernism, both through explicit tribute and implicit literary allusions, H. D. suggests that experimentalism itself can play the role of

Perseus and that modernism can save England from mass cinema if only given the chance.

As an early twentieth-century meditation on film, *Close Up* is exemplary insofar as it demonstrates how the ideology of modernism depends on the concepts of mass and minority—not because these were airtight, perfect categories but rather, precisely, because they were not. Joyce's *Ulysses*, Stein's experimental poems, and Picasso's cubism: all these appealed primarily to a minority and seemed in many ways designed to do so in an age of wildly accessible mass forms. While much has been written on whether modernists defined their individual projects against mass culture, attention to *Close Up* allows us to shift the focus away from a hard and fast dividing line between mass entertainment and modernist aesthetics toward an *ideology* of division that only partially reflects the actual practices of artists and audiences. By taking *Close Up* as a case study, it is possible to trace the development of this ideology through reactions against Hollywood. In their construction of the American Entertainment Empire as both monstrous threat and banal competitor, the core contributors to *Close Up* ultimately reveal the considerable nationalism that underlies their interwar stratification of taste.

Tradition Revisited: Britain in Hollywood

While *Close Up*'s worst fears of Hollywood's destructiveness would never be realized, neither would its cherished hopes for a robust British cinematic modernism. Although British cinema received a material boost from the quotas and recovered an increasing portion of the domestic market throughout the thirties, Hollywood's influence and popularity persisted. While the period following *Close Up*'s final issue in 1934 saw the emergence of the British director Carol Reed as well as the influential partnership of Michael Powell and Emeric Pressburger, it also saw the migration of Alfred Hitchcock to Hollywood in 1939 and the continued absorption of talent from Britain and Europe into the American film industry. Even Aldous Huxley, a few years after penning *Brave New World* (1932), moved to the United States to write for Hollywood. In 1939, Huxley published a satirical novel, *After Many a Summer*, depicting a shallow, youth-obsessed Southern California as viewed through the eyes of a bookish British intellectual. Less than a decade later, Evelyn Waugh, after a trip to Hollywood, was moved to write an even darker satire of Southern California, *The Loved One* (1947), set largely in a garish pet cemetery. Both of these novels serve as further case studies, ones that reveal the importance of Britain's literary heritage to the cultural project of resisting Hollywood.

It is no surprise that Hollywood attracted the attention of two of the most accomplished British satirists of the period. It is intriguing, however, to note the extent to which the two novels depend on a strikingly similar method of transatlantic contrast to produce their devastating cultural critiques. Each novel follows an abundantly literate Englishman into the foreign landscape of Southern California. Moreover, each represents Britishness, in its ties to tradition and literary heritage, as the antithesis of Hollywood. With unusual clarity, these novels reflect the process, begun in the interwar period, of redefining British identity against Hollywood's example. In Waugh's more extended treatment, the feeling that the British have become "a colonial people" in relation to Hollywood is taken to parodic extremes. Whereas Macpherson may have had high hopes for the British cinematic avant-garde, these satirical accounts essentially imagine Britishness as a kind of *arrière-garde*; that is, a reactionary embrace of historical and literary tradition as a bulwark against the dominant yet debased culture that seems capable of making the British feel like colonials.[92]

In the terminology of the day, foreign actors and writers in Hollywood were said to belong to colonies such as the "British colony" and the "Swedish colony." While such idioms sound as if the Europeans have conquered a piece of California, they actually gesture toward the reverse: these foreign talents-for-hire have become colonials at the mercy of a governing force. Evelyn Waugh plays with such reversals in *The Loved One*, focusing on Hollywood's impact on conceptions of British identity and revealing how faith in the British literary tradition comes to take the place of a belief in the superiority of the faltering British Empire. *The Loved One*'s humor rests on its intimate understanding of this rescripting of Britishness in the face of Hollywood. At the same time, *The Loved One* rewrites the British colonial novel, exploiting its generic conventions by remapping British imperial ideologies onto the new landscape of Anglo-American relations.

The Loved One opens in a sublime parody of the colonial setting: unbearable heat, the "rusty fringes of palm-leaf," and the "ever present pulse of music from the neighboring native huts."[93] In this landscape we encounter two Englishmen, "each with his whiskey and soda and outdated magazine," who are the stereotypical embodiments of colonial administrators cut off from what they would call civilization. These Englishmen, however, are not in South Asia but Southern California; they are not administrators enduring the last gasp of empire but are instead desperate writers waiting to be hired in Hollywood.[94] Waugh's characteristic humor emerges in this scene through the sudden unveiling of a chiasmic inversion of power: the Englishmen, who seem poised for governance, find themselves at the mercy of the film studios. Waugh mocks the tenacity of imperial attitudes among the Englishmen: for instance, they disdain a fellow countryman who "went completely native" by leaving the film colony to work in a bar.[95] At the same time, Waugh reveals how thoroughly the American situation interrupts and forecloses the usual narrative of British imperialism. Although several of the Englishmen working for Hollywood have been knighted, they seem less subject to the crown than to the tyranny of the studios. One of the knights, for instance, finds himself at the mercy of the studio executives who recall his existence just long enough to fire him. In fact, when another erstwhile knight compares their situation to that of the British in Africa, he notes with some regret that "We haven't any such rights here, unfortunately."[96] These British knights, Waugh's narrative points out, have no clear place in the Entertainment Empire.

The travails of Waugh's protagonist, the young Englishman Dennis Barlow, reveals a further level to this parody of British imperial narrative. Given that the English have no "rights" or power in Hollywood, living as they do in an aging film colony at the mercy of the fictional giant, Megalopolitan studios, they take recourse in the intangible legacy of their British identities. Not only do the expatriates play cricket and refuse to countenance any deviation from the stereotypical standards of British conduct, but Barlow in particular comes to stand for the last defense of the English against the spread and power of Hollywood: English literature. Barlow has come to Hollywood to write the "life of Shelley for the films" but has found himself instead working for a pet cemetery, the "Happier Hunting Ground," marked by its unbearably maudlin prayers and poems.[97] Ultimately, through his various identifications with English literature, Barlow re-creates himself as a distinctly English person of importance.

Through the figure of Barlow, Waugh suggests that if Britain no longer represents progress and futurity, then it must turn for solace to a different facet of its identity, namely, its long-standing associations with literary tradition. To this end, Barlow woos a caricature of the naive and nubile American girl by presenting himself as an important English poet and, more outrageously, by pretending to have written the classics of English poetry himself. Barlow plunders the *Oxford Book of English Verse*—his prized possession in America—in order to send amorous missives to his unsuspecting target. On the surface, the humor in this scenario derives from both the American girl's staggering ignorance of British literature and Barlow's daring selection of increasingly famous poems; ultimately, he signs his name to the line, "Shall I compare thee to a summer's day." But there is an allegorical flavor to the courtship as well. By putting his name to the great works of English verse, as anthologized by Oxford, Barlow identifies with the British literary tradition at just the moment when he has been rejected by Hollywood.

Barlow and his English compatriots may not have any power or rights in America, Waugh suggests, but at least they have the Shakespearean sonnet. This imaginative recourse to British literature recalls the general tendency in interwar Britain to evoke the greatness of British heritage, and especially literary heritage, when faced with the threat of Hollywood.

Such redefinition of Britishness plays itself out even more starkly in Huxley's satire of Southern California, *After Many a Summer*. The novel as a whole parodies the bloated excesses of the wealthy, aging Jo Stoyte, a character modeled on William Randolph Hearst, the domineering capitalist and American imperialist who would later provide the model for *Citizen Kane*.[98] Stoyte, whose young girlfriend is based on the Hollywood starlet Marion Davies, has invited our hero, the timid British scholar Bodley, to his coastal mansion. Bodley, who possesses the rarified speech of the Oxbridge-educated—his very name an echo of Sir Thomas Bodley, namesake of the Bodleian library—arrives in Hollywood clutching his complete works of Shelley. He is the embodiment of the British intellectual shocked and buffeted by the shallow complacencies of Los Angeles. While Bodley is not, like Barlow, hired to write a screenplay about an English poet, he nonetheless defines himself through his association with poetry. The allegorical picture of the Englishman arriving in Hollywood bearing a volume of Romantic poetry upon his person like a coat of arms is a pithy visual summary of the work that literature does in service of a national identity. Sonnets have replaced swords in the new landscape of mass-reproduced media. At the same time, as Waugh's related parody makes clear, the modern British knight hopes for nothing more than to work for Hollywood.

After crossing the Atlantic in 1937, Huxley spent years screenwriting for Hollywood, perhaps following his own dictum that "for good or for evil . . . the world must be Americanized."[99] It is interesting to note that his labors for Hollywood did not necessarily improve his opinion of the industry. Rather, his expatriate existence drove Huxley to much the same satirical reflections as those of Waugh: the observation that not only was British power slipping in favor of its wealthy former colony across the Atlantic, but that the very meaning of British identity was being defensively reconfigured against the example of Hollywood.

Huxley became a participant in this reconfiguration when he co-wrote the script for MGM's 1940 *Pride and Prejudice*, starring Greer Garson and Lawrence Olivier. As the opening screen of the film announces, this *Pride and Prejudice* is set in that nostalgic place and time known simply as "Old England." Huxley's Old England sounds rather like Keynes's merry England, except of course in this case, Old England has been produced as a commodity within the United States. In Keynes's speech, "merry England" is that nostalgic construct threatened by

Hollywood; in Huxley's film, Old England is actually constructed as a film set in Hollywood. *Pride and Prejudice* is full of haphazard gestures to this curious Old England, from exuberantly flouncy dresses to incongruous Robin Hood-like escapades, at least insofar as Elizabeth Bennet dazzles Mr. Darcy with her bow and arrow during an improbably coy scene of target practice.

Old England thus lives on in the new Hollywood, imprisoned in a kind of perpetual nostalgia. Huxley's *Pride and Prejudice* is a fantasy woven of literary heroes and heroines; bows and arrows; and muddy cobblestone villages full of rustic booksellers, liveried footmen, and ladies in enormous dresses. There is a pathos to the very act of capturing and re-creating this old England on the screen, whether in Huxley's *Pride and Prejudice* or in one of Hollywood's many other anglophile historical pictures of the day. "Old England" has not really been lost, for it never existed. Rather, it has been invented both within and against the American Entertainment Empire. It is curious that Hollywood should blithely wish to pay tribute to what some feel it has destroyed. Yet it is also fitting that at the very moment this phantasmatic past feels utterly irretrievable—beyond the reach even of nostalgia to recall it—it is re-created via technology and disseminated to mass audiences around the English-speaking world.

Huxley's *Pride and Prejudice* thus at the same time reflects and inverts Keynes's death wish for Hollywood. As Keynes noted: "Let every part of Merry England be Merry in its own way."[100] This is in large measure what Hollywood has wrought: a renewed desire for merry Old England, whether within the world of Hollywood film or precisely through its absence. Keynes's call for the local specificity of "every part" of merry England emerges out of the feeling that Hollywood is not local but is rather the sign and furthest determinant of the mass reproduction of leisure. Such an understanding of the modern is shared in Huxley's best-known work: his vision of a dehumanized and dehumanizing brave new world. Keynes's speech embodies one style of resistance to the coming of a particularly American new world. It is a resistance that re-creates England—its art, heritage, and modernism—against what seemed a new world of American ascendancy, of changing types and scales of globalism, and for however many multifarious reasons, a new world that loved to go to the movies.

4. English by Example

F. R. Leavis and the Americanization of Modern England

Raymond Williams tells a story about F. R. Leavis from their years teaching together at Cambridge. At a meeting in 1961 to consider a new course on the novel, Williams recalls, "There was one major argument... The crux was whether the paper should be the English novel, or the novel in general. [Leavis] wanted the English novel only. A majority were against him."[1] After Leavis rejects the inclusion of European novels, in part because of the difficulties of translation, a committee member poses a further question: "Then what about American novelists? Faulkner, for example."[2] Williams notes:

> At this point I have to hold onto my seat. I have the clearest memory of what was said next, and of the mood in which it was said: one of fierce pleasure in the argument but also of surprising conviction. "Faulkner!" Leavis said. "When the Americans moved in on Europe after the War, they had to have a great novelist. That's who they chose, Faulkner." Nobody knew, at the time, what to say after that.[3]

This is more than an opinionated dismissal of a major American writer. Rather, Williams's anecdote highlights the anti-Americanism that Leavis demonstrated from his earliest published work. While such sentiments might seem to participate in general anxieties about American cultural hegemony during the Cold War, Leavis's anxieties can be traced back in time to the interwar years.[4] Moreover, rather than a decorative flourish layered upon deeper insecurities, this reaction to America resides at the heart of Leavis's theories of literature and culture. While Leavis's critics have largely overlooked his abundant references to America, Leavis relies on the example of America, and on transatlantic comparison, as a *method* in his cultural analyses. He wields the term "Americanisation"—a rough synonym for "standardization"—in ways that reveal the national subtext of the "mass civilization" that Leavis understands to menace interwar England. Leavis's position as the self-appointed guardian of Englishness, an image that persists in critical treatments of his work and legacy, derives from the transatlantic connections and reactions underlying his nationalist projects. While Leavis is remembered as guardian of the high, the elite, and the English, these discourses are importantly produced by the twin processes of Americanization and transatlantic comparison.

Before turning to Leavis's work, it is worth noting that a further implication of Leavis's rejection of Faulkner follows from its curious anecdotal recovery by Raymond Williams. As the figure in cultural studies most often placed in opposition to Leavis, Williams actively worked against Leavis's high cultural ideologies, yet he has acknowledged the enormous influence of Leavis's pedagogical aims and methods. While Leavis has been variously called a "genius" and "the single most influential figure in twentieth-century English literary criticism," he has also been accused of "damaging arrogance and skepticism" and dismissed tongue-in-cheek as a "curmudgeon."[5] Leavis, in short, holds a highly contested yet undeniable place in the history of the development of English as a discipline. In turning to his pedagogical writings and social criticism, it becomes clear that Leavis's influential role in the development of English as a discipline follows from his desire to design a field of study that would save England from Americanization. Leavis's anti-Americanism also has had striking ramifications for cultural studies in its influence upon Richard Hoggart's landmark 1957 text *The Uses of Literacy*. Throughout his career, Leavis was not only quick to use American culture as a name for the modernization of England but ultimately relied on the example of America in his reactionary invention of Englishness and his attempts to teach it to the nation.

Leavis and the Threat of Americanization

From his earliest publication, a pamphlet entitled *Mass Civilisation and Minority Culture* (1930), later collected in *For Continuity* (1932), Leavis presents literature and society as mutually constitutive, leading him to make the claim, in all earnestness, that only literary criticism can save modern England.[6] Part Arnoldian lament, part

Spenglerian paean to decline, Leavis's pamphlet announces the need for an educated elite, or a "minority," who can analyze literature fiercely enough to rescue England from popular fiction, advertising, and the burgeoning hegemony of Hollywood. In the pamphlet, Leavis draws his primary example of standardization and machine culture from "a remarkable work of anthropology," the 1929 *Middletown*.[7] Yet the natives in *Middletown* are not English but American.[8] Leavis defends his choice:

> To this someone will reply that Middletown is America and not England. And it is true that in America change has been more rapid, and its effects have been intensified by the fusion of peoples. But the same processes are at work in England and the western world generally, and at an acceleration.[9]

Here America is exemplary in the material sense: it is the embodiment of the modernization and progress that has also begun to transform England. Leavis thus presents the anthropological investigation of America as a prophetic glimpse into England's future. Yet it is a future which appropriate attention to America can forestall. Leavis explains, "It is a commonplace that we are being Americanised, but again a commonplace that seems, as a rule, to carry little understanding with it. Americanisation is often spoken of as if it were something of which the United States is guilty," when in fact, it is that which British proponents of standardization and progress are likely to hasten.[10] Leavis returns to *Middletown* as a touchstone throughout his early writings; in *Culture and Environment* (1933), cowritten with his former student Denys Thompson, he succinctly labels it "an account of the process of dissolution."[11] At the same time, he juxtaposes *Middletown* against one of his other key texts George Sturt's *The Wheelwright's Shop* (1923), which Leavis wistfully analyzes as a tribute to the lost Englishness of the artisan's village.

It is appropriate that *Middletown* should be held up against *The Wheelwright's Shop*, because, as Leavis makes clear in *Mass Civilisation*, part of what marks the dissolution of middle America is the arrival of the automobile. In strong terms Leavis recounts, "we see in detail how the automobile (to take one instance) has, in a few years, radically affected religion, broken up the family, and revolutionised social custom."[12] The problem of the automobile reappears emblematically at the end of *Mass Civilisation* in a discussion of Henry Ford. Ford's matter-of-fact discussion of a future world ruled by machines—"Shall we not some day reach a point where the machine becomes all powerful, and the man of no consequence"—concludes that one "need not bother" about the future.[13] In defense, Leavis intones his hope "that what we value most matters too much to the race to be finally abandoned and that the machine will yet be made a tool."[14] His rejection of Fordist philosophy, as well as what he calls "the official Ford legend," does not lead Leavis, like so many writers in the thirties, to embrace communism.[15] Rather, in a striking ideological conflation, he explains that the paths of both Marx and Ford lead to the machine and disavows any need to choose between them.[16] For Leavis, the primary ideology in need of adherence is Englishness.

In his tributes to Englishness, Leavis turns time and again to what he proposes as its opposite: the modernization and progress that can be seen most clearly in America. In *Culture and Environment*, Leavis draws the example of America directly into his pedagogy. Leavis conceived *Culture and Environment* as a text for teachers of high school and grammar school. Yet rather than detailing classroom methods, this work revisits a number of Leavis's chief cultural concerns, especially standardization and mass culture. *Culture and Environment* explicitly presents "a literary education" as the "substitute" for all that has been lost: the English "folk-songs, folk-dances, Cotswold cottages and handicraft products" that symbolize "the organic community with the living culture it embodied."[17] What threatens the younger generation is not that they will lose their connection to the organic past of English Cotswold cottages—that is already gone—but rather that they will forget how to be properly nostalgic for it. The most direct way to inculcate them with Englishness is to help them define themselves against the worst, and thereby most modern, traits of the Americans. Leavis's attempts to educate via the exercises in *Culture and Environment* reveal his figurative reliance on America even more clearly than *Mass Civilisation*. It is an oft-told tale in colonial studies that Thomas Macaulay's 1835 proposal for civil servant examinations attempted to produce British subjects through literary study.[18] Yet while Macaulay turned directly to English literature, Leavis would train British schoolchildren into Englishness via the negative example of America. The study of literature is Leavis's life work, but his project of cultural preservation depends on the pedagogical value of America as an example.

Culture and Environment thus does not dwell on literature but rather critiques what Leavis calls civilization. To this end, it is divided into short analytic sections with titles such as "Advertising," "Levelling-down," and "The Use of Leisure." At the end of the work, in perhaps its most curious portion, Leavis and Thompson offer a series of exercises for use in the classroom. The genre of the school exercise is ideal for Leavis's purposes because it provides a vehicle for Leavis to reach, and thereby to rescue, the masses. These exercises do not tend to ask students to read or analyze literature; rather, they focus on modern and often explicitly American culture. The exercises themselves are for the most part extraordinarily overdetermined; there is only one suitable response. For instance, Leavis asks students to compare "the Blues" played on the radio with "complicated Elizabethan part-songs" sung in "educated homes" after supper, encouraging them to choose English music in the drawing room over debased American jazz over the wireless.[19] Another exercise presents the Americans themselves for study: "'In fifteen years the American people have changed from essentially a home people to an automobile and movie people.' What other changes have accompanied that described here?"[20] As the ethnographic subjects most suited to Leavis's purposes, the "American people" enter the exercise as a group familiar enough to discuss and yet foreign enough to contrast to the English. Leavis's purpose rests on his dual conviction that English schoolchildren will generate a list of the changes wrought in the lives of modernizing Americans while viewing the Americans objectively, as if from a great distance, and thereby consolidate their Englishness.

Another exercise invokes the American ethnographic subject in even more telling terms. Leavis quotes from a 1928 travel narrative: "In spite of cars and radios the American peasant is still unbelievably in the backwoods; all his reading and writing and listening-in does not make him a whit more mentally up-to-date than the illiterate Spaniard, and leaves him far behind the country Frenchman."[21] Asking the student to consider "what reflections on the nature of education are suggested by this extract," Leavis seems to hope that the student will be savvy enough to follow the implied argument that cars and radios do not lead the American peasant toward mental advancement.[22] Curiously, the identification of the American worker as a "peasant" harbors connotations of the European class system, suggesting the extent to which the passage wishes to underscore a reversal: the American, commonly imagined to be up-to-date, is here a backwoods peasant, defined by the very vocabulary of feudalism. Indeed, as Leavis consistently demonstrates, technological progress and modernization are precisely what render the American culturally backward and easily superseded by the "country Frenchman."

Leavis's rhetorical assimilation of America into his definitions of Englishness has considerable implications for his presentation of social class. In *Culture and Society*, Raymond Williams is at pains to complicate charges of Leavis's elitism, stressing Leavis's position outside the class structure of university dons and highbrow literati. Leavis's middle-class upbringing in the town of Cambridge—his father ran a bicycle shop—put him at odds with both Bloomsbury, which he openly denounced in his writing, as well as the established faculty at Cambridge, where he was never truly institutionally supported.[23] Williams applauds Leavis for attacking "the domination of the world of English by a small interlocking group" and for reducing "to its proper impotence the ordinary conception of a superior minority which happens to coincide with a particular social class."[24] Yet attention to Leavis's invocations of America suggests that he marked class in England, that most important of categories to British cultural studies, in important and sometimes unnoticed ways by a transatlantic sense of national difference. That is to say, there is a way in which, strange as it may seem, Leavis's lament was that the working classes of England had given up their Cotswold cottages and village crafts and *become American*. Interestingly enough, the designations American and English are curiously mobile: T. S. Eliot, American by birth if not by his British citizenship or ambiguous accent in the thirties, promotes Englishness while the English working classes, with their tastes in popular fiction and in cinema, threaten to undermine it.

Not only Leavis but also his collaborators place considerable emphasis on the Americanization of England: in *Scrutiny*, Denys Thompson makes the matter-of-fact observation that "England is less Americanised than America."[25] As the structure of his sentence betrays, England may not be as modern as America, but it is nonetheless vulnerable to being "Americanised." For Leavis, as well as for followers like Thompson, Americanization is the type of thing that can happen to England, because it is not tied to place, but to practices, modalities, and ways of being. Indeed, Leavis occasionally implies that not only England but also America itself might be saved from Americanization. Americanization thus cannot exactly be a process of national hegemony, nor can it be understood as the overlay of one culture upon another. Rather, Americanization, for Leavis, has become a special name for modernization, one that is more concrete in that it invokes its exemplar in its very name.

Thus, although Leavis uses Americanization to mean modernization, the term retains the residue of its nationalist import. So the question urges itself again: if Leavis means standardization, why would he ever need the term *Americanization*? And if Leavis's utmost concern is with the fate of English culture, why the constant reference to the situation in America? One answer is that Leavis has sensed, long before the Cold War debates about American hegemony and English decline, that definitions of modern English culture depend upon understandings of American culture. Throughout his early work, Leavis reveals his investment in tracing how utterly transatlantic English culture threatens to become. As he implies via the exercises in *Culture and Environment*, jazz on the radio has supplanted part-songs in the drawing room. The folk culture that Leavis cherishes, replete with all its homemade and quintessentially English signifiers—and English precisely because they are homemade, made-at-home, of the land itself—is now transformed into a mass culture that is marked not only by mechanization and mass dissemination but also by extranational sources and flows. For Leavis, the idea of American culture remains central because it is what must be negated—literally driven out of England—for English culture to survive.

The English Tradition

Leavis's copious writings on mass culture and America haven't earned him nearly as much attention as his single most influential work *The Great Tradition* (1946). *The Great Tradition*, in which he identifies Jane Austen, George Eliot, Joseph Conrad, and Henry James as the four most important novelists of the English language, helped to elevate the novel to its current standing within modern English letters. Leavis's project is humanist, but it is not exactly universal. As he puts it, "there *is*—and this is the point—an English tradition."[26] Although critics rarely connect this defining act of literary criticism with his earlier writings on America, a broader context brings the unique dimensions of Leavis's humanistic project to the foreground. In *The Great Tradition*, Leavis presents the tradition of the novel as a cure for the ailments of English society that he diagnosed in his earlier writings. In counterpoint to modern dissolution, the great tradition links past and present, anchoring Leavis's aesthetics within a distinctly nationalist framework.

It has often been remarked that two of Leavis's chosen writers are women, casting his turn to the novel as the recuperation of a genre that had been slighted partly because of its associations with the feminine.[27] Yet it is equally notable that Leavis, the champion of Englishness, should select two expatriates as this great tradition's other half. Conrad and James, who each became British citizens, were anglophiles but were hardly English.[28] In the context of Leavis's concerns with England and America, this choice of authors makes considerable sense. For Leavis, the expatriate's spiritual homelessness *is* the modern condition. James and Conrad, as expatriates, have special knowledge of the crisis of modern times and have each made themselves a home within the English language. Leavis calls Conrad "a master of the English language, who chose it for its distinctive qualities and because of the moral tradition associated with it."[29] According to Leavis, the English language has its own morality. Leavis believes James's expatriate condition gave him a "bent for comparison" and taught him how to contrast national cultures.[30] In Leavis's view, it is precisely because they were not born English that James and Conrad are particularly suited to extend the English tradition into the twentieth century.

Leavis insists that James was particularly alienated by modern American life: he was "*déraciné* in his own country."[31] As a perpetual outsider, James is a better cultural critic than Dickens, both in his valuable "criticism of English society" and especially in his "rendering of the portentous effloresences of American civilization."[32] Leavis explains that James's "essential interests were inseparable from an interest in highly civilized manners, in the refinements of civilized intercourse. The social civilization that in America might have yielded him (or seemed to yield) what he needed was…vanishing with his youth. England certainly had more to offer him than America had."[33] The vanishing of civilization, the disappearance of the refinement that James describes with such sensitivity, comes at the turn of the twentieth century—the very moment of Americanization. In Leavis's conception, James fled America "in quest of an ideal society, an ideal civilization."[34] As Leavis assures the reader of *The Great Tradition*, James had better hope of finding such a society in England than in America.[35]

Leavis remained a supporter of anglicized American writers, including another writer he briefly praises in *The Great Tradition*: T. S. Eliot. Leavis referred to Eliot as an "originator" among imitators and ultimately drew on his criticism and his poetry.[36] In *The Great Tradition*, Leavis makes more than a nod to Eliot's 1919 essay, "Tradition and the Individual Talent," when he remarks that Jane Austen "exemplifies beautifully the relations of 'the individual talent' to tradition."[37] Echoing Eliot's essay, Leavis continues, "She creates the tradition we see leading down to her. Her work, like the work of all great creative writers, gives a meaning to the past."[38] Here it is possible to see the great utility of Eliot's construction to Leavis's project. According to Eliot's definition, a tradition keeps the past present. Leavis views the English novel as a lifeline, connecting past and present, imbuing the past with new meaning, vitality, and relevance. Submitting Eliot's theory to practical experiment, Leavis extends Eliot's concept of tradition with the intent of keeping English heritage alive in modern times.

While he never abandoned his appreciation of Eliot, Leavis reserved his highest praise for D. H. Lawrence, who held the kind of nostalgia for preindustrial working-class Englishness that Leavis most admired. In *The Great Tradition*, Leavis announces, "Lawrence, in the English language, was the great genius of our time."[39] To illustrate Lawrence's perspicacity, Leavis quotes from *Lady Chatterley's Lover*, in which Lawrence notes "a gap in the continuity of consciousness almost American, but industrial really."[40] According to Leavis, Lawrence has identified "the major, the inclusive problem of our time": the rupture with the past brought about by modernization.[41] Insisting that " 'industrialism' is only a subheading" of broader national problems summarized by Spengler's *Decline of the West*, Leavis suggests that the problem is the waning of Englishness itself. Lawrence's feel for the English landscape and the horrors of industry offers him pride of place in *The Great Tradition*, allowing him to serve as the literary voice of Leavis's deepest concerns.

Ultimately, Leavis's understanding of the novel—what a novel is, what it is for—emerges out of the same impulses that led him to repudiate the Americanization of

England. In his discussion of George Eliot, Leavis explains how the novel teaches by example. He makes it clear that her works do not offer "primarily an entertainment" by citing James's claim that for Eliot, "the novel was not primarily a picture of life...but a moralized fable, the last word of a philosophy endeavoring to teach by example."[42] Here Leavis reveals his belief in the function of the novel: it doesn't tell the reader how to live but rather shows human beings in moments of genuine moral crisis. Whereas in *Culture and Environment* Leavis presented the negative example of American modern life as a warning to English schoolchildren, in *The Great Tradition* he suggests that it is the role of the truly great novel to offer a meaningful example of how to be English, and therefore how to be human, in the modern world.

Modernism and the Reading Public: Highbrow and Lowbrow

In *The Great Tradition*, Leavis infuses aesthetics with his social mission. It was his hope that even if the masses wouldn't read Henry James, at least their schoolteachers would. Yet Leavis perceived an obstacle, embodied in the word "highbrow," to literature's potential to transform society. In a 1932 essay, Leavis noted that "instead of conventional respect for traditional standards, we have the term, 'high-brow.'"[43] Leavis's frustration with the term stems from the way it was almost always pejorative shorthand for the cultural elite, especially critics and writers. Whereas scholars of modernism have long debated the existence of a great divide between modernist literature and mass culture, Leavis's writings remind us that the experimental writers of the period were called "highbrows" long before they were ever categorized as modernists. Leavis reads the circulation of the slur "highbrow" as a sign of England's loss of its common culture. Through his focus on the reading public, Leavis suggests that the masses greeted modernism not with antagonism but with benign neglect. This neglect, he further contends, helped to produce the particular character of the writing that we now call modernism.

The *Oxford English Dictionary* dates "highbrow," a word of American origin, from the 1880s.[44] Highbrow can be a sensibility, not unlike snobbery, but it can also be a person. Virginia Woolf recuperated the term "highbrow" by applying it to herself with ironic defiance.[45] Woolf also valorized the term "lowbrow," which was sometimes a synonym for the working classes, reserving her scorn for the vast bourgeoisie she called the "middlebrow." Melba Cuddy-Keane calls Woolf a "democratic highbrow" who used the terms but "was able to envision possibilities for moving beyond them in a way that most others involved in the cultural debates could not."[46] While Woolf and Leavis had little more in common than mutual disregard, so worrying was the emergence of the highbrow slur that each felt called upon to respond. In his handbook for teachers, *Culture and Environment*, Leavis credits an American invention, the subscription book club, with helping to produce the concept of the "highbrow" and the divisiveness that accompanied it. Leavis quotes an ad in which a British counterpart to America's Book-of-the-Month Club, the Book Guild, proclaims that its selections are for the "ordinary intelligent reader, not for highbrows."[47] The ad assures its subscribers that they will be safely shielded from the elite literature of modern times. Such protectionist sentiment even extended to writers: Leavis traces a similar message in a circular urging popular writers to keep their "eyebrows well pinned down" and avoid becoming a "superior highbrow."[48]

In a sharp critique of early twentieth-century English society, Leavis contrasts what he sees as the modern repudiation of art and literature embodied in the term "highbrow" with the common culture that he envisions as part of England's past. Leavis turns nostalgically to Shakespearean theater as the height of this common culture. In Elizabethan times, Leavis explains, "*Hamlet* appealed at a number of levels of response, from the highest downward."[49] Leavis quotes his contemporary the scholar Dover Wilson, "Shakespeare...was not a high-brow."[50] For Leavis, this is true because "there were no high-brows in Shakespeare's time," in part because the Book Guild had not seen fit to invent them.[51] With Shakespeare as his primary historical example, Leavis imagines the Elizabethan period as a moment in which culture was stratified into levels—a hierarchy of economics and taste—but in which the material of culture, its objects or even its canon, remained uniformly available. In Leavis's conception, there is no modern equivalent to *Hamlet* because audiences have changed. Paperback best sellers and Hollywood films may be mass entertainment, but they are not a common culture. Leavis's idealized Shakespearean audience has given way to the modern stratification of taste.

Against the prelapsarian fantasy of a Shakespearean public, Leavis summarizes the modern condition: "The same is not true...of *The Waste Land*, *Hugh Selwyn Mauberly*, *Ulysses*, or *To the Lighthouse*. These works are read only by a very small, specialised public and are beyond the reach of the vast majority of those who consider themselves educated."[52] Invoking the pantheon of modernist works by Eliot, Pound, Joyce, and Woolf, Leavis reveals his central concern with the "vast majority" and their ignorance of modernist writing. He emphasizes this point: not only was the majority of the reading public not reading Pound, but many had never even heard the name. Ultimately, Leavis sets up a chicken-and-egg problem that offers a particular slant on the birth of modernist literary production in English. First, Leavis notes that "the age in which the finest creative talent tends to be employed in works of this kind is the age that has given currency to the term, 'high-brow.' "[53] Whereas it might seem that Leavis blames the public's dismissal on the difficulty of the works themselves, Leavis then explains that "it would be as true to say that the attitude implicit in 'high-brow' causes this use of talent as the converse."[54] Here Leavis claims that the attitude that has labeled Joyce and Pound as highbrows actually helps to produce "works of this kind." In other words, Leavis attributes the difficulty, experimentalism, and shock value of such writing to its a priori rejection by the broader reading public. Thus Leavis argues that the masses have themselves created modernism by signaling the extent to which they will refuse to read it. It is with a strange circularity that Leavis suggests that the climate for the new, experimental writing of Eliot, Woolf, Joyce, and Pound was fostered by the public that called them highbrow.

"High modernism," not highbrow, is the contested critical term today. When Fredric Jameson writes in *A Singular Modernity* that high modernism is a "belated construct," he refers to the way in which modernism never emerged like an avant-garde movement, with membership and manifestos, but was rather the invention of a post–World War II moment in literary criticism.[55] Leavis, who was writing just shortly after the height of modernist productivity, offers a distinct viewpoint from that associated with the belated construction of modernism. At the same time, Leavis offers a different perspective than that found in the high-low debates of the past twenty years.[56] In a series of responses to the idea that a "great divide" separated modernism from mass culture, recent critics have done much valuable work demonstrating that writers such as Woolf, Eliot, and Joyce were often favorably disposed toward mass culture and even influenced by it.[57] Leavis, however, tells us more than which writers liked to go to the movies, or even which writers made explicit bids for broader audiences. Using an approach that prefigures cultural studies more than modernist criticism, Leavis shifts the agency from authors to the reading public. Leavis's observations of reading and writing practices remind us that modernist writers were aware of the rebuke embodied in the label high-brow. While it would be going too far to say that modernist writers cultivated their difficulty solely under the sting of this rebuke, it is true that those we now call modernists were writing at a time when most of them had little hope of broad appeal. Leavis thus offers a distinct picture of the cultural "divide" by presenting modernist estrangement from the masses not as the result of elitism and disdain on the part of the authors but rather as the result of a vast indifference on the part of the reading public. Leavis's description does not fully capture the complexity of the interwar writing and reading practices: even the most experimental writers sometimes enjoyed broader appeal. Yet Leavis, in his 1930s writing, offers a unique, early account of the development of what we now call modernism. Unlike the New Critics who followed Leavis and canonized modernism in his wake, Leavis cared passionately about what common readers thought and felt. Thus while the term "modernism" may be a heuristic and a taxonomical afterthought, attention to Leavis's writing reminds us that the ideas of high and low were very much a part of the cultural philosophy of the period when such writing emerged.

Queenie Leavis and the "Reading Habit"

While Leavis's discussions of highbrow, lowbrow, and the example of America have been largely overlooked by critics, Queenie Dorothy Leavis's influential and even more radical interweaving of American culture into the definitions of high and low has received even less attention.[58] Although some critics are quick to differentiate QDL from her husband, rightly suggesting that she deserves her own consideration, it was also the case that the two Leavises influenced each other greatly. QDL was steeped in the literary climate of Cambridge English: I. A. Richards oversaw her thesis; E. M. Forster was one of its readers. Yet QDL was most attentive to the early work of her husband even before their marriage in 1929. In her project, *Fiction and the Reading Public*, published in 1932 by Chatto and Windus, QDL treats many of the concerns of *Mass Civilization* to a fresh approach by focusing more closely on reading practices. The "other" Leavis has sometimes been called a precursor to cultural studies, because she too attempted in makeshift fashion to turn attention from books to their readers, from fiction to the reading public.[59] The accolade is usually ironic because she was as devoted to the repudiation of most popular fiction as her husband.

QDL's Arnoldian aspirations were keen, and in *Fiction and the Reading Public* she tellingly quotes Arnold's 1889 essay, "What is a Great Poet": "Of late there have seemed to me to be certain signs, especially in America, of a revolt of the mob against our literary masters."[60] Noting the exemplary status of America, QDL comments, "We thus have a situation closely resembling that of the United States, marking a new phase in our history and one which, as it is likely to continue indefinitely, is perhaps worth dwelling upon."[61] Even more plainly than her husband, QDL asserts that America simultaneously serves as example and influence because American culture has a unique tendency toward universalism: it can become the bad version of English culture, or the new cultural "situation," because American fiction, magazines, and the movies have both traveled to and transformed England. For QDL, Arnold's comparison was prophetic. Modern England has entered a "new phase" that draws it closer to the situation of America by drawing the masses away from literature.

Before examining QDL's turn to the example of America, it is worth considering the radical way in which she understood English culture to be newly divided into high and low. Marking her method as "anthropological," QDL treats English readers, and in particular the English working classes, as ethnographic subjects, or foreigners within the nation.[62] The missionary impulse runs as high in QDL's work as it did in Arnold's, only in this case, literature has thoroughly supplanted religion. Diagnosing modern English society, QDL observes its division into high and low:

> It is not perhaps surprising that, in a society of forty-three millions so decisively stratified in taste that each stratum is catered for independently by its own novelists and journalists, the lowbrow public should be ignorant of the work and even of the names of the highbrow writers, while to the highbrow public 'Ethel M. Dell' or 'Tarzan' should be convenient symbols, drawn from hearsay rather than first-hand knowledge.[63]

Like Leavis, QDL insists that the reading public exists in ignorance of highbrow writing; she adds that such writers are equally likely to know little of the actual reading practices of the working classes. Following the parlance of the day, QDL treats both highbrow and lowbrow as pejorative. Whereas Tarzan serves as metonym for the low, QDL offers T. S. Eliot's journal *The Criterion* as the epitome of the high: "it is common even in literary circles to fling the epithet 'highbrow' at it."[64]

In *Fiction and the Reading Public*, QDL scrutinizes the reading practices of the working classes even more closely than Leavis does in his essays. She announces that the working classes are reading the wrong books for the wrong reasons and that reading, rather than illiteracy, will imperil England. QDL likens working-class reading practices to a drug habit—she calls it the "reading habit"—that threatens to further impoverish the poor, both intellectually and financially. QDL insists, "In suburban side-streets and even village shops it is common to find a stock of worn and greasy novels let out at 2d. or 3d. a volume; and it is surprising that a clientèle drawn from the poorest class can afford to change the books several times a week, or even daily; but so strong is the reading habit that they do."[65] QDL nearly criminalizes the working-class readers in their eager reliance on popular fiction, "Yank magazines," and best sellers, including those written by the reprehensible American, Ernest Hemingway. The working classes feed their habit through the circulating library as well as "the American firm, Messers. Woolworth," which she disdainfully identifies as the "bookshop of the working-class."[66] Yet while QDL recoils to see her working-class counterparts select their books from among the shelves of stockings and lipstick, she believes her efforts to be firmly on their behalf. QDL may lament the addictive leisure reading that has drawn readers away from great literature, but she has faith in her ability to diagnose the malady sweeping England, much as she has faith in her husband to provide the cure.

In her discussion of the reading habit, QDL identifies a new genre of fiction that epitomizes the malaise. These are novels based on popular films, or what QDL calls, "the book of the talkie."[67] Unlike a literary adaptation, in which a classic text such as *Anna Karenina* becomes an abridged Hollywood picture, a cinematic novelization translates a successful film into paperback fiction. For QDL, the demand for novels that ape the talkies reveals just how debased the English public has become.[68] The "book of the talkie" is thus even more worrying than the bad cinema it echoes because it destroys what literature is, to whom it belongs, and what it is meant to do. The humanizing function of literature, celebrated by both of the Leavises, disappears in the new novels that are meant to remind readers of their favorite Hollywood pictures. Although this genre is rarely mentioned in critical discussions of early twentieth-century mass culture, QDL saw in novelization the threat of Hollywood made flesh, the beginning of English fiction that would be thoroughly Americanized.

The emergence of novelization in the interwar period pushes the Leavisite emphasis on the exemplary status of American culture to its limit. In the instance of novelization, it is not simply that Hollywood films have drawn readers away from their books to sit in the cinema stalls. Rather, in recursive fashion, the films themselves have given rise to a new popular fiction capable of transforming English writing. As QDL laments, the style of these novels, and in particular their transcription of dialogue, follows the form of the cinema rather than more established literary conventions. The case of novelization, then, can be understood to epitomize the cultural change that QDL associates with America. While her anthropological energies remain turned toward England, and particularly toward the habits of the English working class, she is able to study them as if they were foreign in part *because* of the increasing Americanization of English culture. In other words, the working English become the ethnographic subjects of QDL's investigatory lament because their culture, as she evaluates it, is becoming American.

Leavis and the Making of English Studies

Whereas QDL offered a detailed analysis of the problems with modern English culture in *Fiction and the Reading Public*, it was Leavis who would propose the solutions. Leavis's primary solution to society's ills did not emerge directly from critical discussions of the writers or works themselves, but rather grew out of his plan for education. Specifically, Leavis championed the study of the English literary tradition through the development of English as a discipline in the university. Early in his career, Leavis began to link the need for educational reform with the development of literary study. In a 1932 essay, "The Literary Mind," Leavis noted, "to revive or replace a decayed tradition is a desperate undertaking...something in the nature of luck is needed; the luck, let us say, that provides a centre of stimulus and a focus of energy at some university. All that falls under the head of 'English.' "[69] It is quite striking to note the faith that Leavis invests in the university in general and English studies in particular to halt the decay of tradition. Because Leavis understood English to be the university discipline that would prepare teachers for the nation's schools—and Leavis did in fact inspire a number of university youths to become schoolteachers—he imagined English to have the potential to effect change throughout the culture on a massive scale.[70] Commenting on Leavis's influence on the development of the uniquely grand ambitions of English studies, Perry Anderson notes, "Leavis commanded his subject, within his own generation. With him, English literary criticism conceived the ambition to become the vaulting centre of 'humane studies and of the university.' English was 'the chief of the humanities.' This claim was unique to England: no other country has ever produced a critical discipline with these pretensions."[71] Anderson's sweeping claim for the grand, humanist pretensions of English studies reflects Leavis's utter confidence in the potential of English to transform the nation as a whole. While Anderson may exaggerate the uniqueness of the development of literary study in England, overlooking the importance of literary education in the British colonies and elsewhere, it is nonetheless the case that circumstances primed interwar England for an intervention into national education in such a way as to make Leavis's ambitions possible.

In order to contextualize Leavis's radical pedagogical aims—and his desire to inculcate Englishness through literary study—it is necessary to consider the unusual educational climate in England after World War I. In 1918, Prime Minister Lloyd George gave a rousing speech at Manchester in which he pronounced that "an educated man is a better worker, a more formidable warrior, and a better citizen. That was only half-comprehended before the war."[72] Lloyd George's speech reflected, in potent fashion, the pervasive sentiment that England's inadequacies could be illuminated through a comparison of German and English education. What is most interesting about Lloyd George's speech, however, is the extent to which his cry for "a more formidable warrior" led to the reform of English studies in the schools and the reinvention of literary education. At the time, the humanist sentiment was such that it led to the belief that the task of educating children in English literature would produce not only better citizens but also better soldiers. If Lloyd George's exhortation seems like little more than bluff political rhetoric, then it is worth noting the vim with which its precepts were followed over the next few years. On the same platform at Manchester, H. A. L. Fisher, the president of the Board of Education, emphasized the extent to which educational reform was centrally about class. Lamenting in political catchphrase that "the rich learn and the poor earn," Fisher called for a set of reforms that could counter the class divisions in an increasingly mechanized society.[73] While investigations of all subjects were carried out, the two reports on the teaching of English, George Sampson's 1921 *English for the English* and the 1922 *The Teaching of English in England* (commonly known as the Newbolt Report), were among the most influential and enduring. These were the reports that made a case for a new and humanizing approach to English, one that could renew the spirit of nationalism in England and restructure the nation.

Of the two reports, Sampson's is the more readable, although less practical. Above all, it is an exhortation to reform English education in the schools. Denys Thompson notes in a later preface to Sampson's book that English in the schools, before the two reports, was "a somewhat dull and mechanical affair" that treated mostly grammar and composition with the occasional recitation of poetry.[74] Sampson makes his case for the inadequacy of such educational methods by presenting the cultural situation as one of mechanization: "Modern mass-production does not require educated workmen...The lift-man would work his switch no worse if he were quite illiterate and no better if he were a doctor of science."[75] Education, according to Sampson, is misunderstood as preparation for the workplace. In an oft-quoted phrase, Sampson avers, "it is the purpose of education, not to prepare children *for* their occupations, but to prepare children *against* their occupations."[76] Therefore, to return to the worker, "It is not as a lift-man that he is worth educating, but as a man. If the nation exclaims, 'What! All this education, and he only a lift-man!' it is uttering wickedness and stupidity: if the lift-man exclaims, 'What! All this education, and me only a lift-man!' he is uttering wickedness and doubtful grammar."[77] Sampson's phrase gives the nation the ability to protect the worker through its attitude toward education. Sampson further insists that "English is by far the most important subject in elementary schools," which are important because of their ability to reach the greatest number of people.[78] According to Sampson, the purpose of instruction in English is not to indoctrinate youth with grammatical rules but rather to transform society by preparing the masses *against* their future occupations as machine operators or other caretakers of technology. Similarly, the Newbolt Report poses the question, "What has English, and especially English literature, for the wayfaring man who misses the scholar's introduction"?[79] While an answer is not immediately forthcoming, the report assures the reader that such an answer will involve "grave national issues."[80]

In consequence of the Newbolt Report and George Sampson's *English for the English*, English pedagogy in the schools did indeed undergo strenuous reevaluation and change. While schoolchildren did not unanimously embrace Shakespeare and Donne as a lifeline to a lost Englishness, the appearance of English literary studies in its modern and current forms importantly grew out of the climate that produced these reports. The reevaluation of pedagogy at the level of primary and secondary schools was roughly contemporary with changes of a similar sort at the level of the university. Until the mid-nineteenth century, the study of English at Oxford and Cambridge, though not in Scotland, was largely philological; classics held sway as the traditional study of literature and aesthetics.[81] Although classics fought for its place of prominence for some time, it could not fulfill the need for renewed nationalism as could English. Moreover, classics could not speak to as broad a range of class positions nor prepare teachers for the changing primary and secondary classrooms. In the 1880s, the teaching of English was already on the rise, but it was associated with women's education and the Mechanic's Institutes. Although the first professor of English at Oxford was appointed in 1904, the feeling of many there toward this new subject was expressed by a professor of theology who opined that English study was for "women" and the "second and third rate men who were to become schoolmasters."[82]

Leavis entered Cambridge University at a time when the Ph.D. was a recent and somewhat disreputable degree and English studies was still on shaky ground. Whereas Cambridge had since 1883 offered a Litt.D., a doctorate based on the evaluation of published work, it did not introduce the Ph.D. until 1919. Leavis received a Ph.D. in 1924 and was mildly ashamed of having one. He even requested that the Ph.D. not be listed on the title page of *New Bearings in English Poetry* (1932), insisting that it "would raise the worst suspicions, and, anyway, looks comic."[83] While Leavis may have been hampered by his participation in the "modern" Ph.D. system, as well as by the newness of the discipline of English at an old university, he was also responsible for some of the most important changes in teaching English on the university level. As the discussion of *Culture and Environment* revealed, Leavis saw education as the means to curb and counteract the effects of civilization in the form of industrial labor, popular fiction, cinema, and motorcars. In this way, Leavis held beliefs very much in accord with those expressed in the reports of 1921 and 1922. Indeed, Leavis drew an important ideological connection between the reforms in the schools and the creation of English as a discipline in the universities.[84] Because Leavis believed that the function of a university education in English was to produce schoolteachers who would inoculate children with Englishness, protecting them against the mass-produced pleasures and labors of the working class, he understood university English to participate vitally in his project of rescuing society through literary analysis. According to Francis Mulhern, Leavis saw education as the only way to change the social environment, given that industrial progress could not be turned back.[85] It might seem curious that Leavis therefore chose the study of literature and newly developing methods of literary criticism as the means to alter society. Yet for Leavis, literary criticism was the *name* for this vast endeavor of societal change.

In his 1943 work, *Education and the University*, Leavis explains that the English school at Cambridge "emancipated literary studies from the linguistic grinds."[86] With philology marginalized and classics deemphasized, English might emerge as a new species of study, one that is neither rote nor mechanical and yet is socially relevant. Leavis devotes an early portion of the text to a discussion of a theoretical work known as the Experimental College by the American educator, Alexander Meiklejohn. As Leavis quotes Meiklejohn: "Our first aim is not to get liberal thinking done excellently but to get it done at all. In a word, we must recognize that the drift of American life is against those forms of liberal thinking which seem most essential to its welfare."[87] Leavis's commentary is consonant with his early positions on modernity and America. He avers, "For 'drift of American life,' of course, we can read 'drift of modern life': American conditions are the conditions of modern civilization, even if the 'drift' has gone further on the other side of the Atlantic than on this."[88] Here Leavis brings his analysis of society specifically to bear on the development of liberal arts within the university. Leavis's turn to English studies, such comments make clear, grows out of his analysis of Americanization and his attempt to protect England from it. Leavis notes that American universities bear the scars of modernization over English universities: "Even Harvard...appears to have suffered a great deal more from the last half-century of civilization than Oxford and Cambridge have done."[89] This suffering can be counteracted by "liberal thinking" such as that found in the exercises in *Culture and Environment*. For Leavis, the definition of liberal thinking is necessarily transatlantic: it is that which counters the drift of modern Americanized life.

The Americanization of England: Consequences for Cultural Studies

Leavis put such time and effort into writing about education, as well as into teaching itself, because he believed deeply that only educational reform could enact pervasive cultural change and that English was the only discipline to provide the means. Leavis's aims, however curiously condensed, were influential in the creation both of English as a discipline and of literary criticism as a scholarly endeavor. Indeed, Leavis's work on teaching is the only aspect of his scholarship that Raymond Williams deems "wholly valuable."[90] While Williams looks askance at Leavis's belief in the "minority" as the guardians of Englishness, he acknowledges Leavis's importance in the formation of both English and cultural studies at British universities, claiming that *"Minority Culture and Mass Civilisation...* outlined a particular view of culture which has become very widely influential."[91] Although it is true that Leavis influenced English and cultural studies in ways that persist to this day, it is also true that Leavis was prophetic in his anticipation of English reactions to American culture that would become full-blown by the Cold War. While the interwar years saw English uncertainty about the transatlantic shift in power, the years after the Second World War began to make plain the extent to which British imperial decline would be accompanied by the U.S.'s economic, militaristic, and mass cultural rise. In order to consider the ways in which Leavis was *both* influential and far-seeing in his analyses of America, it is worth turning to a different type of example, one drawn from the early development of cultural studies and the writing of one of its foundational figures Richard Hoggart.

Raymond Williams, E. P. Thompson, and Richard Hoggart are often considered the progenitors of cultural studies as it would become institutionalized and practiced in Britain.[92] Although Hoggart opened the possibility for a new kind of academic practice when he founded the Centre for Contemporary Cultural Studies at the University of Birmingham in 1963, it was his first book, *The Uses of Literacy* (1957), that shocked many in England by proposing a new way of studying culture. *The Uses of Literacy*, which Hoggart almost called *The Abuses of Literacy*, details the reading practices of the English working classes. Although *The Uses of Literacy* considers the question of training the working classes in "critical judgement," it earned the disdain of many in midcentury English departments for seriously analyzing material other than literature.[93] Attributing part of his inspiration for *The Uses of Literacy* to the writings of Leavis and the *Scrutiny* group, Hoggart notes the pleasure that came with his realization that "Leavisite methods" such as "close analysis, listening to a text, feeling a text and its texture...were translatable into the study of popular culture."[94] While Hoggart was capable of taking some working-class culture seriously, he was also sufficiently Leavisite to find aspects of mass culture from which the working class must be protected. In a telling scene in *The Uses of Literacy*, the mass culture that menaces a segment of working youths is inextricable from the American culture industries—music and movies—that have produced it. This description of what Andrew Goodwin calls "Hoggart's notion of the working class as victims of American culture" reveals the way in which Leavis's nationalist definitions of culture fed the development of postwar British cultural studies.[95]

In a discussion of popular reading material, Hoggart identifies "the juke box boys," a group of working-class youths who tend to read "comics, gangster novelettes, science and crime magazines."[96] Encoded in the very name of the jukebox boys is the music that entertains them: records that Hoggart notes are "almost all American."[97] Hoggart describes these youths, who "spend their evenings listening in harshly-lighted milk-bars to the 'nickelodeons,'" as "boys aged between fifteen and twenty, with drape-suits, picture ties, and an American slouch."[98] This is a curious description of a segment of the English working class: it Americanizes not only their reading and listening habits but their very corporeal style. As Andrew Goodwin has remarked, "Is the British slouch then a superior posture?"[99] It seems that for Hoggart, an English, or even a British, slouch will not do, because the jukebox boys are marked on a bodily level by their yearnings for American culture. In an even more pointed description, Hoggart observes, "the young men waggle one shoulder or stare, as desperately as Humphrey Bogart, across the tubular chairs."[100] Here one must ask what it means for these markers of American culture to determine the jukebox boys' "stare" or "slouch." Whereas Leavis indicted the working classes in their choice of popular entertainment, Hoggart more forcefully suggests that fantasies of American culture discipline and transform the boys' bodies as well as their material experience of being in the world. As Hoggart surmises, "Many of the customers—their clothes, their hair styles, their facial expressions all indicate—are living to a large extent in a myth-world compounded of a few simple elements which they take to be those of American life."[101]

In terms strikingly similar to those of Leavis, Hoggart distinguishes between America and the "myth-world" of Americanization. Like Leavis, Hoggart makes clear that it is not the lived experience of Americans but the mass cultural processes of Americanization that pose the threat. In the end, Hoggart's indictment of the jukebox boys—he calls them "the directionless and tamed helots of a machine-minding class"—embeds his references to American styles of leisure and habit within the more familiar picture of the modernization of English culture.[102] Certainly, Hoggart is remembered for his work on mass culture in England and not for his occasional references to American music and film. Yet Hoggart's brief discussion of the jukebox boys reveals the permeability of the boundaries between mass culture and American culture, and the easy ideological slippage from one to the other. These references to America can seem an unimportant aspect of Hoggart's writing precisely because American culture and mass culture, by the fifties, had become nearly synonymous in England. Hoggart's central contribution to British cultural studies is, of course, his analysis of *British* culture; yet, it is revealing to note this transatlantic presentation of the working classes, on the model of Leavis's thirties writing, in Hoggart's earliest and best-known work. While Hoggart acknowledges Leavis's influence in both inspiration and method, careful attention to the resemblances between Leavis and Hoggart reveals cultural studies, as well as English studies, to be predicated on a style of Englishness that would resist its own transatlanticity.

Terry Eagleton notes that Leavis not only influenced cultural studies, but that his importance to English literary studies is so fundamental as to be taken for granted. As Eagleton puts it, Leavis's reading practices, cultural ideologies, and intellectual mission have been absorbed into "the bloodstream of English studies in England" and "become a form of spontaneous critical wisdom as deep-seated as our conviction that the earth moves round the sun."[103] While many critics will attest to Leavis's centrality to the development of English studies in England, the transatlantic dimensions of his writings have less frequently been probed. Yet by turning our attention to Leavis's use of the example of America, it is possible to see how his influential development of pedagogical methods and English studies emerged in part through his repudiation of Americanization. Despite Leavis's commitment to developing among the English working classes a literary sensibility tenacious enough to protect them from jazz and Hollywood, Leavis's theories ultimately spread beyond the British Isles, contributing to the rise of American New Criticism. Indeed, the impact of his development of English into a core discipline of the humanities, as well as his commitment to close reading, can still be felt in the United States today. It is thus, perhaps, the greatest irony of Leavis's legacy that English studies in the United States emerged in part out of an intellectual project that defined itself, and the literary culture poised to rescue England, against the example of America.

5. Make It Old

Inventing Englishness in Four Quartets

In one of his most influential and enduring works of social criticism, *Notes towards the Definition of Culture* (1948), T. S. Eliot spares a moment to comment on what he calls American imperialism. America, observes Eliot, practices "a different form of imperialism" than that of the British Empire.[1] This imperialism emerges not through the military conquest of the globe, but rather through the "influence of culture."[2] In a brief passage, Eliot explains his reasoning:

> America has tended to impose its way of life chiefly in the course of doing business, and creating a taste for its commodities. Even the humblest material artefact, which is the product and the symbol of a particular civilisation, is an emissary of the culture out of which it comes: I mention that influential and inflammable article the celluloid film. American economic expansion can be also, in its way, the cause of disintegration of cultures which it touches.[3]

In just a few lines, Eliot sums up and disparages the new U.S. cultural hegemony as signified by the ambassadorial work of its commodities. The American commodity is at once "product" and "symbol," doing the metonymic work of representing the United States even as it destroys the local cultures it encounters. The irony of Eliot's anthropological rhetoric, in which American artifacts serve as emissaries, stems from the way in which it transforms Britain from a site of imperial power into a local culture threatened by the new imperial practices of its former colony. Indeed, earlier in *Notes*, Eliot has matter-of-factly taken the temperature of public opinion in the forties, reporting that British "power is now commonly said to be passing."[4] Yet rather than lamenting this imperial decline, Eliot joins writers from Thomas Hardy to F. R. Leavis in reimagining England as a vibrant collection of local practices, here emblematized by such regional attractions as "the dog races" and "Wensleydale cheese."[5] In the same work in which he decries American commodities, Eliot famously identifies unmistakably English signs of "culture"—from Derby Day to Gothic churches to boiled cabbage—in a genial mixture of high and low. The character of Eliot's examples suggests that at this late date, Eliot is less concerned with elite arts than with English culture, and particularly with the nostalgic protection of Englishness from the modern American forces that threaten its disintegration.

Through works such as *Notes*, Eliot has come to hold a unique place in the pantheon of modern English letters as the American who not only instructed the English on the state of their culture, but to whom they actually listened. Eliot is integral to any discussion of the literary repercussions of Americanization, because his successful renewal of Englishness relies on his negotiation of American culture. Eliot's 1927 adoption of British citizenship and conversion to the Anglican church were the personal marks of his turn from America to England. This striking transatlantic personal history has helped to fuel projects such as Lyndall Gordon's "The American Eliot" and Steve Ellis's *The English Eliot* that explore and even quantify the American and English aspects of Eliot's work. Sometimes, as in David Chinitz's *T.S. Eliot and the Cultural Divide* and Eric Sigg's *The American T.S. Eliot*, this impulse leads authors to emphasize the importance of America to a writer who seemed to have repudiated it. I both build on and depart from these readings by signaling a different relationship between Eliot's treatment of American culture and his literary production of Englishness. Despite Ezra Pound's well-known injunction to "make it new," the mature Eliot was committed in much of his poetry to making it old—so old, in fact, as to predate the United States. With surprising tenacity, Eliot gestures toward the American colonial period and the discovery of the New World, both to a limited extent in his early verse and more fully in his major late work, *Four Quartets*. In so doing, he presents a picture of a transatlantic continuity capable of countering the assault on English culture by the newly "imperial" America.

Among Eliot's major works, only *Four Quartets* offers sustained reference to transatlantic exchange between Britain and America.[6] Even *The Waste Land*, whose opening references to American popular music were famously excised by Pound, alludes much more readily to London's bridges and pubs than to the popular music of the "Shakesperehian rag."[7] Yet there is another set of Eliot's verses, unpublished during his lifetime, which proposes sustained transatlantic engagement. Dubbed the "Columbo-Bolo verses" by Eliot's critics, these poems loosely center on the voyage of Christopher Columbus to the New World and his encounter with native royalty in Cuba. Unearthed in Eliot's early notebooks and in letters he sent to the American poet, Conrad Aiken, the disturbingly racist and misogynistic poems provide insight into Eliot's early understandings of race, colonialism, and the transatlantic. When viewed as a precursor to *Four Quartets*, the Bolo verses suggest the ways in which Eliot's ideas of culture, tradition, and Englishness emerge out of his anxieties about transatlantic relations.

By examining a range of Eliot's writings, from his early unpublished poems to his letters and essays and finally to *Four Quartets*, it is possible to see how his project of remaking Englishness relies upon his rejection of Americanization. For Eliot, Americanization is largely the erasure of culture; it is the modernization that made all the ordinary things Eliot mentions in *Notes*—cheese, cathedrals, and cabbages—precious and worth protecting. At the same time, Eliot's view of Americanization reflects his anxieties about America's racial heritage. In both the Bolo verses and *Four Quartets*, Eliot stages a return to the discovery and settlement of the Americas as a counterpoint to Americanization. In *Four Quartets* in particular, Eliot accomplishes this temporal reversion by nostalgically invoking colonial relations between Britain and America as a means to disavow the modern culture of the United States.

Eliot and Americanization

While Eliot's decision to critique American imperialism in *Notes towards the Definition of Culture* was characteristic of his later years, he had long been aware of the debates around Americanization. When he arrived at Oxford in 1914 to spend a year as a visiting student, Eliot took part in a common-room debate on the "threatened Americanisation of Oxford."[8] In a letter to his American friend, Eleanor Hinkley, Eliot defends his home country, albeit with the slight self-mockery of an exaggerated Southern drawl: "I pointed out to them frankly how much they owed to Amurrican culcher in the drayma (including the movies) in music, in the cocktail, and in the dance."[9] This early encounter with British resistance to Americanization serves as a reminder that Eliot's positions on American popular and mass culture were never simple. Eliot, for instance, was a long-standing jazz fan. As David Chinitz compellingly demonstrated in *T.S. Eliot and the Cultural Divide*, Eliot was much more favorably disposed to elements of popular culture—if not always mass culture—than many of his earlier critics assumed. Moreover, as Chinitz pointed out, even within the category of mass culture, Eliot's position remains complex.[10] Still, Eliot's attitudes toward entertainment become clearer when the dimension of nationality is taken into account, and Chinitz's examples are a case in point. In order to illustrate the range of Eliot's preferences, Chinitz contrasts Eliot's disdain for "the universal picture palace" displaying "Shirley Temple" to Eliot's support for the BBC.[11] Although no paradigm can contain Eliot's complexity, it remains hard to overlook the extent to which Eliot tends to reject icons of Americanization (such as the tap-dancing Temple) in favor of those (the London music hall, the BBC) that promote or emblematize Britishness. To take another example, while Eliot's profound enthusiasm for the music hall singer Marie Lloyd might seem to reposition him as a patron of the popular, it is important to remember that Marie Lloyd was quintessentially English, an iconic part of the local English culture threatened by Americanization.[12] Thus when Eliot holds up Marie Lloyd *against* Hollywood he is not contradicting himself but rather participating in the discourse of American imperialism as he would later describe it in *Notes*.

Eliot's attitudes toward Americanization appear even clearer in one of his lesser-known writings: his 1928 preface to the British imprint of American writer Edgar Mowrer's *This American World*. In this remarkable preface, Eliot reveals the extent to which he has kept up with discussions of what Mowrer repeatedly calls "Americanization." Eliot offers penetrating remarks about the greater "literature of Americanism" within which Mowrer's work should be situated.[13] Eliot is particularly drawn to the section of Mowrer's study that proposes a deep, historical connection between America and Europe. As Eliot explains, Mowrer "inquires into the origin, as well as the nature, of Americanism; traces it back to Europe; and finds that what are supposed to be the specifically American qualities and vices, are merely the European qualities and vices given a new growth in a different soil."[14] In Eliot's system of metaphors, what seems the foreign invasion of the European host is actually the recycling of organic material expelled from Europe in transatlantic migration. Eliot explains that "the majority of foreigners think either of Americanization as something to be welcomed and exploited, or as a plague to be quarantined."[15] Eliot then extends this reference to plague: "Europe, therefore, in accepting American contributions...has contracted a malady the germs of which were bred in her own system."[16] Such a rhetoric of "germs" might seem to recall the language used to express anti-immigrant sentiment in the United States. Yet here the metaphor refers not to the return of peoples to Europe, but to the circulation of communicable habits of work and leisure, of Fordist production and new forms of mass entertainment. In this telling use of biological rhetoric, Eliot expresses the communicability of Americanism in the language both of disease and descent, intimating the concern with transatlantic bloodlines that would obsess him in the period leading up to the writing of *Four Quartets*.

Moreover, Mowrer's text seems strikingly to anticipate the transatlantic concerns that Eliot will enunciate in his later work. At the outset, Mowrer presents his overarching claim: "Something mankind is learning to call Americanism seems destined to spread over much of the earth."[17] This ominous prediction shares its tone with Eliot's prefatory references to "maladies" "germs" and "plague." Indeed, Mowrer is grim in his evaluation of the world's attraction to America, "as when a crowd of bearded statesmen bow before an infant king."[18] Such an unnatural order of things can be cured by revisiting a transatlantic genealogy: "Deep in our racial souls, and again by most of our formal education, we Americans are a prolongation of Europe."[19] This image of Americans proposes a sense of continuity much like that which Eliot will invoke through reference to colonial history in *Four Quartets*. While some of the period's narratives of Americanization focus on industry, progress, and the exploits of Henry Ford, Mowrer is deeply Eliotic in his attention to the organic connection—"deep in our racial souls"—between Europe and America. Mowrer's reference to the "early colonists" makes it clear that the connection between America and Europe has not come with recent waves of immigration but rather dates back to the time period before the formation of the United States. Near the end of the work, after a chapter entitled "Europe Becomes Americanized," Mowrer will reverse the stakes of this connection in a thought experiment that imagines Europe as "an American colony."[20] The point of the experiment is not to deal in fantasies; rather, Mowrer believes the reversal of the colonial relationship to be a possible future state of affairs. Even in the present, he notes, "Europe is anything but independent of the United States. The waves of power are simply running the other way."[21]

The consonances of Eliot's preface with his later transatlantic work *Four Quartets* are remarkable. Not only does the preface reveal Eliot's deep familiarity with discourses of Americanization, but it also reveals the extent to which Mowrer's work provided Eliot with a romantic treatment of the Anglo-American colonial connection. While Eliot may not have shared Mowrer's fantasy that Europe could become a colony of the United States, a fantasy that had British antecedents from the turn of the century, he developed an understanding of American imperialism as a potentially pernicious concatenation of machine culture and economic expansion.[22] At the same time, Mowrer's gesture toward the "racial" connection between England and America seems to anticipate Eliot's own gestures toward such a connection in *Four Quartets*. The consonances between Eliot's 1928 preface and his later writing thus indicates the extent and depth of his engagement with the theories of Americanization that he had encountered in England since the First World War.

Eliot's English Drag: From Nation to Race

In 1927, a year before publishing his comments on Americanism in *This American World*, Eliot announced his personal turn from the United States to Great Britain: he formally adopted British citizenship and converted to the Anglican church. Herbert Read comments that Eliot very nearly disciplined himself into a bodily Englishness: "I was never conscious that he was in any way less English than myself. From the first he fitted naturally into English clothes and English clubs, into English habits generally. In fact, if anything gave him away, it was an Englishness that was a shade too correct to be natural."²³ Virginia Woolf, on the other hand, observed that her friend Tom behaved in a "highly American way."²⁴ Indeed, much as Eliot attempted to shed his American background and embrace English culture, he was constantly reminded of his American origin by those around him. Even after Eliot worked as an editor at Faber for a number of years, his letterhead, quite incredibly, included the identification "U.S.A. origin" after his name.²⁵ Eliot's ability to reinvent himself as English, then, rested on his ability to mask and even repudiate his associations with the United States. Whereas Eliot advertised his connections to America late in life, particularly on lecture tours of the United States, his midlife attempts to become English were marked by his desire to belong not only to the British state but also to the English race. Given his feelings and phobias about race and America, Eliot's longing for Englishness seems to have derived in turn from his vexed racial identifications with the United States.

In an oft-quoted letter of July 1919 that Eliot wrote to a member of the Bloomsbury crowd, Mary Hutchinson, Eliot reflects upon his status as an American in England: "But remember that I am a *metic*—a foreigner, and that I *want* to understand you, and all the background and tradition of you...But I may simply prove to be a savage."²⁶ Here Eliot confesses his great fear that he may be too racially American, too savage, to fathom the civilized tradition of the English. Moreover, almost a decade later, Eliot describes his national and racial identity with a characteristic blend of racism and anxiety:

> Some day...I want to write an essay about the point of view of an American
> who wasn't an American, because he was born in the South and went to school
> in New England as a small boy with a nigger drawl, but wasn't a southerner

in the South because his people were northerners in a border state and looked down upon all southerners and Virginians, and who so was never anything anywhere and who therefore felt himself to be more a Frenchman than an American and more an Englishman than a Frenchman and yet felt that the U.S.A. up to a hundred years ago was a family extension.[27]

Just a year after becoming a British citizen, Eliot is able to diagnose himself with something like American self-loathing and with a sense of self that is inherently tied to his anxieties about sounding like a black American. As in his letter to Hutchinson, Eliot describes his national identity in distinctly racial terms. Yet, Eliot works to counter the description of his tainted childhood through a series of regional and national displacements. Eliot's identification of himself as "an American who wasn't an American," follows from Eliot's regional displacements, his inability to be properly from the South or New England. These regional displacements produce what Eliot describes as an un-American structure of feeling. In the end, it is Eliot's *feeling* of being nationally more French than American, and more English than French, that allows him to disavow his Americanness. He is able to think of the American past—"up to a hundred years ago"—but not the modern American present as consonant with this English identity.

What might be termed Eliot's English drag could also, with some irony, be called an elaborate project of racial passing. Eliot's vexed attempt to fashion himself as an Englishman, in a society that would not let him forget his national origins, grew out of his anxieties about the racial associations of being American. Although Wyndham Lewis referred to Eliot as "the premier poet of Anglo-Saxony," Eliot's letters to Hutchinson and Read reveal that his feelings about his national background were deeply intertwined with his feelings about his own racial mannerisms and dialect.[28] Michael North points out that Eliot encountered such associations in elite circles of English culture.[29] As we have seen, Clive Bell's 1921 essay "Plus de Jazz" accused Eliot of being the kind of writer whose art draws inspiration from "a black and grinning muse"—an association with black America that Eliot would be quick to resist.[30] If to Eliot being American meant an association with savagery and black dialect, then becoming English was also the way to become racially Anglo-Saxon or white. Indeed, Eliot's invention of English culture in his poetry takes part in the racial discourses surrounding Eliot's turn from American to English self-fashioning. As Eliot's appeal and influence attest, it may have taken the anxieties of an American to help produce white, organic Englishness as the palliative nationalism of the late interwar and early postwar periods.

The Columbo-Bolo Verses

The importance of the transatlantic frame to Eliot's racial anxieties can be most clearly seen in a set of early verses that have received somewhat limited critical attention.[31] In 1988, Christopher Ricks published a handful of Eliot's verses as an appendix to a notebook of poetry, *Inventions of the March Hare*, that Eliot had produced in his youth. Unlike the majority of the poems in the notebook, which are earlier drafts of now-familiar representatives of the Eliot canon, the poems in the appendix remained unpublished throughout Eliot's life, despite his persistent attempts to publish them. Wyndham Lewis, rejecting the poems for inclusion in *Blast*, wrote to Pound that he wished to adhere to a policy of avoiding "words ending in –Uck, -Unt, and –Ugger."[32] Indeed, Eliot's Columbo-Bolo verses are not only off-color in vocabulary, but are shockingly racist, misogynistic, and at once homophobic and homoerotic.[33] Specifically, the poems tell the story of Columbus's voyage to the New World, represented by Cuba, and his highly sexualized encounters with the Cuban King Bolo's queen and court. Critical response to the poems has included Lyndall Gordon's insistence on their misogyny and Jonathan Gill's acknowledgement of their racism.[34] Eliot does not deserve any defense for these poems; nevertheless, to ignore them would be to overlook a body of work that reveals much about Eliot's related conceptions of transatlantic relations and racial ideology.

Along with *Four Quartets*, the Columbo-Bolo verses offer Eliot's only extended cycle of poems on the topic of transatlantic voyage and European colonialism. This representation of fifteenth-century Spanish colonialism, interestingly enough, harbors elements of the later endeavors of British colonialism. For instance, although Columbo makes his departure at the bequest of a bawdy Queen Isabella, "that famous Spanish whore," his band of sailors are dubbed "merry men" in an echo of Robin Hood and Robert Louis Stevenson, drink tea in the afternoon, and cry out "avast" in the tradition of British seafarers.[35] The permeability of Spanish and British imperialism in Eliot's poem lends itself to an even starker permutation of the Columbus story. While the Columbo-Bolo poems presume to tell the tale of European discovery of the New World, they identify the Cuban natives as "blacks."[36] Such a strange racial anachronism begins to suggest the way the poems will bring the legacy of Atlantic slavery into a European narrative of first contact. At the same time, a representative verse weaves a reference to rum, an important slave trade commodity, into its scatological tribute to Columbo's travels:

On Sunday morning after prayers
They took their recreation
The crew assembled on the deck
And practiced masturbation.
Columbo being full of rum
He fell down in a stupor
They turned his asshole S.S.W.
And he cried "I'll die a pooper!"[37]

Although the rum in this stanza seems little more than an agent of prurience, rum was a chief product of the British slave trade and, after sugar, a driving force in its perpetuation. This image of a sea captain drunk on Caribbean rum is a caricature of the seventeenth-century British, not the fifteenth-century Spanish. In these bawdy verses, Eliot thus reveals more than a youthful interest in off-color puns; he also reveals the beginnings of his long-standing interest in the British colonization of the Americas.

Much as the Spanish colonists in Eliot's poems betray aspects of a British identity, the Cuban natives seem suspiciously American. Specifically, Eliot's own racial anxieties about being a "savage" in relation to the British seem to surface here. One critic remarked that Eliot's depiction of the Bolos seems to draw on minstrel imagery.[38] Indeed, a hasty sketch that Eliot drew of Bolo in a 1914 letter to Conrad Aiken resembles a comic minstrel caricature even as it presages Eliot's own, fussy English garb. While Eliot's racism here again is unavoidable, there may be an element of national and racial self-loathing in Bolo's pretensions to European manners and fashions. Even when the poems depict Bolo's court as utterly debased, they recall aspects of Anglo-American transatlantic history. As Eliot rhymes in salaciously racist terms:

King Bolo's swarthy bodyguard
They numbered three and thirty
An innocent and playful lot
But most disgustingly dirty.
King Bolo lay down in the shade
His royal breast uncovering
They mounted in a banyan tree
And shat upon their sovereign.[39]

The native adults behave like "innocent and playful" children even as their uncivilized behavior reverses and soils the Western ideal of the monarchy. In a striking parallel, the United States has also historically inverted the monarchical hierarchy of Great Britain, placing "the people" rhetorically above their leader. Such disregard for the "sovereign" in the New World obliquely recalls America's foundational rejection of kings, translating a principle of national pride into a shameful departure from the ideals of civilization. The American associations with racial savagery that characterize Eliot's epistolary tributes to Englishness also guide the Columbo-Bolo poems' depictions of European relations to the New World. In the Bolo poems, Eliot invokes colonial relations between Europe and America in an echo of the racial discourse that helped to prompt his desire to distance himself from the United States.

Make It Old, Make It English: Eliot's *Four Quartets*

Eliot's investment in transatlantic exchange in the Columbo-Bolo verses prefigures one of his best-known and most enduring late works *Four Quartets* (1943). At first glance, *Four Quartets* could not seem more different from the Bolo verses. A product of Eliot's mature years, the *Quartets* speak in austere and elegiac tones about the passing of time and the possibilities for redemption. Whereas the Bolo poems are scatological and disturbingly racist, *Four Quartets* is at once philosophical and deeply metaphysical. Critics have not often been inclined to consider these poems together, perhaps in part because they are so different both in form and content. Yet, along with Eliot's late poem "Marina" (1930), they are the works in which Eliot most clearly offers sustained treatment of the Atlantic region and transatlantic exchange.[40] Considering *Four Quartets* alongside the Columbo verses offers further insight into the ways in which Eliot perceives and presents transatlantic relations. Specifically, both works attempt to turn back time to the colonial period before the emergence of the United States, enabling fantasies of transatlantic continuity. In *Four Quartets*, these fantasies allow Eliot to imagine a nostalgic, preindustrial vision of the land—what Eliot calls "significant soil"—that is at once English and American.

Perhaps because *Four Quartets* is almost disturbingly transatlantic, critics have made a range of arguments for its national affiliations. Jed Esty identifies the *Quartets* as ideologically English, including the third "so-called 'American' quartet," whereas Lyndall Gordon suggests that not only the third quartet but the work as a whole can be understood to be importantly American.[41] Close examination of the poem reveals that *Four Quartets* produces its particular little Englandism *through* its negotiation of a broader transatlantic framework. In *Four Quartets*,

Eliot resolves the dilemma between modern Britain and the United States by refusing them both, returning instead to the moment in colonial history when America was part of Great Britain. In so doing, *Four Quartets* produces a specifically transatlantic nostalgia that recalls the golden age of British imperialism through its colonial relationship with America.

Part of the importance of *Four Quartets*, and of its nationalism, becomes clear in a brief review of its reception. Each of the *Quartets* was published separately in the years 1936 through 1942 before they were collected and published as a single work in 1943. Even before the *Quartets* was published as a single work, the importance of its constituent parts was becoming evident. Eliot's poem spoke much more broadly to the public during the war than *The Waste Land* did in the twenties. While *The Waste Land* can be understood as exemplary of a highbrow, cosmopolitan moment in modernism—the poem's difficulty partially circumscribing its audience—*Four Quartets* presents itself as a philosophical form of succor for a nation in the throes of war. When "East Coker" was first published as a supplement to the *New English Weekly* in March 1940, it had to be reprinted in May and June, and within a year sold almost twelve thousand copies.[42] Later, Eliot read three of the quartets at different times over the BBC, thus reaching an even broader audience.[43] The popularity of "East Coker" and *Four Quartets* more generally, critics have since surmised, follows from the way in which it speaks to the needs of a populace desperate for both an organic form of patriotism and a metaphysical approach to meaning in the face of war. In this way, *Four Quartets* functions as the opposite of *The Waste Land*: rather than lingering on the detritus of modernity, *Four Quartets* suggests that a return to a vital and nationalist past may provide hope for the future. Such sentiments earned *Four Quartets* high critical praise among nationalist literary critics such as F. R. Leavis. In a revealingly titled 1967 lecture at Cambridge, "Why *Four Quartets* Matters in a Technologico-Benthamite Age," F. R. Leavis explained how the *Quartets* are capable of countering the increasing societal modernization that he has elsewhere labeled Americanization. Eliot is among Leavis's most prized living poets in part because, particularly in his late work and above all in *Four Quartets*, Eliot fulfills the Leavisite program of rejecting the modern for a nostalgic vision of old Englishness. An important difference between *Four Quartets* and Leavis's work, however, follows from the way in which Eliot finds it necessary to present an explicitly pre–United States picture of the past in order to produce his imaginative tribute to Englishness.

Each of the *Quartets* takes its title from a place in which Eliot spent time: three in England, and one in America. This state of affairs, coupled with the frequent use of the first person, has motivated much of the biographical criticism that surrounds *Four Quartets*. While such an approach has its limits, it is also deeply relevant to a work whose structure reflects Eliot's personal and ancestral history. Eliot titled the first quartet, "Burnt Norton," after an English place he had briefly visited with his wife. This poem, through its ruminations on "time past and time present," introduces the temporal logic that Eliot continues to draw on throughout *Four Quartets*. The second quartet, "East Coker," recalls in its title the town from which Eliot's ancestors and namesakes left England for Massachusetts. "East Coker," paying attention to Eliot's ends and beginnings, presents an Atlantic genealogy that weaves Eliot's family history into a larger picture of colonial migrations from Britain to America. Yet rather than celebrating this exchange, "East Coker" produces a rustic, little England tied to a racial, bodily Englishness by both invoking and effacing the American side of transatlantic relations. The third quartet, "The Dry Salvages" refers to a spot off the New England coast at the same time that its name recalls European histories of encounters with New World "savages" or "salvages." This poem, more obviously than the other quartets, stages the opposition between ruinous, modern development and the enduring seasons and cycles of nature that are tied at once to race and to the land. The final quartet, "Little Gidding," returns to England and invokes a pre-Cromwellian community of Anglicans who seem to be the spiritual ancestors and guardians of Eliot's vision of Englishness. Yet even this final tribute to Englishness reflects the history of British colonization of the Americas that produces the transatlantic dimension of *Four Quartets*.

"Burnt Norton": The Imaginative Production of the Past

Eliot wrote the first of the quartets, "Burnt Norton," before conceiving the idea of the whole. It stands outside of the transatlantic circuit that will involve the later three quartets, and it appears wedded to a uniquely English place, the country manor house in Gloucestershire that Eliot visited in 1934. Burnt Norton may have captured Eliot's imagination in part because it was named after the baronet who burned it down, while still inside, sometime in the eighteenth century. Yet at the same time, this poem sets up the imaginative production of the past that will ultimately allow Eliot to propose an abiding historical continuity between England and America. "Burnt Norton" begins in meditative conjecture:

"Time present and time past / Are both perhaps present in time future, / And time future contained in time past."[44] This synchronic understanding of time allows Eliot to present his grander claims about meaning and history, as when the poem proposes:

> What might have been and what has been
> Point to one end, which is always present.
> Footfalls echo in the memory
> Down the passage which we did not take
> Towards the door we never opened
> Into the rose-garden. My words echo
> Thus, in your mind.[45]

The importance of these lines follows from the way in which they render equivalent "what might have been" and "what has been," the potential past and the actual past. These twin pasts are "always present" because they exist in the moment by existing in the mind. By equating "what might have been" and "what has been," Eliot insists upon the equivalence of imagination and memory. Indeed, the footfalls that echo in the memory are those which follow "the passage which we did not take / toward the door we never opened." The passage and the door exist as virtual possibilities in memory, yet in the poem, they are as real as any historical past. The poem intertwines memory and imagination, locating them not only in the mind, but also in the written language of the poem itself—"my words echo thus in your mind"— which is also "always present." In the opening of "Burnt Norton," thus, Eliot crafts his own version of the classic conceit of the eternality of poetry through a very specific set of relations that blurs the distinction between imagination and memory.

The effect of this new set of equivalences between imagination and memory is a license on the part of poet and poem not only to recall but also to create the past. Thus, shortly after explaining that the path to the rose garden was never taken, the poem leads the reader into the rose garden. This English rose garden is not the "real" rose garden of past experience, but rather something else just as real: it is the garden produced by the imaginative work of the poem. The poem invites the reader on the journey to this English rose garden, "Through the first gate / Into our first world," as if in a return to an Edenic origin. Through this imaginative return to the rose garden, Eliot creates an alternative history of Englishness that can be *produced* through writerly imagination. This imaginative production can be seen in the presentation of the roses themselves: "the roses / Had the look of flowers that are looked at." In this description, the poem presents the roses as subjective creations rather than objective entities, the stuff of perception rather than the *Ding an sich.*

In a subjectivist conceit, interiority continues to produce the external world: "And the pool was filled with water out of sunlight."[46] Merely looking at the pool through the writerly imagination, the poem seems to suggest, fills it with figurative water, returning the garden to an earlier state. Though this state is hardly permanent—"Then a cloud passed, and the pool was empty"—the moment in the garden is *Four Quartets*'s first example of the imaginative production of the past. The tribute to what the poem calls the "reality" of the sojourn in the garden suggests that the past proposed by the writer's imagination—"what might have been"—is as real and important as any past the mind can recollect. The significance of the rose garden, a symbolically English and Christian space, follows from the way in which Eliot is beginning to suggest that he will create an English past for his readership through the work of the poem. In a historical and cultural moment in which modern technologies were just beginning to suggest the return of the wartime legacy of burnt houses and the ruin of the national landscape, Eliot offers his readership an imaginary English rose garden as the sign of a past that never quite existed, but which can nonetheless be made real by the productive force of his verse.

"East Coker": Atlantic Genealogies

Following his ruminations on "time past" and "what might have been" in "Burnt Norton," Eliot produced an even more decisively nationalist poem in his popular 1940 "East Coker." Whereas "Burnt Norton" begins with an abstract notion of time, "East Coker" opens with a more personal chronology: "In my beginning is my end." Eliot critics tend to read this line biographically, as Eliot titled the poem after the town from which his ancestors left England in 1669 to colonize America, and to which he has now returned as a British citizen. In 1939, Eliot had taken up the topic of his English ancestry with all the vigor of a scholarly project, spending time at the British Museum with a work entitled *A Sketch of the Eliot Family.*[47] Although Eliot discovered a branch of the family that was "respectable squires in Devon," he chose to focus on the namesakes who had made the transatlantic voyage.[48] "East Coker" echoes this sense of Eliot's voyage to England as a spiritual homecoming, reworking its opening line to read later in the poem, "In my end is my beginning." "East Coker" makes clear that Eliot's desire to design a past and genealogy for himself is inextricably tied to his understanding of England's place in a transatlantic framework.

"East Coker" begins with the tension between development and decay that will be further expanded in the next quartet. Here "East Coker" follows its opening tribute to beginnings and ends with an image of change over time:

> In succession
> Houses rise and fall, crumble, are extended,
> Are removed, destroyed, restored, or in their place
> Is an open field, or a factory, or a by-pass.
> Old stone to new building, old timber to new fires
> Old fires to ashes, and ashes to earth
> Which is already flesh, fur and faeces,
> Bone of man and beast, cornstalk and leaf.[49]

In the poem that spurred such positive response from its English audience, Eliot incants a cyclical sense of rise and fall, a scene that quickly transitions from man-made buildings to the earth itself. The bewitchment of the scene follows from the way in which it transports the reader away from modern factories to an idealized old England:

> In that open field
> If you do not come too close, if you do not come too close
> On a Summer midnight, you can hear the music
> Of the weak pipe and the little drum
> And see them dancing around the bonfire
> The association of man and woman
> In dausinge, signifying matrimonie—
> A dignified and commodious sacrament.[50]

Here the poem makes the leap toward which "Burnt Norton" had gestured: it takes the reader back in time to an English past. As he acknowledged in a letter in 1941 to H. W. Hausermann, Eliot copied these lines and several that follow from *The Boke Named the Gouernour* (1531), written by Sir Thomas Elyot.[51] The Anglo-Saxon, which continues for several more lines, imports Eliot's personal ancestry into the poem even as it also invokes a more general sense of antiquated Englishness. Eliot's selection, from Elyot's work, of lines that speak on the topic of marriage seem particularly suited to this tribute to personal genealogy, further betraying Eliot's obsession with the processes that produced him.

Within this section, the image of rustic peasant dancers further allows Eliot to produce an English past in verse. Eliot writes:

> Lifting heavy feet in clumsy shoes,
> Earth feet, loam feet, lifted in country mirth
> Mirth of those long since under earth
> Nourishing the corn. Keeping time,
> Keeping the rhythm in their dancing
> As in their living in the living seasons[52]

The repeated emphasis upon the peasants' earthly feet presents them as the organic synecdoches of Englishness; a legacy not only of antiquated language and folk dancing but of the land itself. Of course, the peasants' bodies intermingle with the land because they are ancient and so have been interred for centuries. But the presentation of the peasants' bodies as organic extensions of the land also reminds the reader of where Englishness should be sought: in ancestry and in the soil, which the peasants doubly embody. Their feet, which also implicate the metrical feet of the poem itself, keep "time," thus presenting them both as in tune with the rhythm of the seasons and, in an alternate reading of the phrase, as the guardians of time for their English audience.

In the sequence of the quartets, "East Coker" is the first poem in which Eliot's personal genealogy so thoroughly mediates his tribute to Englishness. At points, Eliot even slips into the first-person plural, meditating on "all we have been." Such a rhetorical gesture gathers author and reader together within a communal history. Jed Esty has persuasively argued that *Four Quartets* takes part in a broader communitarian impulse in British literature of the late modernist period.[53] "East Coker" remains particularly interesting for the way in which it negotiates both Eliot's personal history and the history of the nation. The almost allegorical set of levels by which these histories coexist suggests how the transatlantic story of Eliot's ancestors is the repressed or unspoken other of the poem's celebratory Englishness. To take a narratological perspective for a moment, it is interesting to note that while Eliot fashions circular time and travel out of beginnings and ends—the departure from and return to the ground of his ancestors—the portion missing from this cycle is, to be plain, the middle. While the banality of such an observation may have precluded its appearance in Eliot criticism, I would like to underscore the way in which the identification of "East Coker" as end and beginning, alpha and omega, leaves out the intermediary history between the settlement of New England and Eliot's return to the land of his ancestors. If "East Coker" is the quartet that brought hope to a nation at war, at least in part through the creation of a particularly English past, then it is telling that it manages to do so by leaving out the violent sundering of Britain and America. The way in which Eliot folded his history into English history, and left the story of the transatlantic journey untold, begins to suggest what the *Quartets* as a whole will much more forcefully reveal, that the poems produce their ideology of Englishness through their negation of the United States.

"The Dry Salvages": Worshippers of the Machine

The negation of the modern United States proposed by "East Coker" manifests most plainly in the subsequent quartet, "The Dry Salvages." Set primarily in America, "The Dry Salvages" stages a return to an earlier period of transatlantic continuity, recalling America's early colonial history in its very title. Like the other quartets, "The Dry Salvages" names a place, specifically a small group of rocks off the coast of Massachusetts. Whereas Eliot proposes the title as a corruption of the French "les trois sauvages," "salvages" was in fact an *English* word for "savage" during the period of New World colonization. Among its examples, The *Oxford English Dictionary* notes Captain John Smith's 1612 assertion that "Wee traded with the Salvages at Dominica" in the *Map of Virginia* and Daniel Defoe's 1719 line, "Among strangers and salvages" in *Robinson Crusoe*.[54] Moreover, the term "dry" was a common English descriptor of rocks not fully submerged by the tide.[55] These etymologies might seem merely decorative if it were not for the way in which Eliot was aware, in somewhat jumbled fashion, of the colonial significance of the Dry Salvages. In 1635, a ship of English colonists wrecked upon the rocks, drowning all the passengers including "Mr William Eliot of New Sarum."[56] According to Helen Gardner, Eliot confused William Eliot for an ancestor, Reverend Andrew Eliot, who did not arrive in New England until somewhat later in the seventeenth century.[57] Eliot thus reprises the themes of "East Coker" by weaving a tribute to English colonization into his depiction of the New England coastline at the same time that he invokes the racial logic of the Bolo poems by conflating savages with the natural landscape of the New World.

"The Dry Salvages," however, does not immediately take up the colonial narrative implied by the New England landmark. Rather, it opens with a tribute to the Mississippi that establishes the poem's rejection of America's modernizing tendencies. The first portion of the opening stanza tells a story of the river:

> I do not know much about gods; but I think that the river
> Is a strong brown god—sullen, untamed and intractable,
> Patient to some degree, at first recognized as a frontier;

Useful, untrustworthy, as a conveyor of commerce;
Then only a problem confronting the builder of bridges.
The problem once solved, the brown god is almost forgotten
By the dwellers in cities—ever, however, implacable
Keeping his seasons and rages, destroyer, reminder
Of what men choose to forget. Unhonoured, unpropitiated
By worshippers of the machine, but waiting, watching and waiting.[58]

From its first lines, "The Dry Salvages," animates the river as a "brown" pagan god. Through this image of the river, this passage introduces the two opposing temporalities—the modern, developmental time of man, and the natural, cyclical time of nature—that centrally concern both "The Dry Salvages" and *Four Quartets* as a whole. The developmental time can be seen in the sequence of temporal modifiers—"at first," "then," "once"—that indicate the diminution of the river's power in contrast to the region's modern development. This threat follows Marshall Berman's conception of development as "the drive to create a homogenous environment, a totally modernized space, in which the look and feel of the old world have disappeared without a trace."[59] The passage overflows with the signs of development, from the particularly American term "frontier," to the parallel constructions "conveyor of commerce," "builder of bridges," and "dwellers in cities." The most telling aspect of this passage comes at the height of developmental arrogance, when the poem asserts that the river is "unhonored, unpropitiated / By worshippers of the machine." The phrase, "worshippers of the machine," stands in precise contradiction to the idea of the river as a local divinity, "a strong, brown god." Such opposition of nature and machine culture can be felt throughout the *Quartets*, yet it is perhaps no accident that the "worshippers of the machine" are located in America. Whereas "East Coker" briefly considered factories and bypasses before enchanting a field into Englishness, "The Dry Salvages" much more explicitly lays out the opposition between machine culture and the recuperative potential of the land.

It is through the figure of the river that the opening of "The Dry Salvages" encodes two kinds of temporality into its language and lyric. The iconic American landmark, the Mississippi, becomes the guardian of natural time for the first portion of the poem. The use of the imperfect tense—"confronting," "keeping," "waiting, watching, and waiting"—only reinforces the abiding sense of permanence that contradicts the linear stages of development. In the lines "ever, however, implacable / Keeping his seasons and rages," a fine Eliotic subtlety embeds and echoes the permanence of "ever," in the very word "however," that turns the poem away from modern development. It is clear that the uniquely American setting of "The

Dry Salvages," with its images of the Mississippi and the New England coast, of frontiers and the worship of machines, will display the conflict between linear, developmental time and cyclical, natural time more fully than Eliot's poems of the English countryside manage to do. In the opening of "The Dry Salvages," it appears, the value of the American setting is the exemplary fashion in which it displays the crises of modernization.

In the second part of the opening section, the Mississippi turns into the Atlantic in a series of images that recall the history of early America. Drawing on nautical imagery to offer an underwater version of the ruin, the poem takes the sea as its subject: "It tosses up our losses, the torn seine, / The shattered lobsterpot, the broken oar / And the gear of foreign, dead men."[60] In rhythmic lines drawn tightly together by internal and end rhymes, the poem presents the sea as the repository of the past, of nautical effluvia, and, more curiously, of "the gear of foreign, dead men." As critics have noted, this image recalls the wartime situation of early 1941 when Eliot published "The Dry Salvages."[61] Certainly the word "gear," is capable of suggesting military as much as nautical apparatus. Yet it is also interesting to note that this gear is tossed up near the New England coast rather than in the European theater of war. Such a geographic displacement highlights the meaning of the word "foreign," in the context of a series of poems that persistently travel back in time to consider the colonial relationship between Britain and America. At base, the foreign gear indicates those who are not American, and who have likely traveled to America by ship, leaving their artifacts to mingle with the oars and lobster pots of the New England fishermen. Yet by presenting the ocean as an archive of "our losses," the poem allows the possessive pronoun to endow the foreign with a sense of belonging, mimicking the early American experience in which, through colonization and immigration, the foreign becomes the national.

This image of the ocean becomes increasingly important to the poem as it begins to represent not only a liminal space but also the primary sign of natural time:

> And under the oppression of the silent fog
> The tolling bell
> Measures time not our time, rung by the unhurried
> Ground swell, a time
> Older than the time of chronometers, older
> Than time counted by anxious worried women
> Lying awake, calculating the future,
> Trying to unweave, unwind, unravel
> And piece together the past and the future,

> The future futureless, before the morning watch
> When time stops and time is never ending;
> And the ground swell, that is and was from the beginning,
> Clangs
> The bell.[62]

In a remarkable passage that repeats the word "time" six times, "The Dry Salvages" introduces the image of the "bell" rung by the "ground swell" of the ocean. The bell and ocean both represent the cyclical time of nature, which exist in contradistinction to "our time" in the modern world. Specifically in these lines, the bell is brought into opposition with a piece of nautical machinery, the "chronometer," which was used from the eighteenth century to measure time and longitude aboard ship. In this juxtaposition of bell and chronometer, the poem presents the bell as capable of superseding the chronometer and its worldly time. In order to do so, the bell, a figure with the Christian overtones of church bells, clangs in an Ecclesiatical echo "that is and was from the beginning." The familiar paradoxes provided by Eliot's poem—"the future futureless" and "When time stops, and time is neverending"—emerge out of this conflict of bell and chronometer, of divine nature and the machine. The presentation of the ocean as the space of timelessness, of the paradoxes of Christian eternity and of the cycles of nature, seems a particularly telling choice in a work that focuses on the import of transatlantic journeys and migrations. It is the geographic identity of the ocean that helps to imbricate Eliot's metaphysical challenge to the "worshippers of the machine" into the transatlantic framework that he sets up in *Four Quartets*. Here in "The Dry Salvages," the compelling reasons for the poem's appeal to cyclical, spiritual time become clear: the wages of modern development and the worship of machines are to be found in America. It is not a cosmopolitan literary pastiche but a lyrical return to Eliot's country of origin that most compellingly argues the need for salvation from this overdeveloped waste land.

From the symbolic imagery of the ocean and the bell, "The Dry Salvages" slides into an exposition that makes even clearer how its philosophy of time reflects discourses of Americanism. In a return to the first-person singular, the speaker muses autobiographically:

> It seems, as one becomes older,
> That the past has another pattern, and ceases to be a mere sequence—
> Or even development: the latter a partial fallacy,
> Encouraged by superficial notions of evolution,
> Which becomes, in the popular mind, a means of disowning the past.[63]

Here the speaker casts doubt on the very idea of "development," with its emphasis on linear sequence and progress over time. This indictment of development recalls the first section of the poem which identified machine-worship as a conceptual error. The poem traces this error to the mistaken teleological thinking "superficial notions of evolution," that reside in the "popular mind." The invocation of the "popular mind" in the "American quartet" is particularly compelling because so many discussions of Americanization circulating in early twentieth-century England invoke popular culture, mass behavior, and mob rule. Here Eliot again reveals all that he is working for in "The Dry Salvages" and in the *Quartets* as a whole. The trouble with the developmental telos of the popular mind, the poem explains, is that it becomes "a means of disowning the past." Eliot's *Quartets*, in contrast, are themselves a means of *owning* the past through their lyrical production of old English dancers and their tribute to the timeless ocean swell that carried ships from England to America.

"Little Gidding": English Endings

Four Quartets returns to an English setting in its last poem "Little Gidding." It is this poem that claims history for England—"History is now and England"—in its well-known closing section. In fact, "Little Gidding" encodes in its name a return to a particular episode in English history. As many critics of the *Quartets* note, Little Gidding is the name of the town in which Nicholas Ferrar founded a religious community, a bastion of Anglicanism and Englishness, visited more than once by Charles I, whom the poem refers to as the "broken king."[64] Little Gidding seems to be an ideal figure for the little Englishness of an enclosed community, thus bringing the transatlantic gestures of the *Quartets* back to England in the end. Yet while this closing quartet is decisively English, the full story of Nicholas Ferrar complicates the picture of what it *means* for the last quartet to be decisively English. Before founding the religious community at Little Gidding, Ferrar played a key role in the struggle to protect the Virginia Company, in which his family was heavily invested. From the early seventeenth century, Ferrar's father had been a shareholder in the Virginia Company as well as the New Bermuda Company.[65] Ferrar and his brother were both important young members of the Council of Virginia, aiding in the attempt to prevent Parliament from canceling the Virginia Company's charter. Despite the work of the Council, on which Ferrar ultimately served as the treasurer and chief adviser of the Earl of Southampton, the Virginia Company was dissolved by Parliament.[66] It was only after this failure in the public sphere of English politics to preserve his family's transatlantic interests that Ferrar formed the separatist community of Little Gidding, which functioned almost as a colony within England itself. In this way, Little Gidding names the English place created when a transatlantic connection has failed. The exemplary Englishness that it provides for the poem rests upon the way in which the communitarian impulse is driven by the loss of the transatlantic connection that characterized the period of English settlement of the New World.

"Little Gidding" spends some time discussing the visits of King Charles to the town, as well as its dispersal at the hands of the Cromwellians. The tragedy of the end of Little Gidding, the poem asserts, renders it exemplary:

> There are other places
> Which also are the world's end, some at the sea jaws
> Or over a dark lake, in a desert or a city—
> But this is the nearest, in place and time,
> Now and in England.[67]

Once again, Eliot's poem brings together time and place. Little Gidding is doubly the world's end: it is both a geographic endpoint and a chronological ending. While the poem insists upon the exemplary nature of Little Gidding as one end among many, Little Gidding is nonetheless the "end" identified by this particular poem of the Atlantic world. It is clear by this final Quartet that this has not been a tale of dark lakes or deserts, but of England and the time of Englishness.

It is the grand ambition of *Four Quartets* to map the relation between the phenomenal world and metaphysical timelessness. As the poem declaims: "Here, the intersection of the timeless moment / Is England and nowhere. Never and always." Yet in this tribute to immateriality, Eliot offers England as a deeply located sense of place, the "where" that rests in contradistinction to "nowhere." On the other side of eternity, Eliot proposes, lies the significant soil that is England. Eliot's invocation of England at this moment encompasses the careful balance this poem strikes between metaphysical immateriality and nationhood. "Little Gidding" thus commits itself from its first section to inserting England into a metaphysical algebra that renders it not merely a national place, but capable of standing for the very idea of place. In the final section, the poem continues:

> The moment of the rose and the moment of the yew-tree
> Are of equal duration. A people without history
> Is not redeemed from time, for history is a pattern

Of timeless moments. So, while the light fails
On a winter's afternoon, in a secluded chapel
History is now and England.[68]

In lines that resurrect images from previous quartets, and in particular from the end of "The Dry Salvages," "Little Gidding" makes its master statement of history and nationalism. "Little Gidding" implicates the histories both of Charles I and the Cromwellians, of the Virginia Company, and colonization of the New World. In the dense fabric of associations common to Eliot's work, and to the *Quartets* as a whole, it seems that the almost metaphysical idea of History is not wholly innocent of the particular histories through which the poem imagines the past. Rather, these particulars continue to betray the international, transatlantic configuration of a work that insists "History is now and England."

Like "East Coker," "Little Gidding" proposes the circularity of beginnings and ends: "What we call the beginning is often the end / And to make an end is to make a beginning / The end is where we start from." This familiar circuit of return and renewal finds its ultimate enunciation in the well-known lines near the end of "Little Gidding": "We shall not cease from exploration / And the end of all our exploring / Will be to arrive where we started / And know the place for the first time." Jed Esty has remarked that these lines may make reference to the way in which the colonial project of exploration has turned back upon England in the late moment of imperial decline. To this insight, it is worth adding that in the context of "Little Gidding," this exploration may specifically implicate Britain's colonial explorations of the Americas. Much as the sense of endings and beginnings in "East Coker" referred to the dual transatlantic migrations of Eliot's ancestors and of Eliot himself, here it seems that the accretion of references to America and the New World, to New England and the Mississippi, to the English town from which the Eliots departed for America, and the English town founded on the failure of the Virginia Charter, reveals the extent to which these explorations may not be of a general imperial type, but rather specifically transatlantic.

While the poem operates most overtly as the bearer of the paradoxes of Christian mysticism in a time of strife, it is a time of nationalist strife that has led Eliot to attempt to reclaim ownership of the past. What the poems together reveal is that the attempt to reclaim ownership of a particularly English past relies upon reference to America. Specifically, the poems persistently gesture toward the colonial relationship between England and America, before the emergence of the United States. This chronology allows the poems to forgo the "worshippers of the machine" and to pursue the more organic connection that Eliot seems to wish to claim as his heritage, his beginning, and his end. This rearrangement of time and space has the effect of imagining an America capable of being returned to an organic, genealogical connection to England, and a restoration of a glorious English past that was concomitant with the newness of its American colony.

Eliot, England, and Tradition

In 1936, years before Eliot finished the *Quartets* or received the Nobel Prize, Virginia Woolf wrote to Julian Bell that Eliot had become "the titular head of English-American letters."[69] While F. R. Leavis, on the first page of *The Great Tradition*, accuses his audience of assuming that he cares for no poet since Donne "except Hopkins and Eliot," his enduring support of Eliot gave ample cause for such an assumption.[70] Although members of the cultural elite as incompatible as Woolf and Leavis were certain of Eliot's importance to English letters, neither would make the mistake of calling him English. Yet Eliot's career as a poet and a critic was marked by a persistent and successful project of instructing the English in the state of their literary, and, later, their national culture. Through the nationalist discourses of the Bolo poems and *Four Quartets*, a set of suggestive parallels emerge between Eliot's career in the invention of Englishness and his literary repudiation of the modern culture of the United States.

In the period between his first Bolo verses and *Four Quartets*, Eliot published the essay that would mark him as a critic dedicated to instructing the English in the state of their literary tradition. This essay, "Tradition and the Individual Talent" (1919), strikingly shares not only the concerns but, more compellingly, the temporal logic of Eliot's two major works of transatlantic poetry. Nonetheless, "Tradition and the Individual Talent" does not mention either America or the United States, presenting itself as a statement of a simultaneously English and European tradition. Eliot opens "Tradition and the Individual Talent" with the statement, "In English writing we seldom speak of tradition."[71] The phrase "English writing" is nicely ambiguous—perhaps referring to literature written in English, but with the unmistakable ring of English nationalism. Moreover, years before his assumption of British citizenship, Eliot's use of the first person intimates his identification, if not thoroughly with the English, at least with "English writing." In case this opening phrase should prove too ambiguous, Eliot continues to deal in a national lexicon, insisting that as for tradition, "you can hardly make the word agreeable to English ears."[72] With this slippage into a corporeal nationality, "English ears" which participate in a common cultural resistance to the word "tradition," Eliot identifies the group to whom he speaks and whom he hopes will attend to his argument.

Eliot soon makes a more general statement that further reveals the nationalist content of a set of ambiguous references to Englishness. He notes, "Every nation, every race, has not only its own creative, but its own critical turn of mind."[73] In striking fashion, Eliot's grammar aligns race with nation and, through the structure of the appositive, produces race as a *synonym* of nation. This structure is deeply telling. While Eliot would insert himself, via first person, into English writing for English ears, he cannot in 1919 make any real claim to be nationally English. He can, however, as he will more fully in *Four Quartets*, make a claim to be *racially* English.[74] Whereas Eliot might have chosen to identify himself strictly with the English language, here he alludes to a larger sense of English culture and community in which he may insert himself without any need to mention his American identity. At moments, this racial Englishness even sounds convincingly national, as when Eliot delineates the way in which "we" tend to define ourselves against "the French," invoking a comparison much more common to the island nation than to Eliot's own.[75]

After Eliot explains the importance of tradition, he proceeds to define it as "the historical sense" that "involves a perception not only of the pastness of the past, but of its presence." Indeed, Eliot notes, "the historical sense compels a man to write not merely with his own generation in his bones, but with a feeling that the whole of the literature of Europe from Homer and within it the whole of the literature of his own country has a simultaneous existence and composes a simultaneous order."[76] The nationalist structure necessary for Eliot's conception of tradition locates the literature of one's "own country" within "the literature of Europe," presenting a European literary tradition which may, but need not, include the United States. Indeed, by gesturing back in time toward Homer, Eliot obviates the need to consider the United States at all.[77] In place of a modern national identification, Eliot offers a different image: "the mind of Europe—the mind of his own country—a mind which [the poet] learns in time to be much more important than his own private mind."[78] This "mind" *is* the tradition; it is the European or national imaginary that the poet must accept as his psychic heritage. By taking part in the supranational mind of the European tradition, Eliot is able to forget himself in a "an extinction of personality" that not only does away with what Eliot dismisses as the poet's personal feelings and sufferings but also subsumes the particularities of his modern national affiliations.[79]

In this tribute to English and European literary heritage, Eliot explains that the "new work of art" is capable of changing the entire tradition. As he puts it, "The existing monuments form an ideal order among themselves, which is modified by the introduction of the new (the really new) work of art among them."[80] Eliot continues, "Whoever has approved this idea of order, of the form of European, of English literature will not find it preposterous that *the past should be altered by the present as much as the present is directed by the past*."[81] (Italics added.) Here, in Eliot's influential and somewhat startling definition of tradition, he renders explicit the inchoate treatment of time and nation that directs both the Bolo verses and *Four Quartets*. The past, which is decisively national, at once "European" and "English," can be produced in the present by the introduction of the new work. Its very newness is that which makes it old, or at least that which makes it capable of changing the meaning of the old, thus rendering the past anew. While in the Bolo verses, Eliot admixes old and new by effacing the United States even as his verses suggest the persistence of American ideologies, it is in *Four Quartets* that Eliot most compellingly enacts the alteration of a nationalist past through a literary work. *Four Quartets* fulfills through literary endeavor the critical rubric that Eliot set up in "Tradition and the Individual Talent."

In the years following "Tradition and the Individual Talent," Eliot managed to speak convincingly to "English ears." F. R. Leavis praised Eliot in 1929: "His poetry is more conscious of the past than any other that is being written in English to-day. This most modern of the moderns is truly more traditional than the 'traditionalists.'"[82] In the forties, via *Notes towards the Definition of Culture* and *Four Quartets*, Eliot fully assumed his now-familiar role as the esteemed pedagogue of culture and tradition. Yet while Eliot became synonymous with the idea of culture in England, he produced this idea in part through his complex negotiations, identifications, and disidentifications with the United States. The spiritual and racial Englishness that was Eliot's gift to his adopted nation could not have been possible without Eliot's persistent desire to gesture toward the colonial and genealogical relations between Britain and America and away from the distressing modernity of the United States.

Afterword

In March 2009, Prime Minister Gordon Brown made a trip to the United States, the first official meeting of Britain and America under the Obama administration. Days before departing, Brown published a piece in the London *Times* celebrating the Anglo-American "special relationship," claiming portentously that "there is no international partnership in recent history that has served the world better."[1] Yet in their accounts of Brown's reception in America, British newspapers flooded with headlines such as "The Special Relationship Is a Joke" and "Humiliated, Hopeless, Paralysed."[2] The perceived rebuffs ranged from a canceled press conference, a working lunch rather than a state dinner, and most especially, the gifts the Obamas presented to the Brown family. Whereas Gordon Brown's gifts to Obama included a pen holder carved from the wood of the HMS *Gannet* and a first edition biography of Churchill,[3] the White House presented the prime minister with a DVD set of old Hollywood movies. Moreover, to Sarah Brown's carefully chosen tony outfits and British children's books for the Obama girls, Michelle Obama reciprocated with plastic models of the presidential helicopter, *Marine One*, for the Brown boys. The British *Observer* called the incident "wounding to British pride," the *Telegraph* lamented that the DVD set "looked like the kind of thing the White House might hand out to the visiting head of a minor African state," and the *Times* noted, "whether deliberate or not, the whole thing feels like a snub."[4]

The chief sentiment recorded in accounts of this incident—British shame at a symbolic dismissal by the Americans—would have been largely unthinkable in the nineteenth century. Whereas Rudyard Kipling could in 1898 proffer paternalistic advice to the newly imperial Americans, the twenty-first century press—in a telling persistence of an imperialist worldview—rhetorically transforms Britain into "a minor African state" in its treatment by the White House. Throughout the nineteenth century, American writers were struggling to step out of the shadows cast by their British counterparts; in 1869, Matthew Arnold expressed a common feeling of the period when he noted "in culture and totality, America, instead of surpassing us all, falls short."[5] Arnold's tributes to America's "intellectual mediocrity" and "general lack of intelligence" might seem consonant with later portrayals of the United States as Britain's crass younger cousin, but it lacks several concerns that would characterize the early twentieth century.[6] First, while Arnold may disparage the United States he, like Kipling, does not anticipate the twentieth-century narratives of American ascendancy on the world stage. Moreover, while Arnold shares the dominant nineteenth-century view of American cultural "mediocrity," he fails to anticipate the early twentieth-century fear of such mediocrity crossing the Atlantic and becoming British.

The discourses developed in the early twentieth century—the period of literary modernism, which is the focus of this book—enabled the transition from the self-assured British complacency toward America in the nineteenth century to the histrionics that have become possible in the twenty-first. The Brown-Obama debacle drew so much media attention in part because of the stark symbolism of its principle effects, many of which have their roots in the early twentieth-century debates. For instance, the cultural weight of the gifts—Hollywood films as a poor contrast to British-authored books—evokes the history of American mass media as a cheap assault on British life as well as the compensatory value of British literary endeavors. A measure of pathos emerges too from the earnest vows of transatlantic partnership in Gordon Brown's *Times* editorial, in which he calls himself an "Atlanticist" and invokes Winston Churchill.[7] As the British media was quick to point out, Obama had removed a bust of Churchill from the Oval Office only weeks before—a move interpreted as further repudiation of Britain. While in the early twentieth century, it was the British who scrambled to protect their media industries against American incursion, some commentators noted that the controversial DVD box set would probably not even play in Britain, due to the protectionist technology of the "region lock."

When John Osborne described the "American Age" as the condition of 1950s Britain, he alluded to a different type of regional relation in which American mass culture was not locked within its local shores but had rather spread contagiously, taking hold of territory across the Atlantic. Osborne's story of the American Age presents itself as the defeated aftermath of the interwar period, a period in which, as we have seen, the shocking possibility of a transatlantic "shift in fortunes" was at once doubted, feared, and occasionally embraced. This was fertile grounds for literary writing that took up a range of modes of being modernist, including those that reflected and reworked the changing power dynamics of the English language. Indeed, while the Brown-Obama debacle most clearly points to issues of politics and diplomacy, other contemporary incidents reveal the persistence of inter-war conceptions of Americanization of art, literature, and culture—and perhaps none more clearly than the kerfuffle over the admission of Americans to the Man Booker Prize.

In 2002, the Booker Prize committee chairwoman, Lisa Jardine, found herself at the center of a media controversy over the possibility that Americans might be considered for the prize.[8] Jardine was against the admission of Americans, but not—as might have been adduced in the nineteenth century—because of any literary inferiority on their part. Rather, she made headlines by suggesting that American writers were so far ahead of their British counterparts that they would render the competition unfair, usurping the Booker Prize with their fresher, deeper, more advanced work in the English language.[9] Such a claim—both echoed and condemned by public figures as the controversy progressed—sets the Americans apart from the other anglophone nations considered for the prize, including those in Africa, South Asia, and the Caribbean. Former Booker Prize winner Arhundhati Roy rejected Jardine's suggestion, though her tone was not one of transatlantic embrace: "I'm certainly not intimidated by American writers...You're pitting your mind against them, not your economy...I don't want to be forced into saying the Americans are the big boys and we need to be protected from the big boys."[10] Echoing her sentiment, prize winner Ian McEwan called fear of American writers, "pathetically weak-minded." Still, Jardine's arguments struck a chord with other Booker Prize winners. David Storey confessed, "Honestly, I don't think British literature at the moment could stand up against the Americans," while Bernice Rubens lamented, "It's true, I don't think we can compete against the Americans. We're pygmies in comparison." The discourses invoked by those on both sides, the image of masculine size and stature embodied in "big boys" as well as that of diminutiveness in the imperialist rhetoric of the British as "pygmies," embeds an Anglo-American contest within the very discussion of adding Americans to the contest. This issue is capable of sparking such strong feelings in part because it touches upon the last British stronghold against Americanization: literature.

As Arhundati Roy's comments suggest, however much literature may have an economic basis, comparisons of national literary merit do not rest upon the size of the gross domestic product. Rather, the Booker Prize debates reveal the extent to which literature has come to embody the last arena of British greatness. Throughout the early twentieth century, as it seemed more and more that the United States might usurp British narratives of progress, the nation of Shakespeare, Keats, and Coleridge took increasing refuge in the value of its literary production. According to F. R. Leavis, literature was the necessary antidote against Americanization; it was the homegrown contender in the contest Britain had urgently to win. This contest was not only fought at home for, as Sara Suleri has pointed out, Britain's literary culture was one of its chief imperial exports.[11] The territorial map of the Booker Prize keeps Britain and its former colonies separate from the United States; it offers a genealogy that implicitly suggests that all the anglophone world, save America, connects umbilically through language and literature to Britain.

Of course, the idea of a strict kinship of Britain, the Commonwealth, and former British colonies is itself a fiction. In *Modernity at Large: The Cultural Dimensions of Globalization,* Arjun Appadurai opens his exploration of the modern world with an account of his personal turn, growing up in India, from imaginative affiliation with Britain to the United States. He recalls, "I gradually lost the England that I had earlier imbibed in my Victorian schoolbooks" and instead "saw and smelled modernity reading *Life* and American college catalogs...seeing B-grade films...from Hollywood at the Eros Theatre."[12] As he succinctly puts it, "Such are the little defeats that explain how England lost the Empire in postcolonial Bombay."[13] U.S. culture and even American English have left their mark on the English-speaking world, a process that primarily dates back to the early twentieth century and the rise of mass entertainment, especially Hollywood film. An account such as Appadurai's—and he is not alone[14]—reflects the fears of those in early twentieth-century Britain who imagined their cultural influence on the wane. In 2002, the decision to exclude the Americans allows the Man Booker Prize to serve as one of the last institutions on the planet that groups Britain, the Commonwealth, and the Republic of Ireland together as a distinct and identifiable anglophone entity.[15] In its way, it is a last stand against the world made new and modern in America's image—a final refusal of Americanization.

Literary culture, and the protection of "British" literature, can evoke such strong feelings in part because, especially since the early twentieth century, literature and Britishness have been imaginatively linked on an international scale. The former British colonies do not continue to use the British pound; they do not generally open public ceremonies with "God Save the Queen." But they do teach and read Shakespeare, Wordsworth, and Jane Austen. It is the "book" in Booker that serves as the guardian of a culture whose global image has changed from that of the imperial ruler of the waves to a much quieter one, generally involving a cup of tea and a fat, old novel. It is therefore no wonder that Gordon and Sarah Brown, in their choice of symbolic presents for the Obamas, selected books: both the biography of Churchill and the British children's books for the girls. Moreover, when the Obamas paid a reciprocal visit to London, now girded with symbolically American gifts such as a vintage baseball bat, the company of esteemed British personalities invited to meet Michelle Obama included none other than British children's book author J. K. Rowling.

Rowling was a particularly suitable guest to present to the Obamas, not only because she happened to be a friend of Sarah Brown's, but also because her books have come to stand for and embody the new globalization of British culture. In this early twenty-first century moment, children's books *are* British culture; writing, fiction, and literature emblematizes Britishness—and ties the nation to its past greatness—in ways that economic, military, or political institutions rarely seem able. Rowling's works in particular, in their stunning worldwide popularity, both rely upon and reproduce a story that can trace its modern heritage to the early twentieth century: a national story about Englishness as an escape from modernity. More clearly than even the Booker Prize debates, the Harry Potter phenomenon rests upon narratives of heritage, history, and little England much like those that began most clearly to be told in the early twentieth century. Hogwarts, with its echoes of both Oxbridge and Eton, is itself a little England. At once quaint and majestic, with its endearing groundskeeper and iconic castle, it is not the sort of place that could be ever found in America.[16]

As the most widely read British fiction at the turn of the twenty-first century, the Harry Potter series is also a crowning response to discourses of Americanization since the turn of the twentieth. The Potter books describe two worlds, one of modern technology and the other of icons of English lore and legend, including castles, fierce dragons, and charming cobblestone villages. Notably, in this second "wizarding" world, magic replaces technology, and curious wizards behave like time travelers, unable to work or even fathom the telephone. If so many of the inventions that lure and baffle the wizards seem to have American associations—the car (Ford), the telephone (Bell), and the airplane (nominally, the Wright brothers)—this is a feature of the books' setting at the tail end of the American Century.[17] Whereas the American Century was characterized by the seemingly magical qualities of new technologies—A box that speaks! Moving pictures! A man on the moon!—in Potter's world, magic replaces machines.

To illustrate this dichotomy, Rowling contrasts the antiquarian wizards with the inhabitants of the world of machines, whom she calls, "Muggles." From the first book of the series, the Muggle relations whom Harry knows best, such as his obese bullying cousin, sound a bit like caricatures of Americans. Unimaginative and boorish, Harry's Muggle relatives dote on technology, talk in loud voices, admire their gigantic car, and tend to overeat. Yet however much this Muggle family may evoke stereotypes about Britain's so-called younger cousin across the Atlantic, they are in fact the Americanized British, at a time when Americanization has *become* British. It is now too late for modern Britain to resist Americanization. Rather, in the world of Harry Potter, it is the old literary England—with touches of a new multicultural Britain—that shelters the spirit and imagination from the disenchanted world of machines.

Moreover, this refuge comes in a form that ties directly into the dialectic of British responses to Americanization. In order to become part of the wizarding world, Harry must learn how to do things with spells. Ranging in influence from Latin verse to Lewis Carroll, these various incantations rule the world of magic, effectively replacing technology with something akin to poetry. In the modern Muggle world, should you wish to see better, you merely flip the switch on the Edison-inspired lightbulb; in Harry's new world, you incant a spell while flicking your magic wand. Much like Aldous Huxley in his 1932 dystopia *Brave New World* outfits John with Shakespeare's "words like magic" in order to arm his resistance to a modern, Americanized nightmare, here the alternative, old English universe of the wizards is itself powered by language. In the Potter books, these spells are everywhere, little metapoems that suggest the power of literature and language—at once written and tied to an oral tradition—even as the books themselves embody the supreme marketing power of the British written word.

J. K. Rowling would probably not cite F. R. Leavis as an inspiration, but her fictional world is surprisingly consonant with Leavis's own nostalgic fiction of Englishness. It is, after all, a world of rustic cottages and many spired strongholds of learning, a world where the word itself is magic. Although the Potter books reflect a wide range of reference, the magical world of Harry Potter would not be possible without the nostalgic visions of Englishness that have flourished in literature and public discourse over the past century. Of course, since 2001, the only Potter phenomenon as big as the books is the films. And while there may be no truth to the rumor that Rowling insisted that the cinematic adaptations of her works not be Hollywood productions and that there be no Americans among the main actors, the Potter films retain their national flavor.[18] Rowling herself, I have no doubt, is as fond of America and Americans as anyone else in Britain; certainly, she has profited hugely from the American market. But in her absorption and reworking of interwar stories of Americanization, she is also the bard of anti-modernity, which the entertainment industry then sells to Americans at theme parks and on DVD.[19] In this way, the Potter films embody one of the trickier (and more profitable) balancing acts of the contemporary moment: the promotion of old Englishness *through* modernization.[20]

At the end of the nineteenth century, German Chancellor Otto von Bismarck commented that the most important item to note of the coming twentieth century was that "North America speaks English."[21] Almost one hundred years later, French theorist Jean Baudrillard glanced backward, remarking, "America is the original version of modernity." Even if modernity is not the sort of thing that can be properly said to have an origin, over the past century, it certainly has had considerable associations with the United States. That other prominent, imperial nation that spoke English, Great Britain, had the highest stakes in early twentieth-century associations of modernity with America. The anecdotes offered in this afterword—the Brown-Obama debacle, the Booker Prize debates, and the Harry Potter phenomenon—illustrate the persistence and reworking of the stories most clearly told in the early twentieth century and especially in the years between the wars. At the same time, these latter-day examples can remind us of the importance of the Anglo-American frame as a scholarly guide. Under the rubric of Americanization, areas of British literary study that have sometimes seemed discrete—the study of nation and empire, of mass entertainment, and of language—fit together as parts of a coherent whole. As twentieth-century studies solidifies as a field, it can draw on the idea of the American Century as a compelling frame for its investigations. Now that many believe the American Century to be coming to a close, as works such as Fareed Zakaria's *The Post-American World* attest, it becomes all the more urgent to look back to and fathom the time when Britain appeared to be slipping and the world seemed poised for Americanization.

Notes

Introduction

1. Rudyard Kipling, "The White Man's Burden," in his *Rudyard Kipling's Verse: Definitive Edition* (Garden City, NY: Doubleday, 1950), 323. Although critics don't always focus on its transatlantic dimensions, Kipling addressed this poem to the United States after the American annexation of the Philippines.

2. John Osborne, *Look Back in Anger*, in *Three Plays* (New York: Criterion Books, 1957), 19.

3. Ibid. Throughout this study, I will follow the practice of British writers of the period who refer to the United States as America. While Great Britain's relations to North America (and indeed to the Americas more broadly) were complex, narratives of Americanization focused on the United States.

4. For representative works, see Laura Doyle, *Freedom's Empire: Race and the Rise of the Novel in Atlantic Modernity, 1640–1940* (Durham, NC: Duke University Press, 2008); Paul Giles, *Atlantic Republic: The American Tradition in English Literature* (Oxford: Oxford University Press, 2006); Sieglinde Lemke, *Primitivist Modernism: Black Culture and the Origins of Transatlantic Modernism* (New York: Oxford University Press, 1998); Michael North, *The Dialect of Modernism: Race, Language, and Twentieth-Century Literature* (New York: Oxford University Press, 1994); Michael North, *1922: A Return to the Scene of the Modern* (New York: Oxford University Press, 1999); Charles Pollard, *New World Modernisms: T.S. Eliot, Derek Walcott, and Kamau Braithwaite* (Charlottesville: University of Virginia Press, 2004); Laura Winkiel, *Modernism, Race, and Manifestos* (Cambridge: Cambridge University Press, 2008); and Alex Zwerdling, *Improvised Europeans: American Literary Expatriates and the Siege of London* (New York: Basic Books, 1998).

5. F. R. Leavis and Denys Thompson, *Culture and Environment: The Training of Critical Awareness* (London: Chatto & Windus, 1933), 35.

6. Quoted in Peter Nicholls, *Modernisms: A Literary Guide* (Berkeley: University of California Press, 1995), 46.

7. Philippe Roger, *The American Enemy: A Story of French Anti-Americanism*, trans. Sharon Bowman (Chicago: University of Chicago Press, 2005), 62.

8. Quoted in Roger, *American Enemy*, 63.

9. In his well-known essay "On Jazz," Adorno laments the "standardized commodity character" of jazz (473), insisting that "the more democratic jazz is, the worse it becomes" (475). See "On Jazz," in *Essays on Music*, ed. Richard Leppert (Berkeley: University of California Press, 2002). On cinema, Adorno famously remarked: "Every visit to the cinema leaves me, against all my vigilance, stupider and worse" (25). See *Minima Moralia*, trans. E. F. N. Jephcott (New York: Verso, 1974).

10. André Siegfried, *America Comes of Age*, trans. H. H. Hemming and Doris Hemming (New York: Harcourt, Brace, 1927), 347.

11. Bertolt Brecht, "Late Lamented Fame of the Giant City of New York," *Poems 1913–1956*, ed. John Willett and Ralph Manheim (London: Eyre Meuthen, Ltd., 1976), 168; 168; 169; 169.

12. Antonio Gramsci, "Americanism and Fordism," *A Gramsci Reader: Selected Writings, 1916–1935*, ed. David Forgacs (London: Lawrence & Wishart, 1999), 297–8.

13. See Richard Stites, *Revolutionary Dreams* (Oxford: Oxford University Press, 1989) 149. Stites notes that according to journalist Maurice Hindus, "in the backwoods, Ford's name was better known than those of most communist figures, excepting Lenin and Trotsky. Some peasants named their children after him; others endowed their new 'iron horses' with human characteristics. An American business reporter in 1930 observed that Lenin was the Russian God and Ford his St. Peter." For further discussion of the Americanization of Europe, see Victoria De Grazia, *Irresistible Empire: America's Advance through Twentieth-Century Europe* (Cambridge, MA: Harvard University Press, 2005).

14. For discussions of little Englandism, see Jed Esty, *A Shrinking Island: Modernism and National Culture in England* (Princeton, NJ: Princeton University Press, 2004), 25–6; and Alison Light, *Forever England: Femininity, Literature, and Conservativism between the Wars* (New York: Routledge, 1991), 8; 153–4.

15. See H. G. Wells, *The Future in America: A Search after Realities* (New York, London: Harper & Brothers, 1906), 17.

16. In referencing the movement back and forth across the Atlantic, Ford refers explicitly to Anglo-American exchange, rather than the European Atlantic. See Ford Madox Ford, *A History of Our Times*, eds. Solon Beinfeld and Sondra J. Stang (Bloomington: Indiana University Press, 1988), 229.

17. W. H. Auden, who became an American citizen in 1946, is an icon of his generation of British expatriates in America.

18. See Giovanni Arrighi, *The Long Twentieth Century: Money, Power, and the Origins of Our Times* (New York: Verso, 1994); A. E. Campbell, *Great Britain and the United States, 1895–1903* (London: Longmans, 1960); Aaron L. Friedberg, *The Weary Titan: Britain and the Experience of Relative Decline, 1895–1905* (Princeton, NJ: Princeton University Press, 1988); Stuart Hall, "Interview with Richard English and Michael Kenny," *Rethinking British Decline*, eds. Richard English and Michael Kenny (New York: St. Martin's Press, 2000), 106–116; and Paul M. Kennedy, *The Rise and Fall of the Great Powers: Economic Change and Military Conflict from 1500 to 2000* (New York: Random House, 1987).

19. As one historian notes of the financial diplomacy between Britain and the United States during World War I: "in the dealings of the Treasury mission can be seen the passing of hegemony from Britain to the United States." See Kathleen Burk, *Britain, America and the Sinews of War, 1914–1918* (London: G. Allen and Unwin, 1985), 5. See Martin Horn, *Britain, France, and the Financing of the First World War* (Montreal: McGill-Queen's University Press, 2002), 183, for an account of the broader implications for Europe.

20. See Kennedy, *The Rise and Fall of the Great Powers*; and Arrighi, *The Long Twentieth Century*.

21. For Kuhn's paradigm shift, see Thomas S. Kuhn, *The Structure of Scientific Revolutions* (Chicago: University of Chicago Press, 1996).

22. T. S. Eliot, *Notes towards the Definition of Culture* (New York: Harcourt, Brace, 1949), 94.

23. See W. T. Colyer, *Americanism: A World Menace* (London: Labour Pub. Co., 1922); A. McKenzie, *The American Invaders* (London: Grant Richards, 1902); and Edgar Ansel Mowrer, *This American World* (London: Faber and Gwyer, 1928).

24. Peter Wollen, "The Last New Wave: Modernism in the British Films of the Thatcher Era" in *The British Avant-Garde Film, 1926 to 1995*, ed. Michael O'Pray (Luton, Bedfordshire, England: University of Luton Press, 1996), 242.

25. Esty, *Shrinking Island*, 35.

26. Fredric Jameson, *A Singular Modernity: Essay on the Ontology of the Present* (NY: Verso, 2002), 164.

27. See Frank Kermode, *Romantic Image* (New York: Macmillan, 1957).

28. For more on the idea of tradition in modernism, see Elizabeth Outka, *Consuming Traditions: Modernity, Modernism, and the Commodified Authentic* (Oxford: Oxford University Press, 2009).

29. After completing this manuscript, I attended a talk (and later read parts of an unpublished manuscript) by Eric Hayot in which he proposes a detailed scheme for reconsidering literature and art, in part through reference to what he calls, "modes of modern literature." While my concept of "modes of being modernist" remains distinct from his meticulous literary taxonomy, we share a desire to move away from author-driven models of modernism in which one's membership in the modernist fold may be mathematically derived from resemblance to a canonical figure. I thank Eric Hayot for sharing his unpublished selections with me.

30. Henry Luce, "The American Century," reprinted in *The Ambiguous Legacy: U.S. Foreign Relations in the "American Century,"* ed. Michael J. Hogan (Cambridge: Cambridge University Press, 1999), 11–29. In the essay Luce writes, "Consider the 20th Century. It is ours not only in the sense that we happen to live in it but ours also because it is America's first century as a dominant power in the world" (22).

31. The "American Century" has endured as a name for the twentieth, as evidenced by the number of texts that take the phrase for a title. See, for instance, David Slater and Peter J. Taylor, eds., *The American Century: Consensus and Coercion in the Projection of American Power* (Malden, MA: Blackwell, 1999); Donald Wallace White, *The American Century: The Rise and Decline of the United States as a World Power* (New Haven, CT: Yale University Press, 1996); and Harold Evans, *The American Century* (New York: Knopf, 1998).

32. Robert Weisbuch, *Atlantic Double Cross: American Literature and British Influence in the Age of Emerson* (Chicago: University of Chicago Press, 1986), xii.

33. Ralph Waldo Emerson, "English Traits," in *Essays and English Traits* (New York: P. F. Collier, 1909), 473.

34. See Ezra Pound, "How to Read," in *Literary Essays*, ed. T. S. Eliot (New York: New Directions Books, 1968), 34. This quote was brought to my attention in Zwerdling, *Improvised Europeans*, 240.

35. See Zwerdling, *Improvised Europeans*, 246–50.

36. Gerald Kennedy, *Imagining Paris: Exile, Writing, and American Identity* (New Haven, CT: Yale University Press, 1993), 41.

37. Virginia Woolf, "On Not Knowing French," *The New Republic*, February 13, 1929, 348.

38. Harriot T. Cooke, "The American Language," in "Correspondance," *The New Republic*, April 24, 1929, 281. James was, of course, actually from New York.

39. Henry James, "The Question of Our Speech," in his *The Question of Our Speech, The Lesson of Balzac, Two Lectures* (New York: Haskell House Publishers, 1972 [1905]), 35. James distinguishes between speaking "well" and speaking "ill" (19) in national terms, discussing "units of sound" that have "a value, which it is open to us, as lovers of our admirable English tradition, to preserve or to destroy" (20).

40. Cooke, "The American Language," 281.

41. Ford Madox Ford, *A History of Our Times*, eds. Solon Beinfeld and Sondra J. Stang. (Bloomington: Indiana University Press, 1988), 229.

42. For his most famous treatment of American English, see H. L. Mencken's *The American Language: A Preliminary Inquiry into the Development of English in the United States* (New York: A. A. Knopf, 1919).

43. See Rachel Blau Du Plessis, "Breaking the Sentence; Breaking the Sequence." in *Essentials of the Theory of Fiction*, eds., Michael J. Hoffman and Patrick D. Murphy (Durham, NC: Duke University Press, 1996), 372–391; and Ellen G. Friedman and Miriam Fuchs, eds., *Breaking the Sequence: Women's Experimental Fiction* (Princeton, NJ: Princeton University Press, 1989). In *A Room of One's Own*, Woolf writes, "First she broke the sentence; now she has broken the sequence." See Virginia Woolf, *A Room of One's Own* (New York: Houghton Mifflin Harcourt, 1991), 88.

44. Edmund Wilson, "The American Language," in "Correspondance," *The New Republic*, April 24, 1929, 281–2; George E. G. Catlin, "The American Language," in "Correspondance," *The New Republic* May 8, 1929, 335.

45. Critique of American English, of course, predates the interwar period. As Michael North notes, "Americanisms had been decried as early as the 1740s." See Michael North, *The Dialect of Modernism: Race, Language, and Twentieth-Century Literature* (New York: Oxford University Press, 1994), 16. I suggest that 1927 represents the modern renewal of this discourse; it differs in its greater fear of the American language invading and transforming England.

46. See chapter 3 for a discussion of the public debates around American English.

47. Dorothy Richardson, "Continuous Performance," *Close Up* 2 (Jan. 1928): 174

48. Many critics have discussed these issues in depth. Alison Light discusses World War I as a cause of British retrenchment; Valentine Cunningham considers the economic crisis and the specter of World War II, among other factors; Jed Esty focuses on imperial decline. See Alison Light, *Forever England: Femininity, Literature, and Conservativism between the Wars* (New York: Routledge, 1991); Valentine Cunningham,

British Writers of the Thirties (Oxford: Oxford University Press, 1988); and Esty, *Shrinking Island*.

49. Tyrus Miller, in his study, *Late Modernism*, identifies the period of late modernism as the late twenties and thirties. See Tyrus Miller, *Late Modernism: Politics, Fiction, and the Arts between the World Wars* (Berkeley: University of California Press, 1999).

50. For a discussion of how American English registered in literary modernism outside both the British and American contexts, and in particular the reactions of James Joyce, see my article, Genevieve Abravanel, "American Encounters in *Dubliners* and *Ulysses.*" *JML: Journal of Modern Literature* 33.4 (Jul, 2010): 153–166.

51. See North, *The Dialect of Modernism*.

52. For important attempts to critique, cross, or otherwise nuance the great divide, see David Chinitz, *T.S. Eliot and the Cultural Divide* (Chicago: University of Chicago Press, 2003); Michael Coyle, *Ezra Pound, Popular Genres, and the Discourse of Culture* (University Park: Penn State University Press, 1995); Kevin J. H. Dettmar and Stephen Watt, eds., *Marketing Modernisms: Self-Promotion, Canonization, Rereading* (Ann Arbor: University of Michigan Press, 1996); Maria DiBattista and Lucy McDiarmid, eds., *High and Low Moderns: Literature and Culture 1889–1939* (New York: Oxford University Press, 1996); Cheryl Herr, *Joyce's Anatomy of Culture* (Urbana: University of Illinois Press, 1986); Michael North, *Reading 1922: A Return to the Scene of the Modern* (New York: Oxford University Press, 1999); Thomas F. Strychacz, *Modernism, Mass Culture, and Professionalism* (New York: Cambridge University Press, 1993); Jennifer Wicke, *Advertising Fictions: Literature, Advertisement and Social Reading* (New York: Columbia University Press, 1988).

53. Miriam Hansen, *Babel and Babylon: Spectatorship in American Silent Film* (Cambridge, MA: Harvard University Press, 1991), 60.

54. Kevin J. H. Dettmar and Stephen Watt, "Introduction: Marketing Modernisms" in *Marketing Modernisms: Self-Promotion, Canonization, Rereading*, ed. Kevin Dettmar and Stephen Watt (Ann Arbor: University of Michigan Press, 1996), 4.

55. Ibid., 3.

56. Melba Cuddy-Keane, *Virginia Woolf, the Intellectual, and the Public Sphere* (New York: Cambridge University Press, 2003), 14.

57. See *The Oxford English Dictionary Online*, s.v. "Highbrow," and s.v. "Lowbrow," http://www.oed.com/ (accessed October 9, 2010).

58. Lawrence Napper, *British Cinema and Middlebrow Culture in the Interwar Years* (Exeter: University of Exeter Press, 2009), 8.

59. See Michael Kammen, *American Culture, American Tastes: Social Change and the Twentieth Century* (New York: Alfred A. Knopf, 1999), 6, 17.

60. The BBC, for instance, frequently broadcast unedited concerts in real time.

61. Radio or the wireless was an important exception to the American ascendency among the new technologies popularized in the early twentieth century.

62. Paddy Scannell and David Cardiff, *A Social History of British Broadcasting* (London: Basil Blackwell, 1991), 278.

63. Ibid., 292.

64. Quoted in ibid., 292.

65. Quoted in ibid., 292.

66. D. L. Mahieu argues that the BBC owes its existence in part to the lowered standards which themselves reflected American mass culture and its "bad" egalitarianism. See D. L. Mahieu, *A Culture for Democracy: Mass Communication and the Cultivated Mind in Britain between the Wars* (Oxford: Oxford University Press, 1988), 3.

67. Historian Jim Godbolt writes, "in the 1930s, Duke Ellington was well received by both Prince George, the Duke of Kent, and by the Prince of Wales." See Jim Godbolt, *A History of Jazz in Britain, 1919–1950* (New York: Quartet Books, 1984), 112. Ellington writes about this favorable reception in his autobiography, *Music Is My Mistress* (Garden City, NY: Doubleday, 1973). Sidney Bechet, a member of the first black American jazz band to play at Buckingham Palace, the Southern Syncopated Orchestra, discusses his experiences in his autobiography. See Sidney Bechet and Rudi Blesh, *Treat It Gentle: An Autobiography* (Cambridge, MA: Da Capo Press, 2002).

68. Wyndham Lewis, *Men without Art* (London: Cassell and Co., 1934), 32.

69. Cited in Margaret Mathieson, *The Preachers of Culture: A Study of English and Its Teachers* (Totowa, N.: Rowman and Littlefield, 1975), 125.

70. For more on Leavis's centrality to the development of English studies, see chapter 4.

71. F. R. Leavis, "Mass Civilisation and Minority Culture," in his *For Continuity* (Cambridge, UK: G. Fraser and The Minority Press, 1933), 18.

72. Joseph Roach, *Cities of the Dead: Circum-Atlantic Performance* (New York: Columbia University Press, 1996), 183.

73. The most important exception to this critical tendency has come about through recent interventions in inter-American, Caribbean and Black Atlantic studies. For instance, Sean Goudie's *Creole America: The West Indies and the Formation of Literature and Culture in the New Republic* (Philadelphia: University of Pennsylvania Press, 2006), while it focuses on interactions between the United States and the Caribbean, discusses the role of Britain in this triangulation. In modernist scholarship, Esty's *Shrinking Island*, while centered on Britain and its twentieth-century colonies, briefly acknowledges the importance of the United States. Other valuable studies of modernism and British imperialism include Ian Baucom, *Out of Place: Englishness, Empire, and the Locations of Identity* (Princeton, NJ: Princeton University Press, 1999); Jane Garrity, *Step-Daughters of England: British Women Modernists and the National Imaginary* (Manchester: Manchester University Press, 2003); Howard J. Booth and Nigel Rigby, eds., *Modernism and Empire* (New York: Manchester University Press, 2000); Peter Childs, *Modernism and the Post-colonial: Literature and Empire, 1885–1930* (London: Continuum, 2007); Richard Begam and Michael Valdez Moses, eds., *Modernism and Colonialism: British and Irish Literature, 1899–1939* (Durham, NC: Duke University Press, 2007). These works, precisely in their attention to England and empire, largely or entirely avoid discussion of the United States.

74. See Terry Eagleton, *Exiles and Emigrés: Studies in Modern Literature* (New York: Schocken Books, 1970).

75. Two historians who helped bring Atlantic studies into the mainstream include David Armitage and Bernard Bailyn. See David Armitage, *Greater Britain, 1516–1776: Essays in Atlantic History* (Aldershot: Ashgate, 2004); and Bernard Bailyn, *Atlantic History: Concept and Contours* (Cambridge: Harvard University Press, 2005). Their earlier work on the subject includes David Armitage, "Greater Britain: A Useful Category of Historical

Analysis?" *American Historical Review* 104, no. 2 (1999); and Bernard Bailyn, "The Idea of Atlantic History," *Itinerario* (1996): 19–44.

76. For his field-altering intervention, see Paul Gilroy, *The Black Atlantic: Modernity and Double Consciousness* (Cambridge, MA: Harvard University Press, 1996).

77. See Giles, *Atlantic Republic;* and Doyle, *Freedom's Empire.*

Chapter One: Ameritopias

1. Fredric Jameson, *Archaeologies of the Future: The Desire Called Utopia and Other Science Fictions* (London & New York: Verso, 2005), xiii.

2. Aldous Huxley, "The Outlook for American Culture: Some Reflections in a Machine Age," in *Complete Essays: 1930–1935*, vol. 3, ed. Robert S. Baker and James Sexton (Chicago: I.R. Dee, 2000), 185.

3. H. G. Wells, *The Autocracy of Mr. Parham, His Remarkable Adventures in This Changing World* (Garden City, NY: Doubleday Doran, 1930), 185.

4. See Trygaeus [pseud.], *The United States of the World: An Utopian Essay* (London: Routledge, 1916); J. F. C. Fuller, *Atlantis: America and the Future* (London: K. Paul, Trench, Trubner, 1926); Richard Michael Fox, *The Triumphant Machine* (London: Leonard & Virginia Woolf at the Hogarth Press, 1928).

5. Marshall Berman, *All That Is Solid Melts into Air: The Experience of Modernity* (New York: Viking Penguin, 1988).

6. Tems Dyvirta [pseudo.], "London's Transformation: A Suggestive Sketch of Days to Come," *Knowledge and Scientific News* (February 1906): 367.

7. "London's Transformation," *Knowledge and Scientific News* (December 1905): 314.

8. "London's Transformation," *Knowledge and Scientific News* (February 1906): 365.

9. As David Trotter points out, some late nineteenth and early twentieth-century British figures used the American frontier as a model for Britain's broader, transoceanic imperialism. This conception follows what I describe in this chapter: the pre–World War I tendency to conceive of American and British imperialism as structurally similar processes of expansion, varying in their particulars as well as their scope. For a detailed discussion of British use of the frontier paradigm, see David Trotter, *The English Novel in History, 1895–1920* (New York: Routledge, 1993), 144–151.

10. Rudyard Kipling, "The White Man's Burden" in his *Rudyard Kipling's Verse: Definitive Edition* (Garden City, NY: Doubleday, 1950), 323.

11. Ibid., 321.

12. Ibid., 322.

13. Patrick Brantlinger, "Kipling's 'The White Man's Burden' and Its Afterlives," *English Literature in Transition* 50 (2007): 172–191.

14. Charles Carrington, *The Life of Rudyard Kipling* (Garden City, NY: Doubleday, 1955), 217.

15. Rudyard Kipling, *American Notes* (New York: Standard Book, 1930), 119–120.

16. Roger Lancelyn Green, *Kipling: The Critical Heritage* (London: Routledge and Kegan Paul, 1971).

17. Rudyard Kipling, "As Easy as A.B.C.," in *Kipling's Science Fiction*, ed. John Brunner (New York: Doherty Associates, 1992), 100. Originally published in Kipling's *A Diversity of Creatures* (Garden City, NY: Doubleday Page, 1917), 45–64.

18. Kipling's hesitations about democracy may also result from changes to the British Parliament. Just one year before "As Easy as A.B.C." was published, the Parliament Act of 1911, which deprived the House of Lords of its absolute veto power, substantially elevated the power of the House of Commons.

19. Rudyard Kipling, "Newspapers and Democracy," in his *The Writings in Prose and Verse of Rudyard Kipling: Letters of Travel* (New York: Charles Scribner's Sons, 1920), 181.

20. Kipling, *American Notes*, 227.

21. Kipling, "As Easy as A.B.C.," 114.

22. See Irving Werstein, *Strangled Voices: The Story of the Haymarket Affair* (New York: Macmillan, 1970), for an account of the affair's symbolic dimensions.

23. Emma Sandon notes that "it was after the 1889 Paris Exhibition that the British exhibitions introduced the reconstructions of native villages within which indigenous performers acted out both quotidian activities as well as staging re-enactments of colonial wars. Often between fifty and two hundred people would live in the villages, and they were given raw materials to build houses and foodstuffs to prepare, and they would be called upon to perform rituals and special activities at particular times. About two hundred Zulus with their families were brought over for the Greater British Exhibition in 1899 and visitors paid to visit their kraals." See Emma Sandon, "Projecting Africa: Two British Travel Films of the 1920s," in *Cultural Encounters: Representing "Otherness,"* ed. Elizabeth Hallam and Brian V. Street (New York: Routledge, 2000), 132. Penelope Harvey similarly notes that "the Franco-British Exhibition held in London in 1908 [displayed] Dahomeyan, Somali, and Senegalese villages" in her *Hybrids of Modernity: Anthropology, the Nation State and the Universal Exhibition* (New York: Routledge, 1996), 71.

24. Kipling, "As Easy as A.B.C.," 110.

25. Jameson, *Archaeologies of the Future*, xiv.

26. Thomas Knock, *To End All Wars: Woodrow Wilson and the Quest for a New World Order* (New York: Oxford University Press, 1992), 195.

27. See ibid., 194–198, for a further discussion of Wilson's reception.

28. Moreover, Wilson's hopes faltered in face of opposition from the U.S. Senate, which refused to ratify the treaty as written and thus kept the United States out of the League of Nations.

29. Margaret MacMillan describes a British reaction to the haste with which the treaty was handed over: " 'So,' wrote Henry Wilson in his diary, 'We are going to hand out terms to the Boches without reading them ourselves first. I don't think in all history this can be matched.' " She further quotes Woodrow Wilson's assertion, "I hope that during the rest of my life I will have enough time to read this whole volume." See Margaret MacMillan, *Paris 1919: Six Months that Changed the World* (New York: Random House, 2003), 459, 460.

30. H. G. Wells, *The Shape of Things to Come* (New York: Macmillan, 1936), 82.

31. Ibid., 82.

32. Ibid., 233.

33. See H. G. Wells, *The Future in America* (New York: Harper and Brothers, 1906) for his early views on the United States. He notes, for instance, his interest in "their Vision, their American Utopia" (16).

34. Wells, *Autocracy of Mr. Parham*, 185.

35. Ibid., 307.

36. Ibid., 40.

37. Eric Hobsbawm, *Uncommon People: Resistance, Rebellion, and Jazz* (London: Weidenfeld & Nicolson, 1998), 265–273. See chapter 2 for further discussion of the arrival of jazz in Europe.

38. Wells, *Autocracy of Mr. Parham*, 67.

39. Ibid., 68.

40. Ibid., 134.

41. Ibid., 171.

42. The Kellogg-Briand Pact was an antiwar agreement developed in part by Senator Joseph Kellogg and approved by over sixty nations, although it was riddled with caveats, unenforceable, and ultimately useless. See Robert H. Ferrell, *Peace in Their Time: The Origins of the Kellogg-Briand Pact* (New Haven, CT: Yale University Press, 1952) for an overview of the treaty. See David Hunter Miller, *The Peace Pact of Paris: A Study of the Briand-Kellogg Treaty* (New York: J.P. Putnam Sons, 1928) for an analysis contemporary with the treaty.

43. Wells, *Autocracy of Mr. Parham*, 185.

44. Ibid., 185.

45. Ibid., 217.

46. Ibid., 313.

47. F. R. Leavis, "Mass Civilisation and Minority Culture," in his *For Continuity* (Cambridge, UK: G. Fraser and The Minority Press, 1933), 40.

48. Ibid., 39.

49. Aldous Huxley, "The New Salvation," in *Complete Essays: 1926–1929*, vol. 2, ed. Robert S. Baker and James Sexton (Chicago: I.R. Dee, 2000), 209.

50. Ibid., 212.

51. Ibid., 212–213.

52. Aldous Huxley, "The Outlook for American Culture: Some Reflections in a Machine Age," in *Complete Essays: 1930–1935*, vol. 3, ed. Robert Baker and James Sexton (Chicago: I. R. Dee, 2001), 185.

53. Ibid., 188.

54. Ibid., 188–189.

55. Ibid., 190.

56. Ibid., 191.

57. Ibid., 191–192.

58. See for instance Peter Edgerly Firchow, *The End of Utopia: A Study of Aldous Huxley's Brave New World* (Lewisburg, PA: Bucknell University Press, 1984).

59. Theodor W. Adorno, *Prisms: Studies in Contemporary German Social Thought* (Cambridge, MA: MIT Press, 1981), 99.

60. See especially D. H. Lawrence, *The Plumed Serpent* (New York: Alfred A Knopf, 1926) for his primitivist fantasies of the Americas.

61. Aldous Huxley, *Brave New World* (New York: Harper Perennial, 1998), 133–134.

62. Ibid., 226.

63. Ibid., 226.

64. See Leavis, "Mass Civilzation and Minority Culture," in his *For Continuity*, 38.

65. Huxley, *Brave New World*, 246.

66. Virginia Woolf, "America Which I Have Never Seen Interests Me Most in This Cosmopolitan World of to-Day," *Hearst's International Combined with Cosmopolitan*, April 1938, 21.

67. *Oxford English Dictionary*, 2nd ed., s.v. "Epitomize," def. 3.

68. See Hugh Kenner, *A Sinking Island: The Modern English Writers* (New York: Knopf, 1988). Although he does not focus on Woolf's piece in *Cosmopolitan*, Jed Esty importantly revises Kenner's conception in his influential *A Shrinking Island: Modernism and National Culture in England* (Princeton, NJ: Princeton University Press, 2004).

69. Woolf, "America Which I Have Never Seen," *Cosmopolitan*, 21.

70. Ibid., 21.

71. Ibid., 21, 144.

72. Virginia Woolf, "America Which I Have Never Seen Interests Me Most in This Cosmopolitan World of Today," in *Virginia Woolf, Major Authors on CD-ROM*, ed. Mark Hussey (Woodbridge, CT: Primary Source Media, 1997). The original can be found at Typescript, M44, page 3, The Berg Collection of English and American Literature, The New York Public Library.

73. Woolf, "America Which I Have Never Seen," *Cosmopolitan*, 144.

74. Ibid., 144.

75. For the allegorical properties of the ruin, see Walter Benjamin, *The Origin of German Tragic Drama* (New York: Verso, 1998), 178, 235.

76. Woolf, "America Which I Have Never Seen," *Cosmopolitan*, 144.

77. Melba Cuddy-Keane, *Virginia Woolf, the Intellectual, and the Public Sphere* (New York: Cambridge University Press, 2003) 13.

78. See Walter Benjamin, "The Work of Art in the Age of Mechanical Reproduction," in his *Illuminations* (New York: Schocken Books, 1969), 221.

79. Woolf, "America Which I Have Never Seen," *Cosmopolitan*, 144.

80. Ibid., 144.

81. Ibid., 144.

82. Ibid., 145.

83. Ibid., 145.

84. Ibid., 144.

85. See Walter Benjamin, "Theses on the Philosophy of History," in his *Illuminations*, 253–64, for his theories of history as messiah, angel, and synchronic vision.

Chapter Two: Jazzing Britain

1. Critics disagree over the "first" signs of jazz in Britain and Europe, in part due to varying definitions of jazz. As R. Reid Badger points out, "In 1919, jazz was a very imprecise term compared to current definitions or even to the popular understanding that emerged over the next decade" (48–9). Hilary Moore explains, "the British public had enjoyed regular contact with a diverse range of black music and musicians prior to the arrival of jazz" (18), noting further that British musicians reproduced ragtime from sheet lyrics as early as 1912. Eric Hobsbawm notes, "the foxtrot, the basic dance routine associated with jazz, first appeared in Britain in the summer of 1914, a few months after its first appearance in the USA" (265). In 1918, James Reese Europe led the 369th Infantry Band of the American Army, performing in France for French, British, and American soldiers (Badger, 56–7); in 1919,

the first American jazz bands arrived in Britain. See R. Reid Badger, "James Reese Europe and the Prehistory of Jazz," *American Music* 7.1 (Spring 1989) 48–67; Eric Hobsbawm, *Uncommon People: Resistance, Rebellion, and Jazz* (New York: The New Press, 1998); and Hilary Moore, *Inside British Jazz: Crossing Borders of Race, Nation, and Class* (Hampshire, England: Ashgate, 2007).

2. Robert William Sigismund Mendl, *The Appeal of Jazz* (London: P. Allan, 1927), 76.

3. Nonetheless, in his 2005 study of jazz in postwar Britain (1940s through 1990s), George McKay notes, "I remain surprised that jazz as a cultural form has been insufficiently considered as a prime export culture," (ix). See George McKay, *Circular Breathing: The Cultural Politics of Jazz in Britain* (Durham, NC: Duke University Press, 2005).

4. "A Tithe Barn, Jazz in the Cotswolds, Past And Present," *Times* (London), September 5, 1923; A8, The Times Digital Archive, http://www.library.upenn.edu.

5. Catherine Parsonage notes, "for several years a flexible policy was maintained whereby American bands could perform in variety halls and in dance halls only when the resident British band was retained" (220) culminating in "the severe restrictions on the appearances of American musicians in Britain from 1935" (252). See Catherine Parsonage, *The Evolution of Jazz in Britain, 1880–1935* (Burlington, VT: Ashgate, 2005).

6. Jim Godbolt, *A History of Jazz in Britain, 1919–1950* (London; New York: Quartet Books, 1984), 9.

7. Hobsbawm, *Uncommon People*, 268.

8. The distinctions among styles were not always clear to the public at large, who tended to identify most upbeat dance music as "jazz." Eric Hobsbawm explains, "No doubt the music to which the plebs danced would not always be considered jazz today…nevertheless, jazz made its mark as a name, an idea, a novel and demotic sound" (269–270). Still, to the most ardent fans, terms such as "hot" and "dirty" signified. Catherine Parsonage explains, "the term 'dirt' often appeared alongside 'hot' to describe the particular timbre of the blues inflections that were incorporated into the melodic line or harmony alongside hot syncopated rhythms" (193). Eric Hobsbawm identifies "hot" jazz as "an art music" (268). Hilary Moore further identifies a racial dimension to the division of styles, " 'Hot' jazz…was seen to represent a black aesthetic…The cooler, whiter style, most commonly known as 'symphonic syncopation,' enjoyed far greater public approval through the early 1920s and was widely perceived as an improvement on and refinement of the original black jazz" (25). See Hobsbawm, *Uncommon People*; Parsonage, *The Evolution of Jazz in Britain*; and Moore, *Inside British Jazz*.

9. James J. Nott, *Music for the People: Popular Music and Dance in Interwar Britain* (Oxford: Oxford University Press, 2002) 151.

10. See Parsonage, *The Evolution of Jazz in Britain*, 45, 47.

11. Nott, *Music for the People*, 148.

12. "Noise" is from Sir H. Harty, "Sir H. Harty on Jazz Music: A Noise for Dancing," *Times* (London), Sept. 1, 1926, 9B. An unnamed contributor alludes to "the plague of jazz and ultra-modernism," quoted in "Art of Brass Bands: Absence of 'Plague of Jazz,' " *Times* (London), July 12, 1933, 12D. "Madness" is quoted in Nott, *Music for the People*, 151.

13. Clive Bell, "Plus De Jazz," *New Republic* (1921): 92–96.

14. W. H. Auden, "Letter to Lord Byron," in his *Collected Longer Poems* (New York: Random House, 1969), 51–52.

15. Ibid., 52.

16. Ibid., 53.

17. *Between the Acts* was published posthumously by Leonard Woolf in 1941.

18. Alfred Appel, *Jazz Modernism: From Ellington and Armstrong to Matisse and Joyce* (New York: Alfred A. Knopf, distributed by Random House, 2002), 14.

19. Virginia Woolf, *Between the Acts* (London: Hogarth, 1990), 81.

20. Ibid., 178.

21. In my piece, "Woolf in Blackface," I suggest that the moment in *The Waves* that describes figures dancing and playing horns may also invoke jazz. See Genevieve Abravanel, "Woolf in Blackface" in *Virginia Woolf Out of Bounds: Selected Papers from the Tenth Annual Virginia Woolf Conference*, ed. Jessica Berman and Jane Goldman (New York, NY: Pace University Press, 2002), 113–119.

22. Woolf, *Between the Acts*, 82.

23. Ibid., 82.

24. Ibid., 178.

25. After the pageant displays the villagers in wigs and turbans, the text relates, in fragmentary fashion, "they signify presumably the League of…" ibid., 182.

26. Ibid., 183.

27. Ibid., 184.

28. Ibid., 188.

29. Ibid., 189.

30. Ibid., 188.

31. Virginia Woolf, "Mr. Bennett and Mrs. Brown," in her *The Captain's Death Bed* (New York: Harcourt Brace Jovanovitch, 1978), 119.

32. Bonnie Kime Scott, "The Subversive Mechanics of Woolf's Gramophone in *Between the Acts*," in *Virginia Woolf in the Age of Mechanical Reproduction*, ed. Pamela L. Caughie (New York: Garland Pub., 2000), 103.

33. Dramatic critic, "A Tithe Barn: Jazz in the Cotswolds," *Times* (London), Sept. 5, 1923, 8A.

34. Ibid.

35. Ibid.

36. Elizabeth Bowen, *The Last September* (New York: Penguin Modern Classics, 1987), x.

37. Ibid., 17.

38. Ibid., x.

39. Ibid., 17.

40. Ibid., 133.

41. Ibid., 24.

42. Ibid., 24.

43. Ibid., 36.

44. Ibid., 68.

45. Ibid., 112.

46. Ibid., 122.

47. Ibid., 123.

48. Ibid., 250; 247.

49. The identification of jazz as at odds with Irish heritage even occasionally worked its way into public discourse: in 1934 a member of the Gaelic League publically attacked

Ireland's minister for finance, "whom he accused of undue devotion to jazz, declaring that his soul was steeped in it." See " 'Undue Devotion to Jazz': Free State Minister Criticized," *Times* (London), Jan. 5, 1934, 12C.

50. W. H. Auden, "Refugee Blues," in his *Collected Shorter Poems, 1927–1957* (New York: Random House, 1967), 64.

51. Ibid., 5.

52. Auden was keenly aware of the plight of German Jews. As one critic notes, in 1936 Auden "married Erika Mann (the daughter of Thomas Mann) solely to provide her with a passport." See John Fuller, *A Reader's Guide to W. H. Auden* (New York: Farrar Straus & Giroux, 1970), 173–74.

53. Although the blues itself is not generally considered dance music, the musical structure of the blues left its imprint on popular dance music of the period. Moreover, songs from the period bearing the name of the "blues" sometimes *were* dance tunes. Describing the performances of James Europe's band in France, Badger writes, "Typical of the dance pieces that…received the greatest public response were Europe's arrangements of 'Army Blues' and Handy's 'Memphis Blues,' which became two of the band's specialties." Badger, "James Reese Europe and the Prehistory of Jazz," 56.

54. "German Ban on Jazz Broadcasts," *Times* (London), October 14, 1935, 13B.

55. Ibid., 13.

56. Ibid., 13.

57. Ibid., 13.

58. One piece, "Foggy Day in London," which they wrote for the Fred Astaire feature, *Damsel in Distress*, may have particularly appealed to British audiences.

59. Cunard's seemingly primitivist interests and her desire for racial justice coexist in complicated fashion. In reference to Cunard, Jane Marcus argues, "The primitivism of her project does not derive from unacted desire but from identification with the downtrodden" (17). Laura Winkiel ties a related point to the neglect of Cunard's massive anthology *Negro*: "Critical protests over Cunard's primitivism have, in part resulted in *Negro* becoming a nearly forgotten anthology" (162). See Jane Marcus, *Hearts of Darkness: White Women Write Race* (New Brunswick, NJ: Rutgers University Press, 2004); and Laura Winkiel, *Modernism, Race, and Manifestos* (New York: Cambridge University Press, 2008).

60. Bell, "Plus de Jazz," *New Republic* (1921): 92–96.

61. See "The Dying 'Jazz,'" *Times* (London), June 9, 1921, 9F. The article quotes a leading figure, who explains that "I am convinced that 'jazz' is practically dead. People are tired of noise, and want real music instead" (9).

62. Bell, "Plus de Jazz," *New Republic* (1921): 95.

63. See Pierre Bourdieu, *Distinction: A Social Critique of the Judgment of Taste* (Cambridge, MA: Harvard University Press, 1984).

64. Bell, "Plus de Jazz," *New Republic* (1921): 94.

65. See Clive Bell, "Negro Sculpture," in his *Since Cézanne* (New York: Harcourt, Brace, 1928). Clive Bell identifies the essay's first appearance in 1919 (113).

66. Bell, "Plus de Jazz," *New Republic* (1921): 93.

67. It is important to note that Bell was not opposed to the idea of American cultural criticism, as long as it supported elite English and European art. In his 1919 essay "Standards," Bell offers a tribute to a transatlantic economy of taste, explaining that "There is no class on this side the Atlantic to insist on quality now. But if, as I am told, we all

owe money to America, has not America acquired, along with her financial supremacy, certain moral obligations? Has she not become the leisured class of the world, and, as such, responsible to civilization for the maintenance of those standards without which the civilization falls? If so, it is for America to insist in fine arts on some measure of talent and intelligence, in society on decent manners, in life on a critical attitude," in *Since Cézanne*, 153.

68. Bell, "Plus de Jazz," *New Republic* (1921): 93. At the same time, jazz's dissemination through the mass sound technologies of gramophone and wireless further complicated its relationship to ideas and fantasies of race. For a discussion of the mass reproduction of racial identity in interwar writing, see Genevieve Abravanel, "How to Have Race without a Body: The Mass-Reproduced Voice and Modern Identity in H.D.'s 'Two Americans,'" *Mosaic* 42, no. 2 (2009): 37–53.

69. Bell, "Plus de Jazz," in *Since Cézanne*, 214.

70. Ibid., 219.

71. Ibid., 221. Bell was not alone in his identification of Stravinsky with jazz. A 1921 article in the *Times* calls Stravinsky's music "highbrow jazz." See "Promenade Concerts: 'Highbrow Jazz,'" *Times* (London), Aug., 22. 1921, 6D. Indeed, Stravinsky's piece, "Ragtime," was widely cited, both positively and negatively, as a highbrow attempt to transform jazz.

72. Bell, "Plus de Jazz," in *Since Cézanne*, 224.

73. Ibid., 222.

74. Ibid., 223.

75. Clive Bell and Vanessa Stephen, the painter, married in 1907.

76. Bell, "Plus de Jazz," in *Since Cézanne*, 224–25.

77. "Sir H. Coward on 'Jazz': The Essence of Vulgarity," *Times* (London), Sept. 20, 1927, 12B.

78. Ibid., 12.

79. Ibid., 12.

80. Wyndham Lewis, *Paleface: The Philosophy of the 'Melting-Pot'* (London: Chatto and Windus, 1929), 65.

81. Ibid., v.

82. Ibid., v.

83. Ibid., 21.

84. Ibid., 58.

85. Ibid., 58.

86. See *Oxford English Dictionary*, 2nd ed., 1989, s.v. "Jazzy."

87. Lewis, *Paleface*, 58.

88. Nonetheless, in 1919, *As You Were*, a revue at the London Pavilion, ragged Shakespeare and other historical figures of the time. According to a review of the show in the *Times*, it reveals that "it was Sir Walter Raleigh who introduced the Jazz into this country" and highlights "the (more or less) dignified spectacle of Queen Elizabeth and her Court dancing something which seems to be a cross between a squirm and a wriggle." See "Queen Elizabeth and the Jazz," *Times* (London), Mar. 3, 1919, 14E.

89. Lewis, *Paleface*, 64.

90. Ibid., 64.

91. Ibid., 65.

92. Ibid., 66.

93. Ibid., 65.

94. In *Blast*, Lewis, with avant-garde precision, arranged those items in his favor under the heading "Bless," and those out of favor under the heading "Blast."

95. Lewis, *Paleface*, 85.

96. According to Douglas Lane Patey, the novel's "final title meant to recall Gibbon's *Decline and Fall* and Oswald Spengler's popular work of oracular historiography, *The Decline of the West*, both of which Waugh had recently been reading." See Douglas Lane Patey, *The Life of Evelyn Waugh: A Critical Biography* (Oxford, UK: Blackwell Publishers, 1998), 25–6.

97. Evelyn Waugh, *Decline and Fall: An Illustrated Novelette* (Boston: Little, Brown, and Company, 1956 [1928]), 103.

98. Ibid., 95.

99. Ibid., 99.

100. Ibid., 100.

101. Ibid., 102.

102. Ibid., 103.

103. Ibid., 103.

104. Ibid., 80. In fact, Wales like the rest of Britain saw the growth of local jazz bands, some of which strikingly recalled the racism of nineteenth-century minstrel performances, including the use of blackface. The *Times* reported on a British "jazz band" contest at the Crystal Palace in 1934, noting that the Welsh "character" bands took top prizes. The *Times* describes the "Aberfan Coons" as follows: "They marched into the arena with glistening black faces, a little straw hat on the side of each woolly wig… They strutted like stage darkeys." The second prize "character band" winners, also from Wales, similarly borrowed its name from American minstrels: "the Abertridwr Chocolate Coons." See "Jazz Bands: A New Kind of Entertainment," *Times* (London), April 23, 1934, 11C.

105. Ibid., 81.

106. The reviews of *Decline and Fall* were generally laudatory; Arnold Bennett called it "an uncompromising and brilliantly malicious satire" (Bennett, "Review," *Evening Standard*, Oct. 11, 1928, 5). Most amusing is the American response in the *New York Times* that called it a "satirical cross-section of very English society" only to express relief at a recognizable figure: "there is a certain joy of recognition in encountering Mrs. Beste Chetwynde [sic] and her colored friend Chokie [sic]." "Unsigned review, April 7, 1929, *New York Times Book Review*," in *Evelyn Waugh: The Critical Heritage*, ed. Martin Stannard (London: Routlege and Kegan Paul, 1984), 6.

107. Waugh, *Decline and Fall*, 103.

108. Ibid., 104.

109. Ibid., 110.

110. Evelyn Waugh, *Vile Bodies* (Boston: Little Brown, 1944), 123.

111. Ibid., 119.

112. Ibid., 119.

113. Ibid., 119.

114. Ibid., 119.

115. Marcus, *Hearts of Darkness: White Women Write Race*, 139.

116. John Banting, "Dancing in Harlem," in *Negro*, ed. Nancy Cunard (London: Published by Nancy Cunard at Wishart & Co., 1934), 203.

117. Robert Goffin, "Hot Jazz," trans. Samuel Beckett, in *Negro*, ed. Cunard, 239.

118. George Antheil, "The Negro on the Spiral, or A Method of Negro Music," in *Negro*, ed. Cunard, 216.

119. Ibid., 216.

120. Kingsley Amis, *Memoirs* (New York: Summit Books, 1991), 65.

121. Kingsley Amis, *Lucky Jim* (London: Victor Gollancz, 1984), 103; 180; 209.

122. Phillip Larkin, *All What Jazz: A Record Diary, 1961–1971* (London: Faber and Faber, 1985) 38.

123. Ibid., 38.

124. Ibid., 100. One historian suggests that by the thirties, "there were more jazz enthusiasts per capita in Britain than in the country of its birth." See Jim Godbolt, *A History of Jazz in Britain 1919–1950* (London: Quartet Books, 1984), 100.

125. Phillip Larkin, "Cool Britannia," in *All What Jazz*, 42. Mrs. Grundy was the unseen neighbor in Thomas Morton's *Speed the Plough* (1798), who set the standard for respectability. Her name later became synonymous with fussy, English conventionality.

126. The pun, "Cool Britannia," famously resurfaced in the 1990s during the Blair administration.

127. Phillip Larkin, *Collected Poems* (London: Faber and Faber, 1989), 83.

Chapter Three: The Entertainment Empire

1. John Maynard Keynes, *The Collected Writings,* ed. Donald Moggridge (Cambridge: Cambridge University Press and the Royal Economic Society, 1982), 371.

A portion of Keynes's quote was drawn to my attention by a footnote in Jed Esty's *A Shrinking Island: Modernism and National Culture in England* (Princeton, NJ: Princeton University Press, 2004), 259.

2. For Taylor's "essential social habit," see Jeffery Richards, "Rethinking British Cinema," in *British Cinema, Past and Present*, ed. Justin Ashby and Andrew Higson (New York: Routledge, 2000), 22. For Lenin's "of all the arts for us cinema is the most important," see Richard Taylor and Derek Spring eds., *Stalinism and Soviet Cinema* (London: Routledge, 1993), ix. Piero Garofalo and Jaqueline Reich tell the notorious tale, "At a 1936 rally announcing massive state intervention in the film industry, Benito Mussolini appeared in front of a large banner that bore the soon-to-be infamous statement: 'Cinema is the strongest weapon'" in Jacqueline Reich and Piero Garofalo, eds., *Re-Viewing Fascism: Italian Cinema, 1922–1943* (Bloomington: Indiana University Press, 2002), vii.

3. Margaret Dickinson and Sarah Street, *Cinema and State: The Film Industry and the Government, 1927–84* (London: BFI Pub., 1985), 5. Note that "up to 1927 the majority of films exhibited in Britain had been American—one estimate calculated that the proportion was as high as 85–90 per cent." Marcus A. Doel suggests that "by 1919 about 80 per cent of all films were being made in California" in "Occult Hollywood," in *The American Century: Consensus and Coercion in the Projection of American Power*, ed., David Slater and Peter J. Taylor (Malden, MA: Blackwell, 1999), 201.

4. Namely, the film acts of 1927 and 1934. For more on these acts, see Dickinson and Street, *Cinema and State*, 5–6; and Lawrence Napper, "A Despicable Tradition? Quota Quickies in the 1930s," in *The British Cinema Book*, 2nd ed., ed. Robert Murphy (London: BFI, 2001), 37–47. As the acts went into effect, British films regained a measure of popularity

at home. Nonetheless, from 1927 into the first years of the thirties, Hollyw
tures were widely condemned for their ruinous impact on British life.

5. Dickinson and Street, *Cinema and State*, 58. A fuller quote from *World Film New*,
Nov. 1937, is revealing: "The American drive to obliterate every vestige of a native British film
industry is succeeding admirably. Cynics are comparing the situation with the Italian conquest
of Abyssinia, and there are indeed certain resemblances. The Americans, with their impressive
supply of Hollywood pictures, have the necessary tank power to put native exhibitors at their
mercy. They are using it remorselessly...So far as films go we are now a colonial people."

6. These lines have gained much currency among film historians. Jeffrey Richards
deserves the credit for resurrecting the quote in *The Age of the Dream Palace: Cinema and
Society in Britain 1930-1939* (London: Routledge and Kegan Paul, 1984), 63. Mark Glancy
provides a detailed discussion of the quote, including its use by film historians, Mark
Glancy, "Temporary American Citizens? British Audiences, Hollywood Films and the
Threat of Americanization in the 1920s," *Historical Journal of Film, Radio and Television* 26,
no. 4 (2006): 461-484. As Glancy points out, the *Daily News* columnist actually opposed the
Film Act, though his words were used to support the act in parliamentary debate.

7. Quoted in Priya Jaikumar, "Hollywood and the Multiple Constituencies of Colonial
India," in *Hollywood Abroad: Audiences and Cultural Exchange*, ed. Richard Maltby and
Melvyn Stokes (London: BFI, 2004), 87.

8. See Christine Gledhill, *Reframing British Cinema, 1918-1928: Between Restraint
and Passion* (London: BFI, 2003), 1-31; 123-180; Richards, *The Age of the Dream Palace*,
44-63; and Sarah Street, *British Cinema in Documents* (London and New York: Routledge,
2000), 10-20. See also Peter Miles and Malcolm Smith, *Cinema, Literature, and Society:
Elite and Mass Culture in Interwar Britain* (New York: Croom Helm, 1987), 164-176.

9. A variety of causes supported Hollywood's periods of ascendancy in Britain and
Europe. As many scholars note, because the United States was largely sheltered from the
effects of the First World War, the American film industry was able to grow more rapidly
than those in Britain and Europe. Moreover, as Lawrence Napper points out, the United
States had the financial advantage of a vast domestic market, allowing foreign markets to
serve up nearly pure profit. American film companies also employed a range of tactics,
from undercutting film-rental charges to booking films in blocks, to secure their hold on
the British market. See Lawrence Napper, *British Cinema and Middlebrow Culture in the
Interwar Years* (Exeter: University of Exeter Press, 2009), 20.

10. See Giovanni Arrighi, *The Long Twentieth Century: Money, Power, and the Origins
of Our Times* (New York: Verso, 1994), 6. Arrighi identifies British and American power as
overlapping in the early twentieth century, dating the end of the British cycle "through the
early twentieth century" and the "U.S. cycle" from "the late nineteenth century."

11. See Victoria De Grazia, *Irresistible Empire: America's Advance through Twentieth-
Century Europe* (Cambridge, MA: Belknap Press of Harvard University Press, 2005), 3.

12. Quoted in Richards, *The Age of the Dream Palace*, 57.

13. For a discussion of the system of quotas limiting Hollywood cinema in Britain,
see Lawrence Napper, "A Despicable Tradition? Quota Quickies in the 1930s" in *The British
Cinema Book*, ed. Murphy, 37-47. For more reflections on attitudes in Parliament, see Walter
Ashley, *Cinema and the Public: A Critical Analysis of the Origin, Constitution and Control of
the British Film Institute* (London: Ivor Nicholson and Watson Ltd., 1934), 6.

14. Tom Ryall, *Alfred Hitchcock and the British Cinema* (Urbana: University of Illinois Press, 1996), 119. Although the viewing public largely accepted *Blackmail* as Britain's first full-length talking film, some scholars suggest that the partial use of sound by previous shorter films belies its status.

15. See Susan McCabe, *Cinematic Modernism: Modernist Poetry and Film* (New York: Cambridge University Press, 2005); and David Trotter, *Cinema and Modernism* (Malden, MA: Blackwell, 2007), 3.

16. For a detailed account of how American cultural institutions, figureheads, and politicians shaped the American film industry, see Peter Decherney, *Hollywood and the Culture Elite: How the Movies Became American* (New York: Columbia University Press, 2005).

17. Jaikumar, "Hollywood and the Multiple Constituencies of Colonial India," in *Hollywood Abroad*, ed. Maltby and Stokes, 78–98; Miriam Hansen, "The Mass Production of the Senses: Classical Cinema as Vernacular Modernism," *Modernism/Modernity* 2 (1999): 68.

18. For key works in audience studies, see Melvyn Stokes and Richard Maltby, eds., *Identifying Hollywood's Audiences: Cultural Identity and the Movies* (London: BFI, 1999); and Maltby and Stokes, eds., *Hollywood Abroad*.

19. Aldous Huxley, *Jesting Pilate: The Diary of a Journey* (London: Chatto & Windus, 1926), 200.

20. This line was part of Cunliffe-Lister's opening address on the second reading of the Cinematograph Films Bill in March, 1927. Quoted in Napper, *British Cinema and Middlebrow Culture in the Interwar Years*, 17.

21. *The Film in National Life: Being the Report of an Enquiry Conducted by the Commission on Educational and Cultural Films into the Service which the Cinematograph May Render to Education and Social Progress* (London: George Allen and Unwin, Ltd., 1932), 126.

22. Ibid., 133.

23. Editors, "Comment and Review," *Close Up* 1 (Oct. 1927): 77.

24. Amelia Defries, "Criticism from Within," *Close Up* 1 (Oct. 1927): 53.

25. "English Films—An American Comment," *Times* (London), February 4, 1926, 8. Times Digital Archive, http://www.library.upenn.edu.

26. Ibid.

27. See Michael North, *The Dialect of Modernism: Race, Language, and Twentieth-Century Literature* (New York: Oxford University Press, 1994), 3–8, for a nuanced discussion of American reactions to *The Jazz Singer*.

28. Christopher Isherwood, *Prater Violet* (Minneapolis: University of Minnesota Press, [1945] 2001), 65.

29. See Napper, *British Cinema and Middlebrow Culture in the Interwar Years*, 20.

30. Quoted in C. K. Ogden, *Debabelization* (London: Kegan Paul, 1931), 147.

31. Ibid., 145. The original quote is attributed to the *Chicago Tribune*, Paris edition, Oct. 20, 1930.

32. The fuller quote is strikingly alarmist: "Why should we offer to discuss the subject at all with America? We do not want to interfere with their language; why should they seek to interfere with ours? That their huge hybrid population, of which only a small minority are even racially Anglo-Saxon, should use English as their chief means of intercommunication is our misfortune, not our fault. They certainly threaten our language, but the only way

in which we can effectively meet that threat is by assuming...that 'Americanisms are foreign words and should be so treated...' The only way to preserve the purity of the English language is to present a steadily hostile resistance to every American innovation" Ibid., 146. Ogden cites *The New Statesman*, June 1927, as his source.

33. Ibid., 78. Ogden cites the *Melbourne Sun*, August 26, 1929, as his source.

34. Ibid., 123. Ogden cites the *Times of India*, May 8, 1929, as his source.

35. A new kind of English, "basic English," resides at the heart of Ogden's proposed solution. He notes, " 'Make everybody speak English' was the four-word peace-slogan suggested by Henry Ford some years ago; 'Basic English for all' is its modern counterpart" (*Debabelization*, 13). Ogden praises the "elastic phraseology" of American slang, recounting its transformation of the average Englishman: "He is slowly learning to 'get busy' and 'put over' his own 'concepts.' 'Right now' his 'co-ed' offspring are 'talkie fans'; they get 'psyched,' and know all the 'dope'—'and then some' " (30; 30–1).

36. Wyndham Lewis, *Men without Art* (London: Cassell and Co., 1934), 32.

37. Ibid., 33.

38. Ibid., 32.

39. Ibid., 32.

40. Ibid., 32.

41. Anne Friedberg, "Introduction: Reading *Close Up*, 1927–1933," in *Close Up, 1927–33: Cinema and Modernism*, ed. James Donald, Anne Friedberg, and Laura Marcus (Princeton, NJ: Princeton University Press, 1998), 10.

42. Ibid.

43. Ibid.

44. British film critic and director Oswell Blakeston expresses his hope that the talking cinema might be able to behave like the silent cinema: "Talkies need not stay in the country of their origin if words are built up in the imagist way." Oswell Blakeston, "Anthology," *Close Up* 7 (July 1930): 75.

45. For "monstrosity," see Kenneth Macpherson, "As Is," *Close Up* 3 (July 1928): 8. For Bryher's comment, see Bryher, "The Hollywood Code," *Close Up* 8 (Sept. 1931): 234.

46. For a detailed discussion of *Close Up*'s response to the rise of the talking cinema, see James Donald's introduction to *Close Up, 1927–33: Cinema and Modernism,* ed., Donald, Friedberg, and Marcus, 79–82.

47. Michael North, *Camera Works: Photography and the Twentieth-Century Word* (Oxford: Oxford University Press, 2005), 85.

48. The English writer Dorothy Richardson notes that during the era of silent film, British children were already beginning to imitate American slang learned from the intertitles. As Richardson put it, "And the American language. Once it was part of the puzzles and bewilderments of 'the pictures,' but is there now a child in London who cannot at the right moment say: 'Oh, boy' and read and delightedly understand each idiom, and grin through the Hollywood caption." Richardson, "Continuous Performance," *Close Up* 2 (Jan. 1928): 174.

49. Macpherson, "As Is," *Close Up* 1 (July 1927): 16.

50. H. D. became a British citizen in 1914 through her marriage to Richard Aldington.

51. See Macpherson, "As Is" *Close Up* 5 (July 1929): 6.

52. Jean Lenauer, "News from the Provinces" *Close Up* 6 (April 1930): 322.

53. Bryher, "Danger in the Cinema," *Close Up* 7 (Nov. 1930): 299–304; 303.

54. Bryher, "The Hollywood Code," *Close Up* 8 (Sept. 1931): 236.

55. Ibid., 236.

56. Bryher, "The Hollywood Code II," *Close Up* 8 (Dec. 1931): 280.

57. Ibid.

58. Ibid.

59. Ibid., 282.

60. Ibid., 281.

61. Ibid.

62. Edmund Quarry argues that the first British talkie was in fact "a short, experi-mental domestic comedy…screened during the winter of 1924–25." Quoted in Tom Ryall, *Blackmail* (London: BFI, 1993), 12.

63. In an interview, Hitchcock explains, "I suspected the producers might change their minds and eventually want an all-sound picture, I worked it out that way." Quoted in Ryall, *Blackmail*, 23–4.

64. Kenneth Macpherson, "As Is," *Close Up* 5 (Oct. 1929): 261.

65. Ibid.

66. "British International Pictures," *Times* (London), July 1, 1929. Times Digital Archive, http://www.library.upenn.edu.

67. "Blackmail: A British International Picture," *Times* (London), June 24, 1929, 12. Times Digital Archive, http://www.library.upenn.edu.

68. Ibid., 12.

69. Truffaut's statement has been widely reprinted. See for instance Jeffery Richards, "Rethinking British Cinema," in *British Cinema, Past and Present*, ed. Justin Ashby and Andrew Higson (New York: Routledge, 2000), 22.

70. Sarah Street notes that certain genres of the British "quota quickie," most notably the farce, were popular with British audiences in the thirties. See Sarah Street, "British Film and the National Interest, 1927–1939," in *The British Cinema Book*, ed. Murphy, 187.

71. H. D., "Russian Films" *Close Up* 3 (Sept. 1928): 28.

72. In response to protective legislation enacted by the British government in 1927 and again in 1938, a growing percentage of films shown in Britain needed to be British in origin. To circumvent this obstacle to their hegemony, Hollywood production companies finan-cially supported the production of inexpensive and often rushed British films, commonly called "quota quickies," to pair with their studio features. See Dickinson and Street, *Cinema and State* 5–29; Napper 37–47.

73. Elizabeth Madox Roberts, "Comment and Review," *Close Up* 1 (Sept. 1927): 66.

74. Bryher, "The War from Three Angles," *Close Up* 1 (July 1927): 18.

75. Robert Herring, "The Latest British Masterpiece," *Close Up* 2 (Jan. 1928): 33.

76. Clifford Howard, "Cinemaphobia," *Close Up* 5 (July 1929): 65.

77. Ibid., 59.

78. An article in *World Film News*, "The Flora and Fauna of the British Film Industry" discusses the ways in which British films were made by Americans to fulfill quota require-ments: "On their deep, inborn sense of our history, our heritage and our customs we depend for the dramatization of our English traditions as well as for the more mun-dane business of fulfilling our British quota." Quoted in Richards, *The Age of the Dream Palace*, 44.

79. Macpherson, "As Is," *Close Up* 1 (July 1927): 5.

80. Macpherson, "As Is" *Close Up* 1 (Aug. 1927): 16.

81. Ibid.

82. In contrast, Virginia Woolf in her 1926 essay, "The Cinema," emphasizes film's difference from literature and laments the adaption of novel to the screen. See Virginia Woolf, "The Cinema," *Collected Essays, Volume II* (New York: Harcourt, Brace, and World, 1967), 268–272.

83. Bryher, "A Survey," *Close Up* 1 (Dec. 1927): 56.

84. The cover wrapper of an early issue of *Close Up* (Oct 1927) reads: "CLOSE UP, an English review, is the first to approach films from the angles of art, experiment, and possibility." Reprinted in *Close Up, 1927–33: Cinema and Modernism,* ed., Donald, Friedberg, and Marcus, 2.

85. For a discussion of H. D., Paul Robeson, and racial identity, see Genevieve Abravanel, "How to Have Race without a Body: The Mass-Reproduced Voice and Modern Identity in H. D.'s 'Two Americans,'" *Mosaic* 42, no. 2 (2009): 37–53.

86. See Annette Debo, "Interracial Modernism in Avant-Garde Film: Paul Robeson and H. D. in the 1930 *Borderline*," in *Quarterly Review of Film and Video* 18 (2001): 371–383, for a discussion of *Borderline*'s reception outside of England. Debo argues that *Borderline*'s reputation as a critical failure overlooks its more favorable reception in Europe.

87. H. D. "*Borderline*: A POOL Film with Paul Robeson," reprinted in *Close Up, 1927–33: Cinema and Modernism,* ed., Donald, Friedberg, and Marcus, 226.

88. Ibid.

89. Ibid., 225.

90. Ibid., 223.

91. In *The Great War and Modern Memory*, Vincent Sherry discusses the uses of the term, "modernism," prior to the mid-twentieth century. Of the two categories he offers—references to a Catholic religious movement and to a temporal modernity—H. D.'s use more closely reflects the latter. Indeed, it is interesting to note the extent to which her use anticipates the mobilization of the term, "modernism," during its canonization after the Second World War. See Vincent Sherry, *The Great War and Modern Memory* (New York: Oxford University Press, 2004), 16–17.

92. Here I use the term, "arrière -garde," in a sense akin to Charles Bernstein's use in a very different context, namely his essay, "Avant-Garde or Arrière-Garde in Recent American Poetry," *Poetics Today* 20, no. 4 (1999): 629–653. In this essay, Bernstein uses the term, "arrière-garde," to refer to the "non-avant-garde," or poetry that, at least at first glance, seems hopelessly conventional (633).

93. Evelyn Waugh, *The Loved One: An Anglo-American Tragedy* (Boston: Little, Brown, 1948), 3.

94. Ibid.

95. Ibid., 11.

96. Ibid., 35.

97. Ibid., 23.

98. Jo Stoyte was apparently based on William Randolph Hearst (as was the character, Kane, in *Citizen Kane*). See John Evangelist Walsh, *Walking Shadows: Orson Welles, William Randolph Hearst, and Citizen Kane* (Madison, WI: University of Wisconsin Press/Popular Press, 2004), 50.

99. Aldous Huxley, "The Outlook for American Culture: Some Reflections in a Machine Age," *Harper's Magazine* (1927); *Complete Essays: Aldous Huxley, Volume III, 1930–1935*, ed. Robert Baker and James Sexton (Chicago: Ivan R. Dee, 2001), 185. See chapter 1 for a discussion of Huxley's position on Americanization.

100. Keynes, *The Collected Writings*, 371.

Chapter Four: English by Example

1. See Raymond Williams, "Seeing a Man Running," in *The Leavises: Recollections and Impressions*, ed. Denys Thompson (Cambridge: Cambridge University Press, 1984), 116.

2. Ibid., 117.

3. Ibid., 117.

4. See Stuart Hall, "Interview with Richard English and Michael Kenny," in *Rethinking British Decline*, ed. Richard English and Michael Kenny (New York: St. Martin's Press, 2000) for a discussion of the "shift in fortunes" (110) from Britain to the United States after the Second World War.

5. For Leavis as "genius" see Sebastian Moore, "F. R. Leavis: A Memoir," in *The Leavises: Recollections and Impressions*, ed. Thompson, 60; for "the single most influential figure in twentieth-century English literary criticism," see Christopher Norris, "Editor's Forward," in *F.R. Leavis* by Michael Bell (London: Routledge, 1988), vii; for "damaging arrogance and skepticism" see Raymond Williams, *Culture and Society, 1780–1950* (New York: Columbia University Press, 1983) 263; for "curmudgeon," see Gerald Graff, *Professing Literature: An Institutional History* (Chicago: University of Chicago Press, 1987), 208.

6. Both book and pamphlet were published by the aptly named Minority Press in Cambridge.

7. F. R. Leavis, "Mass Civilisation and Minority Culture," in his *For Continuity* (Cambridge, UK: G. Fraser, The Minority Press, 1933), 16.

8. As are the authors of *Middletown*, Robert and Helen Lynd.

9. Leavis, "Mass Civilisation," 17.

10. Ibid., 18.

11. F. R. Leavis and Denys Thompson, *Culture and Environment: The Training of Critical Awareness* (London: Chatto & Windus, 1933), 3.

12. Leavis, "Mass Civilisation," 16.

13. Leavis, "Mass Civilisation," 46. See Henry Ford's *To-Day and To-Morrow* (Garden City, NY: Doubleday, Page, 1926). See also Ford's *My Life and Work* (Garden City, NY: Doubleday, Page, 1922).

14. Leavis, "Mass Civilisation," 46.

15. Leavis, "Babbitt Buys the World," in *For Continuity*, 95.

16. See Leavis's essay, "Under Which King, Bezonian?" in *For Continuity*, for an analysis of Trotsky's use of the word "culture" and an announcement that *Scrutiny* will not align itself with Marxism, despite some pressure to do so. In this essay, Leavis ironically suggests that his choice is between "Stalin or the King by Divine Right" (168).

17. Leavis and Thompson, *Culture and Environment*, 1.

18. See Gauri Viswanathan's important *Masks of Conquest: Literary Study and British Rule in India* (New York: Columbia University Press, 1989). For Macaulay's essay, see Thomas Babington Macaulay, "Minute on Indian Education," in his *Selected*

Writings, ed. John Clive and Thomas Pinney (Chicago: University of Chicago Press, 1972), 237–251.

19. Leavis and Thompson, *Culture and Environment*, 126–27.

20. Ibid., 127.

21. Ibid., 143. See Jan and Cora Gordon, *On Wandering Wheels: Through Roadside Camps from Maine to Georgia in an Old Sedan Car* (New York: Dodd, Mead, 1928). Leavis probably consulted the 1929 edition published by J. Lane in London; he notes that he found it in "The Bodley Head" (*Culture and Environment*, 143).

22. Leavis and Thompson, *Culture and Environment*, 143.

23. Leavis's essay, "Keynes, Lawrence, and Cambridge," defends Lawrence against the elitism of Bloomsbury. See F. R. Leavis, "Keynes, Lawrence, and Cambridge," *Scrutiny*, March 1949.

24. Leavis and Thompson, *Culture and Environment*, 262.

25. Denys Thompson, "Advertising God," *Scrutiny* 1, no. 3 (1932): 242.

26. F. R. Leavis, *The Great Tradition: George Eliot, Henry James, Joseph Conrad* (New York: G.W. Stewart, 1948), 9.

27. See Claudia Johnson, "F. R. Leavis: The 'Great Tradition' of the English Novel and the Jewish Part," *Nineteenth Century Literature* 56, no. 2 (2001): 199–227, for a discussion of gender and *The Great Tradition*.

28. Conrad became a British citizen in 1886, James in 1915.

29. Leavis, *The Great Tradition*, 18.

30. Ibid. 128.

31. Ibid., 11.

32. Ibid., 145; 134.

33. Ibid., 162.

34. Ibid., 163.

35. Ibid., 163.

36. See Leavis, *Valuation in Criticism and Other Essays by F. R. Leavis*, ed. G. Singh (Cambridge: Cambridge University Press, 1986), 11. In 1968, Leavis called Eliot "our last great poet" (129).

37. Leavis, *The Great Tradition*, 5.

38. Ibid., 5.

39. Ibid., 23.

40. Ibid., 138.

41. Ibid., 138.

42. Ibid., 28.

43. Leavis, *For Continuity*, 76.

44. *Oxford English Dictionary Online*, s.v. "Highbrow," http://www.oed.com/.

45. Virginia Woolf, "Middlebrow," in *Collected Essays*, vol. 2 (New York: Harcourt, Brace, and World, 1967), 196. Woolf insists, "if I could be more of a highbrow, I would" (196).

46. Melba Cuddy-Keane, *Virginia Woolf, the Intellectual, and the Public Sphere* (New York: Cambridge University Press, 2003), 18.

47. Leavis and Thompson, *Culture and Environment*, 41.

48. Ibid., 38.

49. Ibid., 38.

50. Ibid., 38.

51. Ibid., 38.

52. Ibid., 38–9.

53. Ibid., 39.

54. Ibid., 39.

55. Fredric Jameson, *A Singular Modernity: Essay on the Ontology of the Present* (NY: Verso, 2002), 164.

56. Prominent contributions to the high-low debates can be found in Andreas Huyssen, *After the Great Divide: Modernism, Mass Culture, Postmodernism* (Bloomington: Indiana University Press, 1986); Michael North, *Reading 1922: A Return to the Scene of the Modern* (New York: Oxford University Press, 1986); and Lawrence Rainey, *Institutions of Modernism: Literary Elites and Public Culture* (New Haven, CT.: Yale University Press, 1998).

57. Such work includes David Chinitz, *T. S. Eliot and the Cultural Divide* (Chicago: University of Chicago Press, 2003); Melba Cuddy-Keane, *Virginia Woolf, the Intellectual, and the Public Sphere* (Cambridge: Cambridge University Press, 2003); Kevin J. H. Dettmar and Stephen Watt, eds., *Marketing Modernisms: Self-Promotion, Canonization, Rereading* (Ann Arbor: University of Michigan Press, 1996); Garry Leonard, *Advertising and Commodity Culture in Joyce* (Gainsville: University Press of Florida, 1998); Allison Pease, *Modernism, Mass Culture, and the Aesthetics of Obscenity* (Cambridge: Cambridge University Press, 2000).

58. I shall refer to Queenie Leavis as "QDL" in this section of the chapter to avoid confusion with Frank Raymond Leavis.

59. See Richard Hoggart on the influence of Queenie Leavis on his own work, particularly in John Corner, "Studying Culture—Reflections and Assessments: An Interview with Richard Hoggart" *The Uses of Literacy* (New Brunswick: Transaction, 1998), 269–84.

60. Q. D. Leavis, *Fiction and the Reading Public* (London,: Chatto & Windus, 1932), 190.

61. Ibid., 191–2.

62. Ibid., xv.

63. Ibid., 35.

64. Ibid., 20.

65. Ibid., 7.

66. Ibid., 14.

67. Ibid., 16.

68. Ibid., 15.

69. Leavis, "The Literary Mind," in *For Continuity*, 65.

70. Noting Leavis's ability to inspire Cambridge students to become schoolteachers, Margaret Mathieson writes, "Leavis demanded men 'who would fight,' and many graduates responded to the battle cry by entering schools to teach English as he had taught them" (122).

71. Perry Anderson, "Components of the National Culture," *New Left Review* 3, no. 57 (1968): 50.

72. Cited in Gerald Bernbaum, *Social Change and the Schools* (London: Routledge and Kegan Paul, 1967), 16.

73. Cited in Margaret Mathieson, *The Preachers of Culture: A Study of English and Its Teachers* (Totowa, NJ: Rowman and Littlefield, 1975), 71.

74. Denys Thompson, "Introduction," *English for the English: A Chapter on National Education*, by George Sampson (Cambridge: Cambridge University Press, 1970), 8.

75. Sampson, *English for the English*, 23.

76. Ibid., 27.

77. Ibid., 24.

78. Ibid., 34.

79. Committee on English in the Educational System of England, *The Teaching of English in England; Being the Report of the Departmental Committee Appointed by the President of the Board of Education to Inquire into the Position of English in the Educational System of England* (London: Harcourt Brace, 1922), 252.

80. Ibid., 252.

81. See Robert Crawford, *Devolving English Literature* (Edinburgh: Edinburgh University Press, 2000) for a discussion of the role of Scotland in the development of literary studies in Britain. I would suggest that while it is true that Scotland moved away from classics and philology before England, practicing something closer to contemporary English studies, Scottish practices were not the primary inspiration for the changes coming to England in the twentieth century.

82. Mathieson, *The Preachers of Culture*, 125.

83. Cited in I. D. MacKillop, *F. R. Leavis: A Life in Criticism* (London: Penguin Press, 1995), 73. Leavis's thesis was titled, "The Relationship of Journalism to Literature: Studies in the Rise and Earlier Development of the Press in England."

84. As one critic puts it, "It was Leavis who tightened the link between English studies at university level and the school teacher's responsibility in the outside world," quoted in Mathieson, *The Preachers of Culture*, 122.

85. Francis Mulhern, *The Moment of Scrutiny* (London: NLB, 1979), 100.

86. F. R. Leavis, *Education and the University, a Sketch for an 'English School'* (London: Chatto and Windus, 1948), 7.

87. Ibid., 22.

88. Ibid., 22.

89. Ibid., 28.

90. Williams, *Culture and Society, 1780–1950*, 261.

91. Ibid., 252.

92. See Grant Farred, "Leavisite Cool: The Organic Links between Cultural Studies and *Scrutiny*," *Disposition* 21, no. 48 (1999): 1–19, for a discussion of the place of Leavis in this tradition. Farred notes that although "Leavis.... would seem anachronistic and politically out of place in the company of Raymond Williams, Richard Hoggart, and Edward Thompson" (1), he is an important ancestor to the movement.

93. Richard Hoggart, *The Uses of Literacy* (New Brunswick, NJ: Transaction, 1998) 248.

94. Ibid., 278.

95. Andrew Goodwin, "Preface," in *The Uses of Literacy*, xxiv.

96. Hoggart, *The Uses of Literacy*, 188.

97. Ibid., 189.

98. Ibid., 189.

99. Goodwin, "Preface," in *The Uses of Literacy*, xxiv.

100. Hoggart, *The Uses of Literacy*, 190.

101. Ibid., 190.

102. Ibid., 191.

103. Terry Eagleton, *Literary Theory* (Minneapolis: University of Minnesota Press, 1983), 27.

Chapter Five: Make It Old

1. T. S. Eliot, *Notes towards the Definition of Culture* (New York: Harcourt, Brace, 1949), 94.

2. Ibid., 94.

3. Ibid., 94.

4. Ibid., 38.

5. Ibid., 30.

6. Other poems by Eliot with significant reference to America include early works such as "Preludes" (1917), later works such as "Sweeney Agonistes" (1926–27), "Marina" (1930), and landscape poems such as "Cape Ann" (1935).

7. For *The Waste Land*'s "Shakesperehian rag," Eliot apparently took lines from a musical number, "That Shakesperian Rag" that appeared in the 1912 Ziegfield Follies. David Chinitz, *T.S. Eliot and the Cultural Divide* (Chicago: University of Chicago Press, 2003), 46–47.

8. In 1914, Eliot was a student at Merton College. T. S. Eliot, *The Letters of T.S. Eliot, 1898–1922*, ed. Valerie Eliot (New York: Harcourt Brace Jovanovich, 1988), 70.

9. Ibid., 70.

10. See Chinitz, *T.S. Eliot and the Cultural Divide*, 156.

11. Ibid., 156.

12. See Eliot's essay "Marie Lloyd" (1922).

13. T. S. Eliot, "Preface," in Edgar Ansel Mowrer, *This American World* (London: Faber and Gywer, 1928), ix.

14. Ibid., x–xi.

15. Ibid., x.

16. Ibid., xi.

17. Ibid., 17.

18. Ibid., 19.

19. Ibid., 50.

20. Ibid., 209.

21. Ibid., 220.

22. See my first chapter, particularly the discussion of the anonymous short story "London's Transformation" for reflections on the anxiety that America might colonize England.

23. Herbert Read, "T.S.E.—A Memoir," in *T. S. Eliot: The Man and His Work*, ed. Allen Tate (London: Chatto and Windus, 1967), 6.

24. In a letter to Lytton Strachey of February 23, 1923, Woolf considers the financial plight of "poor Tom," noting, "In fact, the poor man is becoming (in his highly American way, which

is tedious and longwinded to a degree) desperate." See Virginia Woolf, *Letters of Virginia Woolf, Vol III: 1923–1928*, eds. Nigel Nicholson and Joanne Trautmann, (New York: Harcourt, Brace, Jovanovich, 1975), 14. In a diary entry of 1936, Woolf even more starkly contrasts her self-identity as English with Eliot's nationality: "I'm English enough to feel my own past as a peasant...Tom, the American, cant [sic]; feels nothing I suppose." See Virginia Woolf, *Diary of Virginia Woolf*, ed. Anne Olivier Bell (San Diego: Harcourt Brace Jovanovich, 1977), 5.

25. See Alex Zwerdling, *Improvised Europeans: American Literary Expatriates and the Siege of London* (New York: Basic Books, 1998), 306.

26. Eliot, *Letters*, 318. According to the *Oxford English Dictionary* a metic is "a resident alien in a Greek city, having some of the privileges of citizenship." In Eliot's usage, London is the metropole to which he can only partly belong.

27. Cited in Read, *T.S. E.*, 5–6.

28. Lewis is cited in Zwerdling, *Improvised Europeans*, 277.

29. North, *The Dialect of Modernism: Race, Language, and Twentieth-Century Literature* (New York: Oxford University Press, 1994), 10.

30. Clive Bell, "Plus De Jazz," *New Republic* (1921): 92–96, collected in his *Since Cézanne* (New York: Harcourt Brace, 1928), 222.

31. For recent considerations of the Bolo poems, see Loretta Johnson, "T. S. Eliot's Bawdy Verse: Lulu, Bolo and More Ties." *Journal of Modern Literature* 27, no. 1–2 (Fall 2003): 14–25; Gabrielle McIntire, "An Unexpected Beginning: Sex, Race, and History in T. S. Eliot's Columbo and Bolo Poems," *Modernism/Modernity* 9, no. 2 (April 2002): 283–301; Jonathan Gill, "Protective Coloring: Modernism and Blackface Minstrelsy in the Bolo Poems," In *T. S. Eliot's Orchestra: Critical Essays on Poetry and Music* (New York: Garland, 2000); and David Chinitz, "T. S. Eliot's Blue Verses and Their Sources in the Folk Tradition," *Journal of Modern Literature* 23, no. 2 (1999–2000 Winter 1999): 329–333.

32. Lewis notes, "Eliot has sent me Bullshit and the Ballad for Big Louise. They are excellent bits of scholarly ribaldry. I am trying to print them in *Blast*; but stick to my naif determination to have no words ending in -Uck, -Unt, and -Ugger." See Wyndham Lewis, "Letter to Ezra Pound [January 1915?]" *The Letters of Wyndham Lewis*, ed.W. K. Rose (Norfolk, CT: New Directions, 1963), 66–67. In a letter to Pound on February 2, 1915, Eliot recounts, "I have corresponded with Lewis, but his puritanical principles seem to bar my way to Publicity. I fear that King Bolo and his Big Black Kween will never burst into print." Eliot, *Letters*, 86.

33. Along with the several verses published by Ricks, another handful of verses are published in the first volume of Eliot's letters. One is included in *The Faber Book of Blue Verse*. Others are still under copyright protection, along with many of Eliot's papers, and cannot be published before 2014.

34. Lyndall Gordon, *T.S. Eliot: An Imperfect Life* (New York: W.W. Norton, 1998), 77. Gordon further identifies in the poems "an obsessional hatred of women and sex, punitive in its virulence" (77). Jonathan Gill describes the poems as having "a surprisingly racial, even racist, focus" (66). See Gill, "Protective Coloring," 66. Richard Poirier in *The New Republic*, April 28, 1997, noted that "the King Bolo poems reveal nothing of [Eliot's] poetic genius. They could have been written by any number of dirty boys" (37). Ronald Schuchard mentions the poems briefly, "There is much in Eliot's juvenile graffiti that is vulgar and coarsely humorous" (87). See Ronald Schuchard, *Eliot's Dark Angel: Intersections of Life and Art* (New York: Oxford University Press, 1999).

35. T. S. Eliot, *Inventions of the March Hare: Poems 1909–1917*, ed. Christopher Ricks (London: Harcourt Brace, 1996), 315; 318; 318.

36. Ibid., 316.

37. Ibid., 319.

38. Jonathan Gill argues, "Eliot's debt to blackface minstrelsy is most significant, if not immediately visible, in the series of lyrics…about the irreverent and even obscene adventures of a fictional King Bolo and his Big Black Bastard Queen," (66), noting that the Bolo poems are written in "the highly self-conscious literary language that I would call blackface English" (70–71). See Gill, "Protective Coloring."

39. Eliot, *Inventions*, 316.

40. See note 6. Other poems by Eliot with significant reference to America include "Sweeney Agonistes" (1926–27), "Marina" (1930), and landscape poems such as "Cape Ann" (1935).

41. Jed Esty, *A Shrinking Island: Modernism and National Culture in England* (Princeton, NJ: Princeton University Press, 2004), 150; and Lydall Gordon, "The American Eliot and 'The Dry Salvages'" in *Words in Time: New Essays on Eliot's Four Quartets*, ed. Edward Lobb (London: The Athlone Press, 1993), 43–44. Esty's position that in this quartet, "America exemplifies…rapid modernization" (151) is very much in accordance with my own reading of the poem.

42. Gordon, "The American Eliot and 'The Dry Salvages,'" 353.

43. Eliot read "East Coker" on May 26, 1941, on the program "We speak to India" for the Eastern Service (this program was rebroadcast March 17, 1946, for Home Service West of England). On September 1, 1942, Eliot read a series of poems including "Burnt Norton" and extracts from "The Dry Salvages" for the Swedish Service. On October 23, 1942, Eliot read "The Dry Salvages" for the program "We Speak to India" for the Eastern Service. He apparently did not read "Little Gidding" over the BBC. For a list of Eliot's broadcasts, including the above, see Michael Coyle, "Eliot's Radio Broadcasts, 1929–1963," in *T.S. Eliot and Our Turning World*, ed. Jewel Spears Brooker (New York: St. Martin's Press, 2001), 205–213. For further discussion of Eliot's radio broadcasts, see Michael Coyle, "'This rather elusory broadcasting technique': T. S. Eliot and the Genre of the Radio Talk," *ANQ* 11, no. 4 (Fall 1998): 32–42; and Michael Coyle, "T.S. Eliot on the Air: 'Culture' and the Challenges of Mass Communication," in *T.S. Eliot and Our Turning World*, ed. Brooker, 141–154.

44. T. S. Eliot, *Complete Poems and Plays 1909–1950* (New York: Harcourt, Brace and World, 1962), 117.

45. Ibid., 117.

46. Ibid., 117.

47. *A Sketch of the Eliot Family*, written by the American Walter Graeme Eliot, was published in 1887. See Walter Graeme Eliot, *A Sketch of the Eliot Family* (New York: Press of L. Middleditch, 1887).

48. Gordon, *Imperfect*, 348.

49. Eliot, *Complete Poems and Plays*, 123.

50. Ibid., 123–24.

51. Helen Gardner, *The Composition of* Four Quartets (London: Faber and Faber, 1978), 42–3.

52. Ibid., 124.

53. Esty notes, "Through the shared rhetoric of cultural revival, Eliot and other thirties intellectuals (not all of them conservatives) laid claim to national heritage in the name of a resurgent myth of organic community... modernists like Eliot and Woolf called upon traditional and classbound notions of Englishness, but they called upon them in the interest of a more capacious, participatory, and 'ordinary' idea of culture." *Shrinking Island,* 126.

54. *Oxford English Dictionary Online,* s.v. "Savage," http://www.oed.com/ (accessed December 2, 2010).

55. Gardner, *The Composition of* Four Quartets, 53.

56. Ibid., 53.

57. Ibid., 53.

58. Eliot, *Complete Poems and Plays,* 130.

59. Marshall Berman, *All That Is Solid Melts into Air: The Experience of Modernity* (New York: Penguin, 1988), 68.

60. Eliot, *Complete Poems and Plays,* 130.

61. Eliot sent "The Dry Salvages" to John Hayward in January 1941; it was published in *The New English Weekly* in February 1941. It is worth noting that the poem was therefore published well before the attack on Pearl Harbor of December 7, 1941.

62. Eliot, *Complete Poems and Plays,* 131.

63. Ibid., 132.

64. Eliot was apparently motivated to visit Little Gidding in 1936 after reading the draft of a play by his friend George Every on "the subject of King Charles's last visit to Little Gidding." Gardner, *The Composition of* Four Quartets, 62.

65. The New Bermuda Company was an outgrowth of the Virginia Company. Sir Thomas Smythe served as governor of the Bermudas (also known as Somers Islands) and encouraged its financial relations with Virginia.

66. In 1624, Ferrar took office in Parliament and aided in the impeachment of the lord treasurer who had been responsible for the end of the Virginia Company. See *Dictionary of National Biography,* s.v. "Nicolas Ferrar"; and T. T. Carter, ed., *Nicholas Ferrar: His Household and His Friends* (London: Longman's, Green, 1892), 49–79.

67. Eliot, *Complete Poems and Plays,* 139.

68. Ibid., 144–45.

69. In May of 1936, Woolf wrote to Julian Bell, "I get the most astonishing elaborate letters from poet Eliot; who is now the titular head of English-American letters since the death yesterday of A. E. Housman." Woolf, *Letters,* 32.

70. F. R. Leavis, *The Great Tradition: George Eliot, Henry James, Joseph Conrad* (New York: G.W. Stewart, 1948), 1.

71. T. S. Eliot, "Tradition and the Individual Talent," in *Selected Essays, 1917–1932* (London: Faber and Faber, 1932), 37.

72. Ibid., 37.

73. Ibid., 37.

74. For a discussion of the history of European racial ideologies that were similar to but not identical with national identities, see Laura Doyle, "The Racial Sublime," *Romanticism, Race, and Imperial Culture, 1780–1834,* ed. Alan Richardson and Sonia Hofkosh (Bloomington: Indiana University Press, 1996).

75. Eliot, "Tradition," 37.

76. Ibid., 38.

77. It is worth mentioning that Eliot's reference to Homer as the beginning point of the European literary tradition draws on northern Europe's own self-invention through the rhetorical work of claiming the Greeks for the English or the French tradition.

78. Eliot, "Tradition," 39.

79. Ibid., 40.

80. Ibid., 38.

81. Ibid., 39.

82. See F. R. Leavis, "T.S. Eliot—A Reply to the Condescending," in *Valuation in Criticism and Other Essays*, ed. G. Singh (Cambridge: Cambridge University Press, 1986), 12.

Afterword

1. Gordon Brown, "The Special Relationship Is Going Global," *Sunday Times* (London), March 1, 2009, http://www.timesonline.co.uk/tol/comment/columnists/guest_contributors/article5821821.ece (accessed November 22, 2010).

2. See Iain Martin, "The Special Relationship Is a Joke, and It Isn't Funny," *The Telegraph*, March 7, 2009, http://www.telegraph.co.uk/comment/columnists/iainmartin/4954361/The-special-relationship-is-a-joke-and-it-isnt-funny.html (accessed November 22, 2010); and Alice Miles, "Humiliated, Helpless, Paralysed. Time to Go," *Times* (London), March 4, 2009, http://www.timesonline.co.uk/tol/comment/columnists/guest_contributors/article5841400.ece (accessed November 22, 2010).

3. Brown's gift held special significance both because the HMS *Gannet* was an anti-slavery trade ship and because its sister ship provided the wood for the presidential desk in the Oval Office.

4. Andrew Rawnsley, "Obama at Least Didn't Treat Brown Like a Lame Duck," *The Observer*, March 8, 2009, http://www.guardian.co.uk/commentisfree/2009/mar/08/gordon-brown-andrew-rawnsley (accessed November 22, 2010). Tim Shipman, "Barak Obama 'Too Tired' to Give Proper Welcome to Gordon Brown," *The Telegraph*, March 7, 2009, http://www.telegraph.co.uk/news/worldnews/northamerica/usa/barackobama/4953523/Barack-Obama-too-tired-to-give-proper-welcome-to-Gordon-Brown.html (accessed November 22, 2010). Sarah Vine, "First Lady Michelle Obama Shows Even She Has a Gift for the Gaffe," *The Times*, March 5, 2009, http://www.timesonline.co.uk/tol/news/world/us_and_americas/article5848073.ece (accessed November 22, 2010).

5. Matthew Arnold, *Culture and Anarchy*, ed. Samuel Lipman (New Haven, CT: Yale University Press, 1994), 14. For a discussion of nineteenth-century American writers' anxieties about being overshadowed by their British counterparts, see Robert Weisbuch, *Atlantic Double Cross: American Literature and British Influence in the Age of Emerson* (Chicago: University of Chicago Press, 1986).

6. Arnold, *Culture and Anarchy*, 13.

7. Brown, "The Special Relationship Is Going Global," *Sunday Times* (London), March 1, 2009, http://www.timesonline.co.uk/.

8. James English suggests that "the Booker's rumored intention, under new sponsorship, to extend eligibility to U.S. authors" was part of an attempt to manufacture scandal—or

at least was perceived as such (213). See James F. English, *The Economy of Prestige: Prizes, Awards, and the Circulation of Cultural Value* (Cambridge, MA: Harvard University Press, 2005). See also Elaine Showalter, "Coming to Blows over the Booker Prize," *Chronicle of Higher Education*, June 28, 2002, B11.

9. See John Mullan, "Prize Fighters," *The Guardian*, May 23, 2002, http://www.guardian.co.uk/books/2002/may/23/fiction.johnmullan (accessed November 29, 2010).

10. Ibid.

11. See Sara Suleri, *The Rhetoric of English India* (Chicago: University of Chicago Press, 1992).

12. Arjun Appadurai, *Modernity at Large: The Cultural Dimensions of Globalization* (Minneapolis: University of Minnesota Press, 1996), 1.

13. Ibid., 2.

14. In the period following World War II, British colonial and postcolonial writers increasingly identified the United States as an alternative to Great Britain, both imaginatively and materially. Although American imperialism has provoked considerable criticism in recent years, some postcolonial writers explicitly embraced the United States as an escape from Britain. In his 1960 *The Pleasures of Exile*, George Lamming noted, "The West Indies are lucky to be where they are: next door to America"; much later, in an interview in the 1990s, Jamaica Kincaid related, "I think the major thing for me was that I came to America; and not England, or Canada." In his 1986 *Roots*, Kamau Braithwaite quotes Alfred Mendes on the promise, not always fulfilled, of "the States as a new Eldorado." See George Lamming, *The Pleasures of Exile* (Ann Arbor: University of Michigan Press, 1992 [1960]), 152; Jamaica Kincaid, "Interview with Frank Birbalsingh," in *Frontiers of Caribbean Literature in English* (New York: St. Martin's Press, 1996), 139; Kamau Braithwaite, *Roots* (Ann Arbor: University of Michigan Press, 1993), 11.

15. The International Man Booker Prize, established in 2005, considers authors whose work is available in English, either in the original or in translation. American writers' eligibility for this prize thus further classifies them as "international" rather than part of the original Booker's anglophone world.

16. Save, of course, as commodified entertainment. In June, 2010, the "Wizarding World of Harry Potter," a massive and hugely expensive addition to the Islands of Adventure theme park, opened in Orlando, Florida.

17. While it would hardly be accurate to hold Americans responsible for all the technological innovation of the twentieth century, such innovation has often provoked associations with the United States. Nicholas Ostler argues that even when modern technology was not American, such as "Benz's German internal combustion engine, or the French photograph and motion picture, due to pioneers such as Daguerre and Lumière—it was English-speaking developers, such as Henry Ford or the film-makers of Hollywood, who first demonstrated what could be done with the new media on a truly vast scale. This inevitably meant that the key talk about these achievements, how to replicate them and what was to be done with them, took place above all in English" (512). See Nicholas Ostler, *Empires of the Word: A Language History of the World* (New York: Harper Collins, 2005).

18. The *Scotsman* reports, "It took several years for Rowling to allow the books to be made into films by the Warner Bros studio, for fear of 'Americanising' Harry." See Fiona Gray, "And Now for Harry Potter and the Wizard Theme Park," *Scotsman*, April 22, 2007,

http://news.scotsman.com/jkrowlingharrypotter/And-now-for-Harry-Potter.3278867.jp (accessed February 9 2011).

19. The Potter stamp adorns many electronic toys and devices. Without any apparent irony, the American airline, AirTran, even added a Harry Potter themed aircraft to its inventory. See http://travel.usatoday.com/flights/post/2010/06/airtran-adds-harry-potter-1-to-usas-line-up-of-unique-aircraft-designs/96923/1.

20. Such a strategy is not new to transatlantic markets. In my article on the Wessex novels, I describe how Thomas Hardy encouraged the conservation of southwest England's rustic aspects in part to preserve their appeal for American tourists. See Genevieve Abravanel, "Hardy's Transatlantic Wessex: Constructing the Local in *The Mayor of Casterbridge*," *NOVEL: A Forum on Fiction* 39, no. 1 (2005): 97–117.

21. Quoted in Ostler, *Empires of the Word*, 505.

Index